JONGLEUR

A Modified Theory of Oral Improvisation and Its Effects on the Performance and Transmission of Middle English Romance

William A. Quinn
Audley S. Hall

UNIVERSITY
PRESS OF
AMERICA

Library of Congress Catalog Card Number: **81-40643**

To Tricia
and to Grant

iv

ACKNOWLEDGEMENTS

Someday, some scholars may prove--beyond the shadow of a doubt--that all such prefatory acknowledgements as this were once formulaically composed. We hope that the conventionality of our phrasing does not diminish the sincerity of our gratitude.

We would first like to thank Professor Walter Scheps of the State University of New York at Stony Brook, who asked the first questions that led to this study. Our thanks are due next to Professors Alan K. Brown, Stanley J. Kahrl and especially Christian Zacher of The Ohio State University, as well as to Ms. Jane Wemhoener, who guided our initial efforts to achieve a satisfactory answer.

We would also like to thank Professors Leo Van Scyoc, Larry Guinn and Raymond Eichmann here at the University of Arkansas, as well as the Center for Research and Sponsored Programs and the secretaries of our English Department, all of whom helped see this project to its current completion.

Of course, all mistakes in this study remain our own. But without the generous assistance of these and all our other friends and colleagues, such mistakes would have proven far more numerous. Finally, we thank our spouses, to whom this work is dedicated, and to whom we cannot otherwise offer thanks enough.

We must also acknowledge that this study remains very much a work-in-progress. Our basic theory about the improvisational nature of end-rhyme in the medieval romance was deduced from our understanding of its oral performance. But our proof for this theory must be induced on the basis of statistical analyses. We invite all corrigenda both of our data and of our interpretations. And we hope, if our fundamental theory proves sound, that our methodology might be applied to a reconsideration of other Middle English romances.

Fayetteville, Arkansas
December 1981

v

TABLE OF CONTENTS

CHAPTER I

INTRODUCTION

Jongleur is the term now commonly used to designate
the professional reciter of extended narrative poetry
in medieval England. It is a French loanword that may
have once distinguished the public performer of a poem
from its actual author, or trouvere. Such a distinction
may be considered somewhat analogous to that between a
scop and a gleeman in the Old English period--and no
more rigorous.[1] In Middle English, the title jongleur
seems hardly specific and certainly not honorific.
Minstrel and jongleur have frequently been used as
interchangeable names for the medieval performer of
verse, though the former has become more closely
associated with musical entertainment (albeit not
necessarily the white-glove and black-face variety).
As a label, jongleur has the advantage over minstrel
only in that it still indicates a specifically
medieval context. But the definition of jongleur
cannot be restricted to literary performance either.
In addition to singing, recitation and perhaps dramatic
presentations, a jongleur's repetoire may have also
included the playing of a variety of musical instruments,
some magic, a little juggling, or even acrobatics--each
talent as the occasion and his patrons demanded.

The roles that have been variously assigned to the
medieval jongleur, in other words, are far more specific
than that suggested by the probable etymology of his
title (iaculator, "joker" or "jester"), but more varied
than that specified by the word's modern derivative
(juggler). Nevertheless, this study can be concerned
with only one of such a jongleur's many possible skills,
the art of reciting an extended medieval romance like
King Horn "from memory"--and with the implications of
that skill to our understanding of the extant records
of such poetry.

From roughly 1100 to 1500, the jongleurs of England
served as the primary agents for the mass publication
of narrative poetry. To largely illiterate audiences,
the jongleurs provided the only means by which the
romances might be enjoyed. Without doubt, these ro-
mances were intended for aural appreciation, but to
what extent their composition may, therefore, be con-
sidered "oral" remains highly problematic. It seems

1

generally agreed that the jongleur's role in making a
medieval romance public was neither so significant as
that of an oral poet traditionally defined, nor so sla-
vish as that of a modern copyeditor. The primary
intent of this study is to pinpoint the jongleur's
function and to clarify the craft with which he ful-
filled that function. The three surviving manuscripts
of King Horn will be the focus of our analysis; Havelok
the Dane will serve as a contrasting example--or
"control." Whereas the composition of Havelok's single
surviving text seems primarily "written" in nature, the
three extant versions of Horn manifest more clearly the
actual effects of a jongleur's oral performance. Both
romances employ several of the same formal features
that have been designated essentially "oral"; both
represent the same tradition of oral performance--but
they differ significantly as real records of the
jongleur's craft itself.

General debate regarding "The Oral Theory" has be-
come extremely complex because of numerous critical
opinions regarding the far-ranging and divergent mani-
festations of such composition.2 And the statistical
analysis which constitutes the bulk of our own study
may seem equally complex because of its sheer size and
because of the numerous procedural difficulties which
we encountered (cf. "Methodology"). But our own theory
as applied specifically to Middle English romance is
quite straightforward and not entirely new.

The best arguments to date for the operability of
some sort of oral composition in medieval narrative
poetry remain those presented by A.C. Baugh.3 We know
that jongleurs performed their romances from memory.
This situation in itself, Baugh argued, demands some
sort of improvisational system in order for the per-
former to sustain the formal requirements of his long
narrative poem--in the case of King Horn, its couplets.
Furthermore, whenever two or more manuscripts of a
medieval romance survive, the variations within these
texts are frequently such that they may not simply be
attributed to scribal error. Baugh interpreted such
discrepancies among manuscripts as proof of their oral
transmission. And such transmission seems necessary
to imply oral composition. Deliberately following the
precedent studies of Magoun, Parry, Lord et al, Baugh
sought two features that have been designated fund-
amentally "oral": the repetition of conventional themes,
and the recurrence of formally interchangeable phrases,
or formulae. Milman Parry has provided the standard
definition of a formula as "a group of words which is

2

regularly employed under the same metrical conditions to express a given essential idea."4 Similarly, A.B. Lord has defined theme as "a recurrent element of narration or description in traditional oral poetry"; unlike formulae, however, themes are not restricted in their use by metrical considerations.5 Baugh found a good deal of evidence for both oral features in medieval romance, and suggested--by analogy--the improvisational nature of a jongleur's performance. Since the focus of this study is primarily prosodic, recurrent themes in medieval romance will be of little further interest.

    Baugh's evidence of the formulaic phrasing in Middle English romances has not proven so convincing as that provided by studies of either ancient compositions (like Beowulf and the Iliad) or of quite recent recordings of oral poetry (such as performed in Cyprus, Yugoslavia or the Soviet Union). Several opponents of Baugh's theory have demonstrated most convincingly that such conventional expression is common in clearly "written" compositions from the same period as well. But Baugh's evidence, as we shall see, has not proven invalid as an indication of his basic theory, so much as it has proven statistically insufficient to compel scholarly agreement. Most medievalists are willing to acknowledge that the boundary between oral and written composition is not so clear--neither historically nor critically--as was once thought. Furthermore, as Ruth Finnegan has stated, "The three ways in which a poem can most readily be called oral are in terms of (1) its composition, (2) its mode of transmission, and (3) (related to (2)) its performance."6 Though Baugh's primary intent was to demonstrate the jongleur's significance in these second and third contexts, his use of the term formula introduced unavoidable implications about the first. No one accepts a straightforward analogy between the composition of a work like King Horn and one like the Iliad--nor was any truly intended by Baugh.

    Our own modified theory about a jongleur's improvised performance and its effects on the final rendition of a medieval romance began with a reconsideration of this concept of the formula in Baugh's original analogy. Formulae, as defined by Parry, may be taken as concrete evidence for oral performance-- this Baugh argued. But such metrically controlled, recurrent phrasing should also imply a very specific type of oral poetry composed entirely of formulaic elements--a theory not intended by Baugh, nor supported by his evidence, though a logical implication of his analogy. In other words, Baugh would have us recognize formulae as the effects of oral composition in medieval romances, but not assume that they truly functioned as such in their composition. This original analogy requires, therefore, significant modification.

First, in one type of oral poetry—that is, in formulaic composition proper—there can be no valid distinction made between the poet and the performer; such an oral poet actually remakes his poem with each recital. He may preserve some conceptual outline of his narration, which he will no doubt edit or expand to suit his immediate audience, but there seems to be no real concern on the poet-performer's part for preserving a "fixed text." An alternative type of oral poetry is preserved by means of a performer's rigorous memorization; the performer of such poetry strives to avoid any modification of his inherited poem. But normally the length of such poetry is a good deal shorter than that of the average medieval romance. Furthermore, either of these two well-known types of oral poetry tends to require the extensive training of the professional performer in a more or less stable poetic medium. As far as we can now tell, the medieval jongleur in England did not enjoy such an apprenticeship.

Nevertheless, the jongleur's performance of an extended narrative poem must first be considered (however flawed) a product of his memory. Most Middle English romances have French or Anglo-Normal precedents; Baugh acknowledged that the first English redactors of such poems were probably not just bilingual, but literate, and that they (re)produced an original text—most of which are now presumed to be lost, while copies of copies survive. It is not necessary to assume that a jongleur then read such a first copy (i.e., that the performer was also literate); he may have simply listened to its recitation repeatedly. Still, an original of the poem did theoretically exist, and formulaic composition rigorously defined seems, therefore, precluded. In which case, a clear distinction can be made between the functions of the poet and the performer—even if they happen to have been, on occasion, one and the same person. Subsequent memorization of a pre-established text is, therefore, required by the performer. But Baugh did demonstrate that the typical jongleur's memory of any such original composition can hardly be considered "rigorous."

If we could imagine an English jongleur with
eidetic recall, such a performer would have orally
reproduced the original text of his poem with as per-
fect fidelity as a taperecorder today (or, perhaps, as
a Welsh bard in his own time). In England from 1100 to
1500, there seems to have lived no such "perfect" per-
former. We reiterate Baugh's premise that some sort of
improvisation seems both formally necessary and
actually operative in the transmission of several
medieval romances. But if a modified "oral theory" is
to be applied to this Middle English poetry at all--as
we hope to demonstrate that it may--it must focus ex-
clusively on the effects of oral performances, and yet
not imply a specific mode of composition. Baugh's
formulaic analogy did not permit such a distinction be-
cause, as Raymond Eichmann has most recently
reiterated, such "oral poetry is not to be thought of
in terms of poetry that was written to be recited but
rather conversely as poetry that was recited and even-
tually put down in writing in some 'typical' form."[7]
Since Middle English romances were often indeed
"written" (i.e., translated) to be later performed,
they may not be considered "oral" in this formulaic
sense.

But the two major types of oral poetry noted above
need not provide the only models for our consideration
of the medieval romances in England--which indeed seem
to have been written, then recited, then recopied in
the extant manuscripts. The jongleur's system may be
entirely unique. It is, at least, theoretically pos-
sible therefore for any given manuscript of a Middle
English romance to represent a complex of three quite
different processes:

> 1) an original composition, probably written;
>   in other words, an "autograph copy"--ex-
>   tant examples of which are considered most
>   rare.
>
> 2) a scribal copy as traditionally defined--
>   that is, the scribe reads one text (be it
>   the original or some other copy produced
>   by however many stages of written trans-
>   mission) and duplicates another text. The
>   "scribal errors" that are introduced in
>   such transmission must be considered
>   either "slips of the hand" or deliberate
>   editorial revisions.

5

or 3)   a text taken by dictation--that is, a
        written copy of an oral performance; it is
        possible, but not necessary to assume that
        the jongleur and the copyist were the same
        individual on occasion.

Consistent oral improvisation by a jongleur might be
evident as such only in medieval manuscripts that pre-
serve a scribal record of the third process, dictation.
But it is also possible (and probably more common) for
an extant manuscript to represent in part the effects
of both written and oral transmission. For example, a
written copy of a written copy of an oral performance
of a written copy of an original composition could dif-
fer from another version of the same poem because of
both scribal modification and oral improvisation. "The
basic point then," as Ruth Finnegan observed, "is the
continuity of 'oral' and 'written' elements."8 Only
the formulaic and the written modes of composition, as
A.B. Lord insists, need be considered mutually exclusive
concepts.9

     The primary challenge confronting a proponent of
the medieval jongleur's importance as an oral impro-
viser, therefore, is to discover a system that will
substitute for the formal functions fulfilled by
formulae and, yet, not prescribe the mode of com-
position with which they are so inextricably connected.
Our own theory departs from Baugh's and from all stan-
dard theories about the "oral" nature of medieval
romance in that we diminish the significance of the
(formulaic) phrase as the key element in a jongleur's
improvisational system; rather, we promote an alter-
native system based primarily on the jongleur's
recurrent use of certain pre-determined rhyme words.

     With only minor aberrations in one of its three
manuscripts, the romance of King Horn was recited (or
chanted, or sung, or whatever--but not read) entirely
in couplets. It has generally been assumed by advoca-
tes of the significance of a jongleur's improvisation
that his pairing of one line to another should be con-
sidered analogous to the matching of certain half-lines
selected from a plethora of semantically interchangeable
formulae according to the formal demands of the line as
a whole (e.g., the alliterative and stress patterns of
Old English poetry, or the metrical regularity of dac-
tylic hexameters in Homeric composition). Though this
supposition seemed eminently logical in theory, we now
consider it to have been a misdirection in terms of the
formal demands actually placed on the performer of

Middle English romance. Perhaps, the analogy was
simply too rigorously applied; it presupposes a clearly
defined verse line in the Middle English romance which
must be composed of equally formal phrases. This
frustrating focus on formulaic phrasing in medieval
romance may have also been fostered by the pervasive
modern preconception of regular end-rhyme as an orna-
mental supplement to, but not an adequate formal surro-
gate for regular rhythm. As has often been noted, how-
ever, the highly irregular stress pattern of King Horn
makes its end-rhymes alone the primary formal feature
that defines its couplets as such. And it is this for-
mal feature alone that would have to be satisfied by
surrogate system for the "formulaic" analogy. Whereas
the verse form of a bard or scop required some system
of formulaic phrases, the couplet form of a medieval
jongleur may have been satisfied by a system that im-
provised around certain recurrent rhyme words. (The
metrical regularity of Havelok the Dane may, however,
represent a significant modification of this tradition
of jongleur improvisation.)

In the following pages, we hope to demonstrate and
clarify precisely what a jongleur's improvisational
system was by analyzing the three surviving versions
of King Horn as records of its oral performance. An
"oral" theory may, thus, be resurrected for medieval
romance if and only if: a) it remains clear that,
although the truly formulaic line is a function of
phrasing, the jongleur's couplet is a function of his
rhyming vocabulary; and b) it is remembered that a
jongleur's improvisational system might supplement the
presentation of a, more or less, memorized model, but
does not generate an entirely new poem.

A bare outline of our modified theory about the
method with which a medieval jongleur performed King
Horn would be as follows:

1. The jongleur attempted to commit the work to
    memory.

2. He often forgot its exact phrasing, but was
    committed during performance to preserve its
    established form--i.e., its couplets, defined
    as such by their aurally exact end-rhymes.

3. In order to avoid any awkward hesitation
    during his public performance, the jongleur
    had also memorized several remarkably small
    sub-groups of words,--one sub-group (normally

no more than three to five words) for each of
his most recurrent rhyme sounds. The words
included in these sub-groups of a romance's
entire rhyming vocabulary were generally quite
flexible in meaning, and thus could be em-
ployed in a variety of contexts.

4. The performing jongleur anticipated his entire
   couplet (i.e., both of its end-rhymes) as a
   formal unit. Both rhymes were determined
   before either was spoken.

5. When the jongleur committed himself to a par-
   ticular statement and to a particular rhyme
   sound, he would also (most often) select a
   semantically suitable word from the appro-
   priate, preestablished rhyming vocabulary.
   Such a word he, thus, used SYSTEMATICALLY
   to conclude either line of his couplet--or
   both.

6. The jongleur could then improvise the exact
   phrasing of the lines themselves; he was ap-
   parently permitted much stress variance to
   "reach his rhyme--especially in those lines
   that contained a systematic rhyme word.

7. One couplet of King Horn was, thus, formally
   completed, and the jongleur could proceed to
   his next statement.

These seven "steps" would, of course, take place in an
instant during an actual performance. We will attempt
to demonstrate inductively that they comprise a
jongleur's standard operating procedure; in short, such
improvisational skill was part of the profession for
which he was paid.

We might here note briefly that two types of
exceptions are permitted in such an improvisational
system since it only aids a performance, but does not
formulaically compose the poem. Both types of excep-
tions may be considered examples of the fact that an
experienced jongleur's memory could override any need
to improvise his narration so systematically.

First, it makes no sense that a skilled jongleur
would have deliberately avoided "innovative" rhyme
links (i.e., couplets in which neither rhyme word was
drawn from his predetermined vocabulary). The jongleur
could have either reproduced such couplets exactly from

8

his memorized text, or he could have been suddenly "inspired" by novel combinations during his actual performance.10 Such "innovative" exceptions are extraordinarily rare in King Horn. But they do remind us that the proposed system of improvisation was supplemental to performance, and not absolute in terms of composition.

The second type of exception is, more precisely, an elaboration of "step" six in the proposed system. Rather than always improvising his wording, a jongleur might occasionally recall the specific phrasing of an entire line or couplet (as well as its concomitant end-rhymes) that had worked quite well before. We consider such repetitive and conventional expressions to be a logical by-product of the jongleur's improvisational system, but not the system itself. Yet, it is precisely these lines that have been labelled "formulaic" and, as such, have become the center of a debate surrounding the "oral" nature of medieval romance; so, in the next chapter, we shall review that debate in more detail.

Notes to Chapter One:

[1]Kemp Melone, for example, assures us that the author of Widsith "would hardly have understood the distinction we make" between composer and performer, in "The Oral Tradition: Courtly Poetry," in Albert C. Baugh, ed., A Literary History of England, 2nd Ed. (New York: Appleton-Century-Crofts, 1967), p. 46.

[2]For one of the best introductory surveys of the diversity of "oral poetry," cf. Ruth Finnegan, Oral Poetry: Its Nature, Significance and Social Context (Cambridge: Cambridge Univ. Press, 1977).

[3]Albert C. Baugh's two most important articles on the subject are "Improvisation in the Middle English Romance," Proceedings of the American Philosophical Society 103 (1959), 418-54, and "The Middle English Romance: Some Questions of Creation, Presentation, and Preservation," Speculum 42 (1967), 1-31. Baugh's studies were confined to the context of medieval narrative poetry that rhymed--as shall be our own. For another, major perspective on Middle English poetry, cf. Ronald A. Waldron, "Oral Formulaic Technique and Alliterative Poetry," Speculum, 32 (1957), 792-804.

[4]Milman Parry, "Studies in the Epic Technique of Oral Verse-Making. I: Homer and Homeric Style," HSCP, 41:80 (1930), as quoted by Albert B. Lord, The Singer of Tales (Cambridge, Mass.: Harvard Univ. Press, 1960), p. 30.

[5]Lord, p. 73

[6]Finnegan, p. 16.

[7]Raymond Eichmann, "Oral Composition: A Recapitulary View of its Nature and Impact," Neuphilologische Mitteilungen 80 (1979), 108.

[8]Finnegan, p. 24.

[9]Lord, p. 220.

[10]Most often, as we shall see, such "inspiration" seems to result more from the relative availability of certain rhyme sounds in English than from a careful selection of novel combinations for the sake of variety.

CHAPTER II

THE ORAL THEORY AND MEDIEVAL LITERATURE

In 1936, Ruth Crosby outlined what seemed an entirely new perspective for the appreciation of much Middle English poetry. Her article "Oral Delivery in the Middle Ages" concluded that "oral delivery of popular literature was the rule rather than the exception in the Middle Ages . . ." and "such popular literature came to have some striking peculiarities."[1] Two years later, Crosby expanded her studies to demonstrate the effects of this oral tradition on the fourteenth-century versecraft of England. In "Chaucer and the Custom of Oral Delivery," Crosby reiterated the underlying critical significance of her initial observations, but implicitly noted a major (albeit elusive) transition in the craft of "oral delivery": "Writers of Chaucer's time realizing that their works would become known to the public through the ear fully as much as through the eye, addressed both classes of audience."[2] Though Crosby limited her analyses to demonstrating the evidence for oral delivery in Middle English poetry, her observations naturally invited speculation about the oral composition of this same poetry.

As noted in the previous chapter, the entire pursuit of an "oral theory" that may inform the popular verse of post-Conquest England gained further impetus from certain presupposed analogies with the more conclusive evidence for the "oral" traditions of Homeric and Old English poetry. But several more recent critics, notably Michael Curschmann, have questioned whether the original analogies still hold.[3]

The critical challenge that confronts a modern reader of the medieval romances remains the formulation of an aesthetic justification for their excessive repetitiousness. The simplest, though least satisfactory, justification has been to make certain generic excuses for the exigencies of narrative verse. Although we seldom demand a romance of some 2000 lines to employ the same compression of poetic expression which may be found in, for example, a sonnet, to confess that extended narrative verse may, for no other reason, be justifiably less crafted or "polished" than the lyric seems both unpalatable and untenable as a valid critical principle in terms of medieval narrative. Chaucer, for example--not to mention Vergil or Milton-- applied no less of his talent to his extended pieces than to his short poems; we must remember that the

11

shorter pieces, in fact, were often considered merely
apprentice exercises that prepared the poet for his
magnum opus, and Chaucer frequently left his early
efforts incomplete.

Ruth Crosby's studies were geared towards demon-
strating that the intended mode of appreciation (and
not the mere length) of a poem may most clearly ex-
plain what seem (by modern standards) certain imagina-
tive shortcomings of much medieval verse:

> Direct address to an audience is then the
> surest evidence of the intention of oral
> delivery. In most works bearing such
> evidence however, certain other accompanying
> characteristics are to be found. The first
> of these is excessive repetition . . . Today
> we attempt to avoid repetition . . . It was
> not so, apparently, with the medieval poet.
> We must bear in mind that this literature
> we are discussing was meant to be spoken.[4]

Crosby's review of the evidence for oral delivery in
medieval verse, thus, focused on certain recurrent
syntatic units--that is, on repetitious phrases in any
given poem. She divided such repetitions into two
groups. Simply to demonstrate the existence of a tra-
dition of oral delivery in most medieval verse, Crosby
considered her second group more significant, "since
it consists of those types of phrases which actually
further the purpose of oral delivery by showing the
relation of poet or minstrel to his audience. This
group consists of transitions, asseverations and
oaths."[5]

But it seems to have been Crosby's first grouping
of repetitious phrases that proved more provocative to
proponents of an "oral" theory" which may have informed
the productions of the jongleurs' craft. "Four varie-
ties of phrases make up this group: introductory
phrases, descriptive phrases, expletives, and formu-
las."[6] Crosby reduced such repetitions to secondary
status because they offer no direct indication of
uniting the poet and his listeners during a live perfor-
mance, but rather appeal to a certain "fondness for
familiarity" on the part of the audience, a taste which
modern audiences do not share.

But since Crosby's studies, the overriding critical
question has become: to what extent can such syntactic
repetitions in medieval romance be considered function-

ally equivalent to the formulaic half-lines, set-pieces
and topoi of poetry orally composed? As potential
formulae, it has not proven feasible to keep Crosby's
original two groupings completely distinct in their
functions; so, we have chosen to conjoin them under the
single designation "tag-lines." No completely acceptable
explanation for the formal function of such recurrent
"tag-lines" in medieval English romances has yet been
achieved. Yet, we believe, there remains an urgent
need to do so--or, most medieval romances might be dis-
missed prematurely as the products of "weak" imagina-
tions that were somehow afflicted by conventionality.
As A.C. Baugh observed, "The attitude of modern critics
towards this feature of romance style is on the whole
unfavorable, although there have been apologists."[7]

Before any valid critical assessments of the art-
istry of a given medieval romance can be clearly es-
tablished, the craft that informs the artifact must
first be comprehended. Though what critical principles
may or may not apply to "oral" versus "written" poetry
remains hotly debated, it is generally acknowledged
that the presence of repetitive formulae should be con-
sidered a positive aesthetic contribution to the formal
appreciation of poetry presented in an oral mode,
whereas the excessive repetition of such formulae (di-
vorced from their original formal function) in a written
composition quickly generates only tedium.

The precise effects of a probable transition from
"oral" to "written" formats on the appreciation of
Middle English romances has for some time baffled
critics. Margaret Schlauch has summarized the pre-
valent understanding of the suspected transition's
effects on the art of the jongleurs:

> In the earlier part of the period being
> considered (ca. 1250-1400), the long ro-
> mances were evidently composed for direct
> oral delivery by poet-entertainers in the
> halls of noble patrons. By the end of
> that period, the mode of production and
> consumption had, so to speak, undergone
> an economic transformation. The English
> aristocracy had grown in numbers, in
> wealth, and in literacy. Its represe ita-
> tives no longer depended exclusively on
> oral entertainment; they began to aspire
> to ownership of romance texts for private
> reading.[8]

13

It seems only logical that prose romances should begin
to appear at the end of this period, and so they do.
At present, however, it remains impossible for a critic
to determine (from the internal evidence alone) more
than that a specific Middle English verse romance <u>seems</u>
to be "the work of a minstrel."

       Little recent scholarship has considered this sub-
ject specifically in terms of the anonymous romance of
<u>King Horn</u>, which will be the focus of our own study.
But the debate has raged on all sides of it. For
example, Mildred Pope in her introduction to <u>The Romance</u>
<u>of Horn</u> <u>by</u> <u>Thomas</u> analyzes the divergences among four
of its apparently independent manuscripts in order to
determine a common source (Y); she suggests:

                    The interest of these divergences, so slight
               in themselves, is, however, great, for they
               indicate that in Y we have to do with a
               versifier who was basing his version of the
               poem not on a manuscript copy but on his
               <u>memory</u> of the version that he had acquired,
               for it is in works preserved in this manner
               that one finds similar unpremeditated changes
               of detail. They are the outcome of a memory
               that is in possession of the poem and well
               stored with the clichés of traditional verse,
               but careless about exactitude. And, as may
               be seen so often in Middle English romances,
               the result is unfortunate, for the changes--
               so slight often in themselves--in their cumu-
               lative effect impair, as always, the individ-
               uality of the poem, dilute its terseness,
               destroy the crispness of phrase.[9]

Contrariwise, John Speirs has argued that the recurrent
"tag-lines" of Middle English romances need not be con-
sidered a detriment to their artistic quality; rather,
"Those English romances which reflect a greater degree
of literacy in poet and audience are not always those
which show greater art."[10] Speirs implicitly seeks to
justify this general impression by distinguishing
medieval English romances from their French equivalents
according to the differing modes of their respective
composition. "Whereas the finer French romances are
already literary poems, the finer English romances
(apart from Chaucer's) are mostly poems that are, at
least to a much greater degree, of the nature of the
older oral poetry."[11]

       Speirs and Pope may be considered critically anti-

podal in their respective assessments of the "tag-lines"
that Crosby demonstrated were indicative of oral deliv-
ery. These "clear" signs of oral delivery have not,
however, given any definite indication of the actual
procedures involved in the composition of much Middle
English literature. On the presence of "tag-lines"
alone, it has been proven critically impossible to dis-
tinguish an orally preserved text from mere hack-work.

Even Albert C. Baugh conceded that "one of the
easiest assumptions to make, it would seem, and one of
the hardest to prove, is that the romances were com-
posed by minstrels."[12] In A Manual of the Writings in
Middle English: 1050-1500, Helaine Newstead has under-
lined the fact that the surviving manuscripts of
medieval romances hardly represent a homogenous craft.
Some follow their written French sources most faith-
fully; others seem to suggest that an English jongleur
is adapting his tale much more freely from memory. "The
literary quality of English romances varies as strik-
ingly as the other features, and it is difficult to
discern any consistent trend towards improvement or de-
generation."[13] And, in 1969, Dieter Mehl expressed a
"new" critical caution about the applicability of any
"oral theory" to our appreciation of the Middle English
romances because "It is not even certain that most of
these poems were ever recited by minstrels."[14] In short,
the date of a given romance's "original composition" in
itself gives no clear indication of its mode of composi-
tion.

In 1967, two years before Mehl's caveat, A.C. Baugh
himself had qualified, but did not abandon his "oral"
theory. Baugh reasserted his postulate that the tex-
tual variants, which can be everywhere perceived when
multiple manuscripts survive for a single Middle English
romance, cannot be explained solely on the basis of
scribal errors:

> Such deliberate changes occur not in a few
> places but throughout a romance. They involve
> not just the substitution of a better word,
> but the rephrasing of a line or several lines
> and often the substitution of new rime-words.
> The scribe is no longer copyist; he has be-
> come a poet . . . The explanation, however,
> presents a still greater difficulty. How are
> we to account for the fact that many of these
> 'improvements' consist in substituting
> banalities, clichés, and rime-tags.[15]

Baugh goes on to emphasize the jongleur's role in the
oral reproduction of the Middle English romances. As
he transmitted the text, the minstrel frequently impro-
vised from a convenient stock of phrases. Thus, though
not precisely the "work of minstrels," the surviving
manuscripts of medieval romance may represent the
effects of their reworkings. It was such reworking
that Baugh considered somewhat "formulaic."

In 1959, Baugh had provided the fullest demonstra-
tion for the validity of his theory. In a thirty-six
page article for the American Philosophical Society,
Baugh cited hundreds of examples of what he considered
formulaic phrasing and themes from the six romances
that comprise "The Matter of England" (i.e., Beves of
Hampton, Guy of Warwick, Richard the Lion-Hearted,
Athelston, Havelok, and--our own primary concern--King
Horn). Although Baugh did not commit himself to the
specific theses of Parry, Lord, Rychner, Bonjour, or
Magoun, he did maintain that his own theory regarding
Middle English romance was based on an analogy to some
synthesis of their collective ideas:

> . . .since the practice of improvisation can
> be observed in our own day, since it results
> in the necessary use of formulaic elements,
> and since formulaic elements are found exten-
> sively in the epic poems of Greece, medieval
> France, and Anglo-Saxon England, the possi-
> bility cannot be denied that here also they
> have resulted from comparable circumstances
> of oral presentation. It would seem reason-
> able, therefore, to ask whether the Middle
> English romances as they have come down to us
> are to any extent the product of similar
> practices.[16]

Baugh then reviewed a myriad of adverbial, prepositional,
infinitive, participial, and other such phrases that may
be considered metrically equivalent substitutes. "In
other words, they meet the requirements of the formu-
la."[17] Baugh also analyzed the recurrence of certain
conventional themes, such as the knight taking his wea-
pon, or identifying himself, or--"the most extended
theme"--the fight, which Baugh showed might consist of
some combination of forty-nine recurrent elements.

To this evidence for the use of both formulae and
themes (phenomena which "The Matter of England" seems
to share with other "oral" poetry), Baugh added a study
of the indications of a third feature, called "the

16

predictable complement"--a type of conventionality that might be peculiar to the verse form of medieval romance. Such complements are paired statements that may be considered "a kind of conditioned reflex" on the part of the poet or reciter:

> Generally the statement and its predictable complement form a couplet, and this feature of the composition is the result of the fact that the couplet is the basic unit of most English romances, even the stanzaic romances.[18]

It was this fundamental observation by Baugh that gave our own study its first impetus--in addition to his (albeit ambiguous) emphasis on improvised performance as distinguished from actual composition. Baugh's qualified theory acknowledged that the known literary sources for several Middle English romances make their "situation. . .quite different"[19] from that proposed for the Iliad, Beowulf, or Roland. Our own modifications of Baugh's ideas, however, will derive primarily from a rejection of his assertion that "Considerations of rime are doubtless responsible for many a predictable complement, but are not the complete explanation."[20] Implicitly, Baugh conceived of these predictable complements as a unique category of formulae, in that they too seem to provide "a stock of ready-made phrases which vary only enough to provide a choice of rimes."[21] Baugh, thus, more or less postulated that a jongleur's rhyme words must be considered supplemental to the phrases in which they occur. Our theory, simply inverts this relationship; we propose, rather, a stock of "ready-made" rhymes.

It seems to us that Baugh's analysis of the predictable complement (like his treatment of formulae in general) asks for too straightforward an analogy between the improvisational techniques employed by a medieval jongleur and the compositional devices of a bard or scop. In other words, though Baugh himself recognized the theoretical limitations inherent in his fundamental analogy, his terminology forced too precise an application of it. Though we acknowledge that our own modified theory of a jongleur's oral improvisation may offer no more than a confirmation and clarification of Baugh's most basic insights, we reject his analysis of the actual method used by a jongleur during public performance. We are hardly the first to do so.

Baugh based his entire theory primarily on the

evidence of what we have generically labelled "tag-lines" (be they themes or formulae). But it was Laura Hibbard Loomis who had already indicated that such conventional phrasing could recur just as often in medieval poetry which must still be considered essentially written (albeit with poetic results that are generally considered regretable). Loomis based her study on the acknowledged hack-work of the Auchinleck MS.,[22] and implicitly demonstrated that its "written" compositions employ the same stylistic features that Baugh would assert are essentially "oral." Likewise, Margaret Schlauch has observed that, in contrast to King Horn, "one of the Auchinleck romances called Horn Childe and Maiden Rimnild reduces the simplicity to banality, and the language to stereotyped artificiality."[23] All this, then, underlines the point that "tag-lines" alone offer no clear indication of the mode of production, or reproduction, for any given Middle English romance.

The theoretically clear distinction between "oral" and "written" composition, and consequently the analysis of their respective effects on the art of Middle English romances, has grown increasingly complex. Dieter Mehl has attempted to clarify at least the cause of the resultant confusion:

> The possibility that minstrels had some share in the process or that some scribes also acted as entertainers can, of course, not be ruled out; nor can it be denied that many of those scribes just turned out haphazard, patched-up collections of tags, ready-made rhyming couplets, half-stanzas and motifs gleaned from some other romance. Moreover, it would be unwise to make a cut-and-dried distinction between 'oral' and 'literary' composition. The processes of copying, translating, and adapting were on the whole far less 'literary' than the modern reader might easily imagine. They left ample room for improvisation, the use of clichés and other features which we tend to associate with oral composition.[24]

Nor is this confusion about the manuscript preservation of a given poem confined to Middle English literature. Michael Curschmann, in reviewing the applicability of an "oral theory" to the Nibelungenlied, asserts, "We have forgotten. . . that in a culture which is still predominantly oral, in the general sense, there is no room for an absolute juxtaposition of oral and written, in a specific sense."[25]

Curschmann, therefore, suggests that we consider the concept of the "transitional text"--that is, one which manifests the techniques of both oral and written composition--in our analysis of most medieval literature.[26] And Raymond Eichmann argues further that, "Understandably, not every work in its totality, has to belong to only one of these two extremes; the aforementioned elements /i.e., formulae and themes_/ might well serve as a gauge, not so much as an indicator of the exact proportion of these two traditions but as to whether or not, and to what extent the oral nature of the work is still in evidence."[27]

Two objections to such a "transitional theory" might be raised. First, Lord objected to the designation of an actual composition as "transitional" because the techniques employed in the production of a truly oral (i.e., formulaic) poem as opposed to those used in a truly written poem seem fundamentally immiscible as such--though the latter may imitate certain stylistic features of the former.[28] Second, whereas Eichmann suggests that we recognize the survival of oral phenomena modified by later written revision, the Middle English romances may represent essentially written compositions (i.e., translations that become oral —as it were, after the fact— through the subsequent improvisation of jongleurs). Nevertheless, this "transitional theory"--as fostered by Mehl, Curschmann and Eichmann, among others--seems particularly applicable in theory to the surviving records of much medieval literature. And this theory seems, therefore, to have become the prevalent critical opinion at present: certain, originally oral works became to varying extents written during scribal transmission; the degree of this "transition" depends entirely on the type of revisions imposed by each individual copyist on his text.

We do not wish to refute such a "transitional theory" entirely. It makes eminent sense as an abstract overview, and it may often provide the only valid assessment of a specific medieval poem's style. The "transitional theory" acknowledges quite straightforwardly that, since the actual distinction between "oral" and "written" became blurred in the reproduction of manuscripts during the Middle Ages, so must be our own critical application of that distinction. In so far as the "transitional theory" merely strives to rectify a prior oversimplification--that is, an either/or fallacy regarding the "oral" vs. "written" nature of a medieval work--it seems fundamentally correct. This theory itself does not, or should not, suggest that oral composition somehow "evolved into" written composition. Furthermore, the "transitional theory" does not itself preclude the possibility of making more precise distinctions within the extreme parameters set by its obscure termini-that remain designated "oral" and "written"--if new evidence should be discovered.

We believe that an analysis of the rhyme words employed in King Horn will provide such evidence, and that such an analysis is necessary prior to the critical assessment of any Middle English romance's formal artistry.

One unfortunate corollary implied by the ambivalence of the "transitional theory" itself has been a certain critical arbitrariness regarding the actual, formal merits of much medieval verse. We may return to the debate about "taglines" for a prime example of the dilemma that implicitly confronts all students of Middle English romance. If such repetitiousness may not be formally explained, it must be aesthetically "excused." Since the presence of "tag-lines" alone has proven insufficient for determining whether a given manuscript of a given romance should be considered either an orally transmitted reproduction or a textual transcription, subsequent critical evaluations of that work of art often appear quite contradictory--as we shall see in our next chapter. Baugh, for example, insists that King Horn was sung (probably to the accompaniment of a harp) and should, therefore, be considered the record of a memorized, oral performance.[29] And its repetitiousness and conventionality should be appraised accordingly. Mehl argues, however, that Horn's "skillful compression and accentuation of the story-material betrays the hand of a careful and conscious artist."[30] We concede that the presence of "tag-lines" in itself does not disprove Mehl's assessment of Horn's composition, but we do not believe that its oral performance would necessarily preclude such skillful compression.

We hope to demonstrate in our fourth chapter that the recurrent rhyming vocabulary employed in all three manuscripts of King Horn may, to a certain extent, be considered indicative of the jongleur's true skill. The manuscripts of King Horn, in other words, seem to be more or less faithful transcriptions of oral performances--and should be assessed accordingly.[31] The scribe who recorded Havelok the Dane, however, was at least its redactor, if not the actual author of this romance.

20

We will suggest that the often-noted "tag-lines" or ready-made couplets of many Middle English romances may indeed be a contingent result of their oral performance--one effect of the far more inclusive system of recurrent end-rhymes. But we also acknowledge that "tag-lines" alone may simply indicate written hackwork. The critical distinction must be made, and we believe that for many Middle English romances it can be made-- empiricallly. It is the recurrence rate of a romance's rhyming vocabulary (the statistical frequency of such repetitions, and not just the existence of repetitive phrasing) that distinguishes one type of manuscript from another--and that might, therefore, specify the "oral" or "written" or "transitional" nature of a given romance's final form.

Notes to Chapter II

[1]Ruth Crosby, "Oral Delivery in the Middle Ages,"
Speculum 11 (1936), p. 110.

[2]Ruth Crosby, "Chaucer and the Custom of Oral Delivery,"
Speculum 13 (1938), p. 414.

[3]Michael Chruschmann, "The Concept of the Oral Formula
as an Impediment to Our Understanding of Medieval Oral
Poetry," Medievalia et Humanistica (Cambridge: Cambridge
Univ. Press, 1977), N.S. 8, pp. 63-67. Curschmann offers
an excellent synopsis of the growth of the "oral
theory's" influence on the analysis of medieval litera-
ture in general.

[4]Crosby, "Oral Delivery," p. 102.

[5]Crosby, "Oral Delivery," p. 106.

[6]Crosby, "Oral Delivery," p. 102.

[7]Albert C. Baugh, "Improvisation in the Middle English
Romance," Proceedings of the American Philosophical
Society 103 (1959), p. 420.

[8]Margaret Schlauch, English Medieval Literature and Its
Social Foundations (rpt. 1967; London: Oxford Univ.
Press, 1956), pp. 175-6.

[9]Mildred K. Pope, ed., The Romance of Horn by Thomas,
Anglo-Norman Text Society 9-10 (Oxford: Basil Black-
well, 1955), p. xlv.

[10]John Speirs, Medieval English Poetry: The Non-Chaucer-
ian Tradition (London: Faber & Faber, 1957), p. 107.

[11]Speirs, p. 109.

[12]Albert C. Baugh, "The Middle English Romance: Some
Questions of Creation, Presentation, and Preservation,"
Speculum 42 (1967), p. 3.

[13]Helaine Newstead, "Romances: General," in J. Burke

22

Severs, ed., A Manual of the Writings in Middle English: 1050-1500 (New Haven, Conn.: The Connecticut Academy of Arts and Sciences, 1967), p. 12.

[14]Dieter Mehl, The Middle English Romances of the Thirteenth and Fourteenth Centuries (London: Routledge & Kegan Paul, 1969), p. 7.

[15]Baugh, "The Middle English Romance," p. 29.

[16]Baugh, "Improvisation," p. 420.

[17]Baugh, "Improvisation," p. 421.

[18]Baugh, "Improvisation," p. 428.

[19]Baugh, "Improvisation," p. 431.

[20]Baugh, "Improvisation," p. 428.

[21]Baugh, "Improvisation," p. 431.

[22]Laura Hibbard Loomis, "The Auchinleck Manuscript and a Possible London Bookshop of 1330-1340," PMLA 57 (1942), 595-627.

[23]Schlauch, p. 177.

[24]Mehl, p. 10.

[25]Curschmann, p. 71.

[26]Curschmann, p. 75.

[27]Raymond Eichmann, "Oral Composition: A Recapitulary View of its Nature and Impact," Neuphilologische Mitteilungen 80 (1979), p. 101.

[28]Albert B. Lord, The Singer of Tales (Cambridge, Mass.: Harvard Univ. Press, 1960), p. 129.

[29]Baugh, "The Middle English Romance," p. 18.

[30]Mehl, p. 50.

[31]In the strictest possible sense, it is difficult to
imagine any manuscript being an exact duplication of
a jongleur's oral performance because it is difficult
(though not impossible) to imagine a scribe keeping up
with a normal recitation. It seems more likely that
a jongleur, even if he himself were the scribe as well,
would have to slow his pace somewhat for the copying
process. The pauses that such a slowing might intro-
duce would provide the jongleur with opportunities for
revision that a live performance would not. But, in so
far as the performer refused to exploit these opportuni-
ties--that is, in so far as the jongleur approximated
a normal performance--manuscripts may represent "accur-
ate records" of "actual performance." We believe King
Horn's three manuscripts are such records; they are, in
other words, very close approximations of live perfor-
mances, and any exceptions in their improvised couplets
may indeed be exceptional.

CHAPTER III

SPECIFIC BACKGROUNDS: <u>KING HORN</u> AND <u>HAVELOK</u> <u>THE</u> <u>DANE</u>

In terms of plot, characterization and setting, many points of comparison between <u>King Horn</u> and <u>Havelok the Dane</u> can be found. And, as John Speirs has noted, "It seems natural for modern readers to associate the two romances."[1] Both tales seem to incorporate fiction-alized recollections of the period of the Viking invasions against Britain. Both romances were composed in rhymed couplets. And the association of these two romances with one another does not seem to be an entirely modern convention; <u>Horn</u> was transcribed immedi-ately after <u>Havelok</u> in the <u>Laud Miscellany</u> 108/II (Summary Catalogue No. 1486). Although the narrative craft of these two romances is not the primary focus of our study, a preliminary review of the tales themselves should prove useful to the analyses of their respective uses of end-rhyme that will follow.

i. <u>King Horn</u>

<u>King Horn</u> is generally recognized as the oldest surviving Middle English romance; there are three extant manuscripts of it which vary in length from 1530 to 1569 lines. No one of these manuscripts can be clearly demonstrated to have been a source for the other two. There are countless differences in detail among the three manuscripts of <u>Horn</u>. Yet, the narrative diver-gences among them are generally considered to be slight. <u>King Horn</u> seems to have been originally composed c. 1225 in a Southwestern or South Midland dialect. The stress pattern of its individual lines is highly irregular and can vary from two to four or more beats per line.[3] Karl Brunner has, in fact, suggested that "Perhaps <u>King Horn</u> was first told in alliterative verse by itinerant minstrels."[4]

The folkloristic elements of the story of <u>King Horn</u> are clear:

> Horn, the rightful heir to the throne of
> Suddenne, is cast adrift by the pirates who have
> invaded the kingdom and slain his father. As
> an exile of apparent, though unknown nobility,
> Horn inspires the love of Rymenhild, daughter
> to the king of Westernesse. The treachery of
> his faithless companion, Ffikenhild, however,
> forces Horn into exile again. Having fled to
> Ireland, Horn wins great honor by slaying an

invading Saracen giant who had slain his father.
Horn is offered the daughter of the king of
Ireland in marriage, but refuses. He returns in
disguise to Westernesse after he learns that
Rymenhild has been promised to King Mody of
Reynis. Horn promptly kills Mody, denounces
Ffikenhild and sets off to reconquer Suddenne.
Meanwhile, Ffikenhild has captured Rymenhild and
attempts to force her into marriage. Horn
returns, again in disguise, kills Ffikenhild,
and is reunited with Rymenhild. Together with
their loyal friends, they thus obtain dominion
over Westernesse, Reynis, Ireland and Suddenne.
And live happily ever after.[5]

The proper names used in the above summary are based on
those found in the C MS. of Horn, and they have become
the norm for most modern editions. This nomenclature
differs, however, from manuscript to manuscript--at
times, markedly. Joseph Hall has charted the signif-
icant differences for us:

C	O	L
Murry	Morye	Allof
Godhild	Godild	Godild
Halpulf	Ayol	Apulf
Fikenild	Fokenild	Fykenild
Almair	Aylmer	Eylmer
Ailbrus, Apelbrus	Aylbrous	Apelbrus
Rymenild	Rimenild, Reymild	Rymenyld
Cutberd	Cubert	Godmod
Reymild	Hermenyl	Ermenild
Harild	Ayld	Apyld
Berild	Byrild	Beryld
Purston	Purston	Purston
Modi	Mody	Mody

And Hall considers these consistent variations a clear
proof that "no one of the versions is a slavish adaption
of any other."[6] Yet, no "adaption" substantially alters
the story of Horn or its artistic appeal.

The basic pleasure that any version of King Horn
seems to have offered its original audiences has been
best summarized by Margaret Schlauch: "the tale was
probably an effective item in the repertoire of a
professional minstrel earning his living by oral
recitation."[7] Horn's narration is generally fast-paced

26

and often quite moving. Its plot remains remarkably
faithful to the Anglo-Norman romance of Horn and
Rimenhild (c. 1175).[8] But Mestre Thomas' tale comprises
some 5250 alexandrines rhymed in tirades; King Horn
compresses much the same material into less than one-
third of the space. Charles Dunn concludes that "What-
ever its source, King Horn is artistically most success-
ful" primarily because of the exemplary "economy" of its
well-knit plot, its charming love-story and its con-
vincing psychology.[9] The craft of King Horn's end-
rhymes--that is, the most conspicuous formal skill of
its performance--has, however, been largely either
ignored as insignificant or dismissed as awkward. The
couplets themselves seem to offer little for a modern
appreciation of the poem's art.

ii. Havelok the Dane

     A complete rendition of Havelok the Dane survives
in only one manuscript, Laud Misc. 108, Bodleian Lib-
rary, Oxford. Its date of composition has been proposed
to be as early as 1203 or as late as the beginning of
the fourteenth century.[10] George B. Jack has recently
argued that c. 1272 seems to be the most probable date
for the original composition of Havelok--perhaps only
fifty years after Horn.[11] The text of the more or less
complete Bodleian Havelok plus an additional eleven
lines from a Cambridge fragment comes to 3001 lines--
about twice the size of Horn.[12] The four-stress verse
lines of Havelok are generally quite regular. Its
original dialect seems to have been Northeast Midland.

     The adventures of Havelok begin after:

               The kings of both England and Denmark die,
               leaving children as heirs. Goldborough of
               England is entrusted to Godrich, Earl of
               Cornwall; and Havelok the Dane becomes a
               ward of Earl Godard. Both guardians prove
               unfaithful. Godard assigns the fisherman
               Grim to kill Havelok, but Grim recognizes
               the child's kingship by a birthmark and a
               miraculous light that shines from Horn's
               mouth. Grim flees to England where Havelok
               grows to be an exceptionally strong scullion
               in the castle of Godrich. Meanwhile, Godrich
               had promised Goldborough's father that she
               would marry the strongest man in England.
               The Earl of Cornwall attempts to usurp
               Goldborough's claim on the throne by joining

her with a mere scullion (i.e., Havelok).
At Grim's house, however, Goldborough also
witnesses Havelok's luan, and an angel as-
sures her of his noble destiny. Havelok
eventually defeats both Godard and Godrich,
and rules as king of both England and
Denmark, with Goldborough as his queen--
happily ever after.[13]

A comparison of the basic plots presented in both Horn
and Havelok suggests that their stories are essentially
the same; they both incorporate several common folklore
motifs and may both be considered examples of the rite
du passage tradition as well as of the expulsion-and-
return formula.

Though Charles Dunn considers Havelok "one of the
freshest, most timeless, and most appealing of the
early Middle English romances,"[14] its popularity seems
to have been far more limited than Horn's. Two Anglo-
Norman narrations of the story of Havelok, both in
octosyllabic couplets, predate the composition of the
Middle English romance. Gaimar included the tale of
a Havelok, who rules for twenty years after the defeat
of Arthur, in his Estoire des Engles (11. 47-818);
Gaimar's work is dated c. 1140. Furthermore, an
anonymous Lai d'Haveloc (1106 lines) was written c.
1200 in imitation of Marie de France's Breton lays.
Thus, in complete contrast to King Horn, Havelok the
Dane is a more extended composition than its Anglo-
Norman precedents. But there is no real evidence (i.e.,
that of multiple manuscripts) to indicate its wide ap-
peal in England.

Various, and often contradictory, critical assess-
ments of Havelok suggest that it is, at once, both more
literary and more vulgar than Horn. Karl Brunner has
observed that Havelok "is far less courtly and knightly
than King Horn. The existing text is probably one
recited by a minstrel on market days in town squares
(cf. 11. 13-16 and the end)."[15] Dunn suggests further
that the less aristocratic status of the audience for
which Havelok was apparently first intended may have
yielded certain "social limitations" which hampered its
dissemination.[16] On the other hand, Albert C. Baugh has
noted that Havelok was apparently written by a far more
conscientious artist than the composer (or, at least,
recorder) of King Horn; "the closing lines of Havelok
ask a silent prayer for the author: 'Say a paternoster
stille/For him þat haueth þe rym maked,/And þerfore

fele nihtes waked.' Now no Middle English romance
has a better claim to be the work of a minstrel than
Havelok, and yet staying awake many nights to compose
the rime surely implies writing."[17] We would qualify
Baugh's comment with at least one exception--King Horn.
We will argue that Horn has a better claim to be an
accurate record of the "work of a minstrel" than does
Havelok the Dane, and we hope to justify this claim by
a detailed analysis· of their respective end-rhyme
techniques. Though the critical temptation to evaluate
the artistry of Horn and Havelok by comparing one to the
other remains strong, it is at least possible that they
are the products of two entirely different versecrafts,
and that the formal skill required for each might be
differentiated from the other.

Notes to Chapter III

[1] John Speirs, *Medieval English Poetry: The Non-Chaucerian Tradition* (London: Faber & Faber, 1957), p. 191.

[2] The three manuscripts of *King Horn*: 1) MS. Harleian 2253, British Museum, London (L); 2) MS. Laud Misc. 108, Bodleian Library, Oxford (O); and 3) MS. Gg. iv. 27. 2, University Library, Cambridge (C). All line references to and quotations from this romance will be taken from Joseph Hall's *King Horn: A Middle English Romance* (Oxford: Clarendon University Press, 1901).

[3] For a detailed, though somewhat outdated description of *King Horn*'s irregular stress patterns, cf. "Metre," pp. xlv-l, in Hall's edition.

[4] Karl Brunner, "Middle English Metrical Romances and Their Audiences," in *Studies in Medieval Literature in Honor of Professor Albert Croll Baugh*, ed. MacEdward Leach (Philadelphia: Univ. of Pennsylvania Press, 1961), p. 221.

[5] For a more detailed synopsis of *King Horn*'s narrative, cf. J. Burke Severs, ed., *A Manual of the Writings in Middle English: 1050-1500* (New Haven, Conn.: The Connecticut Academy of Arts and Sciences, 1967), p. 19.

[6] Hall, p. liii.

[7] Margaret Schlauch, *English Medieval Literature and Its Social Foundations* (rpt. 1967; London: Oxford Univ. Press, 1956), p. 177.

[8] Mildred K. Pope, ed., *The Romance of Horn by Thomas*, Anglo-Norman Text Society 9-10 (Oxford: Basil Blackwell, 1955).

[9] Charles W. Dunn, "Romances Derived from English Legends," in J. Burke Severs, ed., *A Manual*, p. 20.

[10] Speirs, p. 109. The MS. itself has been dated from 1300 to 1325.

[11] George B. Jack, "The Date of *Havelok*," *Anglia* 95 (1977), 20-33.

[12] The Bodleian MS. of *Havelok* seems to have suffered from an abnormal number of graphemic irregularities in

its copying--often ascribed to its Anglo-Normal scribe's
inability to spell English. In order to avoid our own
(perhaps prejudiced) revisions of this romance's ortho-
graphy (and of its end-rhymes thereby), all citations
of Havelok will be taken from Donald B. Sands's reg-
ularized edition in his Middle English Verse Romances
(New York: Holt, Rinehart & Winston, Inc., 1966), pp.
55-129.

[13]For a more detailed synopsis of Havelok's narrative,
cf. J. Burke Severs, ed., A Manual, pp. 22-23.

[14]Dunn, p. 25.

[15]Brunner, p. 23.

[16]Dunn, p. 24.

[17]Albert C. Baugh, "The Middle English Romance: Some
Questions of Creation, Presentation, and Preservation,"
Speculum XLII No. 1 (January, 1967), p. 7. "Maked"
does not necessarily imply a written composition, nor
does staying up all night. Compare Egil's Saga in
which Egil Skalagrimsson stays up all night mentally
composing his drapa for Eirik--a command performance
if there ever was one. Baugh, with his typical
thoroughness, is conceding the objection (i.e., that
Havelok may be a written composition). We too shall
argue that Havelok may be an essentially written
composition, but not on the basis of its colophon alone.

CHAPTER IV

A MODIFIED ORAL THEORY: THE THEORY IN THEORY

A. C. Baugh has already drawn our attention to the fact that the author of Havelok the Dane claims to have been up all night "writing" rhymes. This claim might in itself suggest that any "oral" features in the composition of this romance would be merely imitative. King Horn, however, was apparently sung, or chanted, or recited. It remains dubious that the performer's melody--if he had one at all--varied extensively from one couplet to the next, but such a performance might have masked certain metrical irregularities that instantly become evident to a modern prosodist as he reads the manuscripts.

In any event, it is likely that the text of King Horn was actually performed (and perhaps transmitted) from memory, whereas it is possible that the author (or scribe) of Havelok ultimately thought of his own text of the romance as a written entity.[1] And the poem could be read as such--if only by (or to) a jongleur prior to his own oral performance. This hypothetical distinction between the extant texts of these two romances, so slight in itself, could prove significant if the manuscript of Havelok--though perhaps intended for oral performance--is not in fact an accurate record of such performance, while the three manuscripts of King Horn are. It is this difference that may explain the stylistic superiority which has often been attributed to Havelok at the expense of Horn. It is this distinction which may also be indicative of the fact that the two romances represent in their extant forms two quite different arts of rhyme.

There have been two traditional means by which the prosodic quality of these two medieval romances has been compared. The critic can either obtain a general impression from "normal" reading, or he may carefully attempt to scan specific lines;[2] there are merits to both approaches. And both methods have determined that the versification of Havelok is, by far, more regular than that of King Horn. George Kane has even suggested that the prosody of King Horn "sometimes looks and possibly is incompetent."[3] The somewhat baffling irregularity of King Horn's meter has indeed been interpreted as s symptom of its incomplete transition from the prosody of the Old English alliterative system to that of the newer French versecraft. Yet Donald

33

Sands, who otherwise seems none too enamoured of the
stylistic merits of Horn when contrasted to Havelok,
does suggest that "Horn reads aloud quite as well as
many other Middle English narrative poems,"[5] although
he insists on the superior metricality of Havelok's
"genuine iambic tetrameter."[6]

Any random sampling of Havelok the Dane should
demonstrate its metrical regularity. We offer a
scansion of its first six lines--hardly a random
selection--simply to concede Sand's observation:

> Herkneth to me, gode men,
> Wives, maidnes and alle men,
> Of a tale that ich you wile telle,
> Who-so it wile here and ther-to dwelle.
> The tale is of Havelok y-maked;
> Whil he was litel, he yede full naked.

Trochees seem to substitute freely for iambs--especially
in order to achieve rhetorical emphasis. Unstressed
syllables may accumulate in what seem, by modern stan-
dards, somewhat excessive numbers. But the observation
that each line of Havelok contains four and only four
primary stresses ("iambic tetrameter") seems fundamen-
tally correct. We assume, of course, that the two
secondary stresses of lines four and six provide valid
equivalents for one primary.

We do not insist that the above analysis of
Havelok's rhythm be considered definitive--only that
it be recognized as both valid and sufficiently regular.
No doubt alternative (but equivalent) scansions of
these lines are possible. And, no doubt, a thorough
scansion of Havelok in its entirety would reveal
numerous flaws. But in the first six lines of Havelok
a formal principle has clearly been established--a
metrical norm that should be maintained by every line
of the entire romance. In fact, the line itself of
Havelok can be (and, as noted, has been) defined in
terms of this meter; the lines of Havelok are either
iambic tetrameter or flawed. Against this definition,
the prosody of King Horn seems outrageously poor.

A comparable selection of the opening lines from
the three manuscripts of Horn soon reveals the fre-
quently observed "irregularity" of its lines in any
extant version. We have chosen the introductory lines
of Horn so as to confront directly two alternate
explanations of the discrepancies that exist among its
manuscripts. These alternative theories are derived

34

from answering "yes" to either of the following two
questions:

Either 1) Did the scribe actively revise the
romance as he recopied it?

Or 2) If the scribe merely recorded an oral
performance, did the _jongleur_ recreate
the work _solely_ from memory?

If either case were true, it seems to us most logical
that the opening lines of the three manuscripts of
King Horn should represent the poem's "best"--that
is, in terms of its prosody. Either the romance's
opening lines would have been revised most or for-
gotten least in order to attain or maintain
maximum metricality. Otherwise, "alle men" might not
"herneth." Neither the (perhaps detrimental) emenda-
tions of a scribe nor the (not too) rigorous recall
of a _jongleur_ offers an adequate explanation of the
divergences encountered in a detailed comparison of
the three manuscripts of King Horn.

We offer, therefore, the following scansions of
the first eighteen lines of the C MS. of King Horn
followed by the first twenty lines of MSS, L and O.[7]
We wish thereby to highlight both the stress variance
of lines _within_ each version of the romance and the
differences _among_ comparable lines of the three trans-
criptions. For-example, the fourth line of the C MS.
seems to contain only two primary stresses, but its
ninth line may have as many as five. Furthermore,
the fourth line of the L MS. seems to add a third
stress by adding the adjective "gode," but comparable
statements in both the C and O MSS. lack this addi-
tion. Other such discrepancies in phrasing (be they
insertions, omissions or transpositions)-that cannot,
we believe, be simply attributed to the dialectical
differences among the manuscripts--have been indicated
typographically. We would particularly like to high-
light the omission of any statement in these lines
from MS. C that would parallel the specification of
Horn's age in MSS. O and L (ll. 17-18), as well as
the apparent transposition in MS. C of the lines that
comprise the final couplet of this sampling.

Alle beon he bliþe
þat to my song lyþe:
A sang ihc schal ȝou singe   4
Of Murry þe kinge.
King he was biweste
So longe so hit laste.
Godhild het his quen,
Fairé ne miȝte non ben.   8
He hadde a sone þat het horn,
Fairér ne miste non beo born.
Ne no rein vpon birine,
Ne sunne vpon bischine:
Fairér nis non þane he was,   12
He was briȝt so þe glas,
He was whit so þe flur; }
Rose red was his colur. }   16

In none kinge riche }
Nas non his iliche. }

Alle heo ben blyþe
þat to my song ylyþe,
a song ychulle ou singe
of Allof þe gode kynge   4
kyng he wes by weste
þe whiles hit yleste
ant godylt his gode quene
no feyrore myhte bene   8
ant huere sone hihte horn
feyrore child ne myhte be born
for reyn ne myhte by ryne
ne sonne myhte shyne   12
feyrore child þen he was
bryht so euer eny glas
so whit so eny lylye flour
so rose red wes his colour   16
He wes feyr & eke bold
ant of fyftene wynter old
Nis non his yliche
in none kinges ryche.   20

```
Alle ben he bliþe
þat to me wilen liþe
A song ich wille you singe
of morye þe kinge                    4
King he was bi westen
Wel þat hise dayes lesten
And godild hise gode quene           8
Feyrer non micte bene
Here sone hauede to name horn
Feyrer child ne micte ben born
Ne reyn ne micte upon reyne
Ne no fonne by schine                12
Fayrer child þanne he was
Brict so euere any glas
Whit so any lili flour
So rose red was hys colur            16
He was fayr and eke bold
And of fiftene winter hold
Was noman him yliche
Bi none kinges riche.                20
```

Rather than assuming that the extremely popular romance of King Horn represents a particularly poor example of the jongleur's craft, or that the poem itself underwent some incomplete metamorphosis from its performance as an alliterative piece to its preservation in a rhymed verse form, we assume that the manuscripts of King Horn represent (with only minor scribal errors) the romance as it was actually performed, and that these performances were once artistically appealing as such. Thus, rather than asserting that Horn did not meet one formal definition of the verse line (i.e., its metrical regularity as evident in Havelok), we suggest that its jongleur did not have this definition of the form that he would strive to maintain during an oral performance.

Although it seems universally agreed today that the couplet should be defined as "a pair of rhymed lines,"[8] the medieval jongleur may have defined his couplet as "a pair of end-rhymes." The distinction is one of formal priority between the line and the couplet. Normally, we assume that the stress pattern of a line determines the proper placement of its final rhyme; this rule seems applicable to a critique of Havelok. But--rather than assuming (and then trying to explain why) King Horn fails to satisfy this rule-- let us assume that the rule was simply inoperative

37

during the romance's oral performance.[9] The jongleur
of King Horn, we suggest, defined the length of his
lines according to the placement of his end-rhymes--
not vice versa. The rhyme itself defined the "end" of
each line; the end of each "line" did not determine the
position of its rhyme.

If we accept this concept of the couplet as King
Horn's indivisable formal unit (and not as a conjunc-
tion of two, still more basic formal units--its lines),
a pair of closely related principles may be deduced re-
garding the discrepancies that have been observed both
within and among each version of King Horn. Both prin-
ciples relate directly to a comprehension of the
jongleur's improvisational method.

First, the improvisational method of a jongleur
would probably have to have been one that provided some
systematic recall of rhyme words, since it is these
very words that alone define the aurally perceptible
form of Horn.

Second, the exact phrasing of each line in Horn
might be mutable (at least in so far as the jongleur
himself was concerned, during his live performance).
The line's specific phrasing was apparently not pre-
determined by a rigorous system of meter or stress
placement. It is this second principle that signi-
ficantly distinguishes the jongleur's improvisational
method from the formulaic analogy offered by Baugh.
Although a jongleur's lines should not violate the
rules of normal syntax or sense, there was no role to
fix their precise wording.[10] The jongleur seems to have
recalled a meaning, but not necessarily one specific
statement of that meaning.

In short, if the Middle English jongleur had an
improvisational system at all, it should be one
actually geared to the formal requirements of King
Horn--not to those of The Iliad or of Beowulf. If an
analogy exists between these three oral modes, it per-
tains to a comparison of the artistic effects attained
by three different methods--not to an analysis of the
methods themselves. Therefore, rather than a "stock of
interchangeable phrases," we postulate that the medieval
jongleur may have had a "stock of interchangeable rhyme
words"--a memorized lexicon of prefabricated end-rhymes,
as it were. This mental rhyming dictionary would com-
pare to formulae properly defined only to the extent
that both generate discernible repetitions for the sake

of maintaining poetic form. We should, thus, expect
some sort of repetitious pattern in the use of a system-
atic rhyming vocabulary to be observable in the sur-
viving records of King Horn. The purpose of the next
two chapters is to test the validity of this expecta-
tion.

There has never been any doubt that the rhyming
vocabulary of King Horn is "repetitious." Repetition,
most broadly defined, may indicate mere incompetence
in a written composition; but "It has also been taken
by some scholars as constituting one of the differen-
tiating characteristics of oral as distinct from
written literature."[11] Nevertheless, it is also true
that the rhyming vocabulary of Havelok the Dane (our
allegedly written romance) may validly be labelled
"repetitious." The end-rhymes of King Horn have just
seemed more "repetitious" (i.e., "incompetent") than
those of Havelok--this is one comparison that we hope
our theory will disqualify. The all-too-common sub-
ordination of end-rhyme to meter in modern prosodic
studies has made it easy to assume (by analogy) that
the end-rhymes of Horn (like its meter) are less art-
ful than those of Havelok. Indeed, the language of
Horn has been called "bald and unimaginative."[12] But
the repetitiousness of rhyme words in King Horn may be
substantially different from--not just relatively in-
ferior to--a similar feature in Havelok. The average
reader normally finds the couplet links of King Horn
far more predictable than those of Havelok; we believe
that this general impression has been essentially cor-
rect. We add only that Horn's jongleur may have had an
artistically justifiable reason for this apparent
"monotony." We hope to demonstrate that the repetitive
rhymes of King Horn are truly systematic (a feature of
performance), while those of Havelok are merely con-
ventional (a shortcoming of written composition).

In order to clarify this distinction between two
types of repetition--prior to analyzing the evidence
for one type in Horn--we have extracted all the coup-
lets in both Havelok and MS. C of King Horn which link
lines by means of a specific rhyme sound,-edde, which
we will henceforth designate the couplets' common
rhyme element. The gathering of all couplets in a sin-
gle manuscript that share the same rhyme element we call
a cluster. Thus, the -edde cluster in MS. C of King
Horn consists of the following couplets:

Heo sette him on bedde;
Wiþ Aþulf child he wedde. (299-300)

& Cutberd ros of bedde
Wiþ armes he him schredde; (839-40)

A king hire wile wedde
& bringe to his bedde, (949-50)

Heo feol on hire bedde,
þer heo knif hudde, (1195-6).

The recurrence of bedde in each of the above couplets
obviously does not determine the phrasing of Horn's
lines as such. But its recurrence does seem to sat-
isfy the real formal requirements of a jongleur's
performance by consistently providing a readily re-
called end-rhyme. It is this type of repetition that
we designate systematic.

The equivalent -edde cluster in Havelok the Dane
consists of the following eleven couplets:

He hem clothede right ne fedde,
Ne hem dede richelike bedde. (420-1)

Thus-gate Grim him faire ledde;
Him and he genge well he fedde (785-6)

That hire sholde noman wedde,
Ne noman bringen hire to bedde, (1113-4)

To-morwe sholen ye been weddeth,
And, maugre thin, togidere beddeth. (1127-8)

For-thy from Denmark hider he fledde,
And me full faire and full well fedde, (1431-
2)

Fro Denemark full sone he fledde
Intill Englond and ther him fedde (2236-7)

Whan the othre sawen that, he fledden,
And Godard swithe loude gredde (2416-7)

And that the king hire havede wedded
And haveden been samen bedded, (2770-1)

That me forth broughte and well fedde
And ut of denemark with me fledde, (2868-9)

40

And dide him there sone wedde
Hire that was full swete in bedde. (2926-7)

Hou he weren boren and hu fedde
And hou he worn with wronge ledde (2986-7).

From this single example (which is not entirely rep-
resentative since it has been chosen to highlight one
of the romance's minimal uses of rhyme variety and,
thus, its maximum potential for improvised composi-
tion), Havelok seems in fact to be more "repetitious"
in its selection of end-rhymes than Horn. Whereas
Horn employs five different words (eight would have
provided the cluster's maximum variety) to generate
its four couplets, Havelok uses only one word more
in its eleven couplets (when twenty-two would have
produced the maximum variety); proportionately,
Havelok's end-rhymes seem here to be twice as "mono-
tonous" as Horn's. Yet, the primary difference between
a suspected improvisational system and mere monotony
is that the former can be demonstrated to fulfill some
formal purpose, whereas the latter cannot; the latter
is easy, but the former is necessary to performance.

In the -edde cluster extracted from King Horn,
the excessive repetition of one element in the cluster
permits almost maximum variety among the other words
used to compose its couplets (only wedde repeats it-
self twice). In Havelok the Dane, however, all but
two of its six rhyme words may be called conventional--
fedded repeats six times; bedde, five times; wedde and
fledde both four times each. In Havelok's cluster,
67% of the rhyming vocabulary repeats itself exces-
sively; whereas, in Horn's, only 20% (not counting
wedde) does so. Furthermore, there is a certain
semantic monotony to the rhyme-links in Havelok (e.g.,
the wedde/bedde and fedde/fledde statements) that is
not so evident in Horn.

Nevertheless, most readers of both romances are
normally convinced that the rhymes of King Horn are
far more predictable than Havelok's, and we would argue
that this impression is essentially correct because one
may anticipate the recurrence of bedde in the couplet
of Horn's -edde cluster far more readily than the re-
currence of any single word in Havelok's cluster.
The above comparison, we will argue demonstrates the
art of end-rhymes in King Horn at their best, but the
quite different craft of Havelok's rhymes at their
worst. Whereas the performer of the former generally

41

improvised his couplet with a systematic vocabulary
of available end-rhymes (a process that did tend to
generate conventional lines), the author of the lat-
ter--confronted by the additional formal demands of
the iambic tetrameter line--may have frequently used
the same standard rhymes and "tag-lines," but did not
truly employ the same improvisational art that first
produced them. Havelok's conventional rhymes are a
sign of the composer's sloth, not of the performer's
skill. Later, in Chapter VII, we will attempt to
balance this unduly harsh assessment of Havelok's
conventional rhymes by considering its other stylistic
achievements--features that have often been taken to
indicate the romance's artistic superiority to King
Horn, but which we will interpret as further signs of
its quite different "written" (i.e., revisable) trans-
cription.

In Appendix D, we offer further evidence and
clarification of the distinction between the con-
ventional rhymes to be found in Havelok and the sys-
tematic rhymes that our theory anticipates may be
found in King Horn. Again, it should be noted that
the examples we provide in Appendix D have been
selected to demonstrate Havelok's most conventional
use of end-rhymes--a decision that gives a somewhat
distorted perception of the romance's generally more
"varied" rhyme-craft, but that also provides the most
rigorous touchstone for determining if a given manu-
script accurately records a jongleur's actual im-
provisation. Havelok does not, though its end-rhymes
(and phrasing) do seem very "repetitious" to modern
readers. We concede that the repetition of a romance's
rhyming vocabulary in itself does not seem to offer
sufficient proof of its oral improvisation, any more
than did that of "tag-lines."

The above hysteron proteron in our discussion--
our brief attempt to disprove that Havelok's end-
rhymes indicate oral improvisation, prior to demon-
strating that Horn's do--does force us to reconsider
exactly what sort of repetition might function best in
maintaining a jongleur's actual performance. If we
continue to take the -edde cluster from MS. C of King
Horn as our model, we may note again that the con-
sistent repetition of one word, bedde, in all of the
couplets that share this common rhyme element permits
a good deal of variety among the other words with which
it rhymes (including an apparent off-rhyme with hudde);
only wedde repeats twice. We may also observe that

bedde may appear at the end of either line in a
couplet, and that the phrasing (as well as stress
pattern) which leads to it is often quite flexible.
From these observations, we may hypothesize that the
repetitive rhyme-words which a jongleur would actually
employ to improvise his couplets should be a relatively
small subgroup of each cluster's total rhyming vocab-
ulary. It is such a subgroup--and not, as in Havelok,
the full range of a cluster's actual rhyme words--that
would have provided the jongleur with a truly useful
improvisational system. The recallability of such a
system of end-rhymes--that is, its improvisational
usefulness--would increase in inverse proportion to
the size of "the stock of interchangeable words" that
a jongleur was actually forced to remember. Quite
simply--the fewer, the better. In theory, therefore,
we should expect the maximum repetition of a minimum
number of words in each cluster of King Horn (though
seldom just a single word as seems to be the case in
the -edde cluster above). It is this phenomenon that
we designate systematic end-rhyme. And its pervasive
use in a Middle English romance may be taken as an
indication of oral improvisation. And it is such im-
provisation that best explains the discrepancies ob-
served among the three extant manuscripts of King Horn.

Our theory, for example, would best explain the
transposition of lines 17-18 in MS. C of King Horn as
opposed to the readings of lines 19-20 in the L and O
MSS.; the improvising jongleur simply inverted his
end-rhyme--but did not thereby disrupt the form of
his couplet. Similarly, we might expect the omission
or addition of entire couplets by a jongleur, but not
of individual lines.[13] This principle might best ex-
plain why MS. C fails to specify Horn's age; the
jongleurs forgot or remembered such an entire state-
ment entirely--not half of it. We shall also see
that one systematic rhyme word may substitute for any
other in the same cluster. And we have already ex-
plained that minor phrasal emendations might be
frequent in a jongleur's performance because the line
itself was not his fixed form.

We reiterate A.C. Baugh's premise that the main
challenge confronting a Middle English jongleur when
he performed his poem from memory was simply not to
falter formally--or stop. "To a minstrel verbal ac-
curacy is not so important so long as he keeps the
meter . . . . The important thing for him is to keep
going."[14] But our redefinition of the jongleur's
"couplet" requires a substitution of "aurally exact

43

end-rhyme" for Baugh's "meter." A truly useful system
that would allow the medieval jongleur to perform this
craft should provide him with an improvisational means
of maintaining the aurally conspicuous form of his
poem. It would supplement his presentation from memory
of the narration, but no more. On the one hand, the
jongleur's system should prove not entirely "composi-
tional" in the traditional sense proposed by oral
theorists-a "text" has been composed prior to per-
formance. On the other hand, a jongleur's memory
seldom struggled for the exact preservation of his
narration's specific wording.

We believe, therefore, that the improvisational
system of end-rhymes employed in King Horn can be con-
sidered neither completely "oral" nor completely
"written," and to consider the system simply an
"evolutionary transition" between the two seems a
historical oversimplification. The earliest English
jongleurs may have found themselves facing a rather
unique formal challenge:

- The rhyming demands of a foreign
  versecraft were rather suddenly imposed
  on their native language, the largely
  uninflected vocabulary of which made the
  achievement of these demands that much
  more difficult.

- They lacked the elaborate training that
  produced a Welsh bard or, for that mat-
  ter, a scop.

- They also lacked the "literary" means for
  revisable composition that more soph-
  isticated French poets of the time al-
  ready had at their disposal.

If the three surviving manuscripts of King Horn
are, indeed, representative of a much larger (though
largely lost) field of improvised romance, it must be
admitted that the itinerant poets who first employed
regular end-rhyme in English poetry adapted to the new
formal demands of their "imported" versecraft in some
rather peculiar ways. Nevertheless, it was these
jongleurs who established the tradition of regular
end-rhyme in English verse and who, thereby, estab-
lished the first principles for its appreciation.

44

It is quite beyond the range of our study to offer an apologia for the art of end-rhyme in general.[16] We do not wonder why the Middle English jongleurs maintained their couplets so rigorously--just how. But we will suggest that the craft of using regular end-rhyme in English poetry has been appreciated--from its very inception--as a difficult skill; if difficult to write, then all the more difficult, it would seem, to perform. Only a detailed analysis of King Horn's systematic end-rhymes will clarify the specific method used by a jongleur to overcome these difficulties.

Notes to Chapter IV

[1] The "chapbook" nature of the Laud Miscellany, in-
cluding its several saints' lives, might suggest that
the small folio represents a collector's reading
material, rather than a jongleur's repetoire. But,
of course, this same argument would then apply to the
O MS. of King Horn contained therein--which, we shall
see, does seem the most "written" version of the ro-
mance.

[2] In our opinion, any rigorous scansions of either King
Horn or Havelok must remain somewhat hypothetical be-
cause of controversies about specific pronunciations
that dialect questions and musical performance may
introduce.

[3] George Kane, Middle English Literature (London, 1951,
p. 49.

[4] Joseph Hall, ed., King Horn (Oxford, Clarendon Univ.
Press, 1901), pp. xIv-xlvi.

[5] Donald B. Sands, ed., Middle English Verse Romances
(New York: Holt, Rinehart & Winston, Inc., 1966), p. 16.

[6] Sands, p. 55.

[7] The format is Joseph Hall's.

[8] The concept is commonplace, but this particular
wording comes from M.H. Abrams, A Glossary of
Literary Terms, 3rd Ed. (New York: Holt, Rinehart &
Winston, Inc., 1971), p. 161.

[9] Absolute rules of metrical regularity may have not
become fully operative in English verse until Chaucer's
time. But we do not mean to suggest that a jongleur's
performance should be considered "ametrical." We hope
to indicate alternative features of aural form in King
Horn, not a total lack of them.

[10] Again, this statement is not intended to suggest that
a jongleur performed prose narratives that rhymed. But
rather than being restricted to one normative line in
which there can be relatively limited metrical sub-
stitutions, the jongleur was apparently permitted a
far more flexible system of stress patterns which his
performance (i.e., his pace, his intonation or his
melody) might very well have "regularized."

[11]Ruth Finnegan, <u>Oral</u> <u>Poetry</u>: <u>Its</u> <u>Nature</u>, <u>Significance</u>
<u>and</u> <u>Social</u> <u>Context</u> (Cambridge: Cambridge Univ. Press,
1977), p. 90. Finnegan suggests that the concept of
<u>repetition</u> itself may be too amorphous a theory to be
<u>critically</u> useful in practice.

[12]Hall, p. lvi.

[13]MSS. C and L of <u>King</u> <u>Horn</u> satisfy this expectation
with little qualifi̲c̲a̲t̲i̲o̲n̲, but the "odd lines" of MS.
0 present certain difficulties. We would divide these
"odd lines" into two distinct categories, however. If
the given "odd line" falls between two couplets (i.e.,
aa b cc--in which scheme "b" designates the "odd line"),
then we would suspect a textual emendation; the <u>scribe</u>
has inserted or omitted a line. But if an "odd <u>line</u>"
rhymes with either adjacent couplet (either aaabb or
aabbb), it is possible that a jongleur improvised the
"triplet"--just showing off. Furthermore, there are
numerous examples of double couplets (aa aa) in all
three manuscripts; if a "triplet" is suspected of
failing to complete the second couplet in such a
sequence, the omission may be attributed to either a
scribe or a jongleur. In short, each "odd line" must
be analyzed in terms of its own context and syntax.

[14]Albert C. Baugh, "The Middle English Romance: Some
Questions of Creation, Presentation, and Preservation,"
<u>Speculum</u> XLII No. 1 (January, 1967), p. 29; our italics.

[16]We would like to suggest, however--as an indication
of the continuing need for a reevaluation of the
functions of end-rhyme--that W.K. Wimsatt's theory
(which assumes that rhyme makes its "special contribu-
tion to poetic structure in virtue of its studiously
and accurately semantic character") has little or no
relevance to our appreciation of a <u>jongleur</u>'s skill;
Wimsatt, of course, was thinking on̲l̲y̲ o̲f̲ t̲h̲e̲ <u>poet</u>. Cf.
"One Relation of Rhyme to Reason" in <u>The</u> <u>Verbal</u> <u>Icon</u>:
<u>Studies</u> <u>in</u> <u>the</u> <u>Meaning</u> <u>of</u> <u>Poetry</u> (Univ̲.̲ o̲f̲ K̲e̲n̲t̲u̲c̲k̲y̲:
U̲n̲i̲v̲.̲ o̲f̲ K̲e̲n̲t̲u̲c̲k̲y̲ P̲r̲e̲s̲s̲,̲ 1954), pp. 153-185.

CHAPTER V

JONGLEUR PERFORMANCE: INTRATEXTUAL ANALYSES

i. When critics evaluate a poet's use of end-rhyme,
variety is normally applauded as one of the best and
most difficult skills to be attained. Indeed, praise
for variety may actually apply to at least three, quite
different features of end-rhyme: its sound, its place-
ment or its vocabulary. But the medieval jongleur seems
to have been blissfully oblivious to the joys of variety
in any of its manifestations. Rather, the performer of
a Middle English romance seems to have preferred--and
with good reason--aural exactness in his selection of
end-rhymes.

The C MS. of King Horn, which Joseph Hall con-
sidered to be prosodically the most primitive of the
romance's three extant versions,[1] consists of 1530 lines.
If maximum variety of sound were an operative principle
in its author's selection of end-rhymes, 735 different
rhyme sounds should have been employed--that is, one for
each couplet. Yet, the C MS. actually uses only 167
separate rhyme sounds. Similarly, the 1546 lines that
comprise the L MS. of King Horn allow, in theory, 773
different rhyme sounds, but only 194 are, in fact, used.
Likewise, the O MS. of Horn uses only 199 different
rhyme sounds to link its 1569 lines.

Although maximum variety of rhyme sound seems
irrelevant to the selection of end-rhymes in King Horn,
its poet might still have sought variety in two other
ways: by the selection of a completely non-repetitive
rhyming vocabulary with which to make his relatively
limited number of rhyme sounds, or by the maximum dis-
persal of these repetitive rhyme sounds throughout the
romance (i.e., their placement). If each rhyme sound
that recurs in King Horn would do so with equal regular-
ity--as they "should" for the sake of maximum distri-
bution--as many as 300 lines could intervene before each
of the given rhyme sounds "had to" repeat itself in two
couplets. Such maximum distribution for the sake of
variety is not at all true as a description of King
Horn's end-rhymes. Likewise, if each and every rhyme
sound used in King Horn recurred "on average"[2] in five
couplets of MS. C or in only four couplets of MSS. L
and O, as few as eight or ten words would achieve maxi-
mum variety in the selection of a rhyming vocabulary
for each. But this hypothetical virtue of selecting
a unique pair of rhyme words for each and every couplet
is not true of King Horn, either. So, these "overall

49

averages" give, in fact, an entirely erroneous impression Horn's repetitiveness in the selection of both rhyme sounds and rhyme words.

Prior to analyzing the recurrence patterns of King Horn's rhyming vocabulary, therefore, we found it necessary to divide the different rhyme sounds of its various manuscripts into three categories according to the relative frequency of their own recurrence (cf. Appendices A, B & C). By distinguishing those rhyme sounds that recur in only one or two couplets of King Horn ("Category I" entries in each appendix) from those that recur in three to nine couplets ("Category II") and by sorting, in turn, these rhyme sounds from those that recur in ten or more couplets of each manuscript ("Category III"), we were able to discern that a majority of Horn's different rhyme sounds were actually employed in a disproportionately small number of its lines. The statistics and ratios for each category of each manuscript may be charted as follows:

TABLE I

	# of Rhyme Elements	% of Total # of Rhyme Elements	# of Lines	% of Total # of Lines
MS. C				
Category I	87	52%	212	14%
Category II	62	37%	628	41%
Category III	18	11%	690	45%
TOTAL	167		1530	
MS. L				
Category I	121	62%	320	21%
Category II	56	29%	606	39%
Category III	17	9%	620	40%
TOTAL	194		1546	
MS. O				
Category I	122	61%	314	20%
Category II	54	27%	536	34%
Category III	23	12%	719	46%
TOTAL	199		1569	
COMPOSITE				
Category I		58%		18%
Category II		31%		38%
Category III		11%		44%

The main statistic that Table I is intended to
highlight is the discrepancy that exists between Cate-
gories I and III regarding their respective percentages
of the romance's total number of rhyme elements and
total number of lines. The fact that almost 60% of
the total number of rhyme sounds employed in King Horn
are confined to less than 20% of its lines suggests
that the remaining 80% of the poem may be far less
varied in this respect than could be indicated by an
overall average. From this observation about the "re-
petitiousness" of rhyme sounds in King Horn, we can move
to the question of its systematic rhyming vocabulary for
each of these limited number of sounds.

It is in our first three appendices that we actu-
ally survey the total rhyming vocabulary used in each
version of King Horn in order to determine any recurr-
ences of rhyme words for every rhyme sound. The rhyme
words that comprise the non-recurrent rhyme sounds in
each manuscript of King Horn are all listed in Category
I of the appropriate appendix. But this category proved
to be of no relevance to our proposed theory.[5] On the
one hand, the lack of recurrence of these rhyme elements
in Category I makes it quite impossible to discern any
clear repetition of a rhyming vocabulary within them.
On the other hand, this category's lack of evidence
that would support our theory need not be interpreted
as evidence that contradicts it. We simply need to
acknowledge that approximately 20% of each manuscript
cannot be subjected to an inductive analysis of rhyme
word recurrence--and, therefore, this 20% of the romance
can give no indication of its jongleur's systematically
improvised performance. Although it is true that the
Category I entries do indicate a certain variety of
rhyme sounds in King Horn, and that such (limited)
variety may be considered at odds with the rigorous
repetition normally associated with formulaic composi-
tion, there is--because there can be--no real evidence
for a lack of repetitiousness in the rhyming vocabulary
of Category I. Our study focuses, however, on that 80%
of each manuscript of King Horn in which rhyme word
repetitions might be discerned within significant rhyme
sound recurrences.

By sorting all the rhyme words used in each of the
romance's three manuscripts into clusters according to
their common rhyme elements (sound), we have sought to
discern any patterns of repetition in King Horn's
rhyming vocabulary which may have comprised its jong-
leur's improvisational system. Our intent was to dis-
cover the minimum number of words employed to complete

a maximum number of couplets within each of these clusters. In Table II, which follows, we list the actual rhyme words that may have provided the jongleur of King Horn with a readily recalled system for improvising its couplets.

Again, it should be noted that all data given below has been extracted from the more detailed, individual analyses of each cluster in Categories II and III of Appendices A through C. To check the accuracy or rationale for any statistic given below, reference may be readily made to the appropriate rhyme element of the appropriate category for the appropriate manuscript. In Table II, we list our findings for each manuscript in parallel columns. The rhyme elements of Category II are presented first--in alphabetical order--and then those of Category III. Occasionally, a specific rhyme element will appear as a Category II entry for one or two of the manuscripts, but as a Category III entry for the other(s). Such instances will be cross-referenced. A few rhyme elements simply have no parallel in one or both of the other two manuscripts.[4]

We have adopted the term subgroup to designate the rhyme words of each cluster that the jongleur seems to have used systematically to complete a majority of its couplets; according to our theory, these subgroups should be relatively small subsets of the actual rhyming vocabulary used in their respective clusters.[5] The heading "SG/11" below indicates the ratio between the size of each subgroup (i.e, the total number of words that need to be recalled) and the size of its own cluster (i.e., its number of lines--a figure that determines the cluster's hypothetical maximum variety of vocabulary). The smaller the ratio indicated by "SG/11," the more convincing--we argue--is its usefullness as an improvisational system.

Under "VOCAB" below are listed the words themselves that comprise each subgroup.[6] Following each of these listings, a percentage is given parenthetically. This figure indicates the ratio between the number of couplets in each cluster that actually employ the subgroup's vocabulary--systematic end-rhyme as proposed by our theory--and the total number of couplets in that same cluster. And the higher this percentage, the more convincing--we argue--is the evidence that King Horn's jongleur actually employed such a system of repetitive end-rhymes to improvise his performance. In other words, if there is anything "oral" about the extant manuscripts of King Horn, we believe it must be induced from the following data.

TABLE II

Category II

Rhyme Element	MS. C SG/11.	MS. C VOCAB.	MS. L SG/11.	MS. L VOCAB.	MS. O SG/11.	MS. O VOCAB.
ADDE	1/8	HADDE (100)	- - -	- - -	1/8	HADDE (100)
ADE	- - -	- - -	1/6	MADE (100)	- - -	- - -
AGE	6/6	∅	6/6	∅	6/6	∅
AKE	2/14	TAKE, SAKE (86)	2/14	TAKE, MAKE (86)	3/18	TAKE, rake forsake (100)
ARE	2/10	ƷARE, AYLMARE (100)	2/6	BARE/YFARE (67)	- - -	- - -
ASTE	2/8	CASTE, LASTE (100)	1/6	CASTE (100)	1/6	CASTE (67)
AUCTE	- - -	- - -	- - -	- - -	1/6	LAUCTE (100)
AWE	2/10	DRAƷE, FELAƷE (100)	3/18	FELAWE, DRAWE, slawe (100)	2/12	DRAWE, FELAWE (100)
AY	3/8	LAY, DAY/MAY (100)	2/14	DAY (/may), lay (100)	1/6	DAY (67)
AYLE	- - -	- - -	- - -	- - -	1/8	FAYLE (100)
E	- - -	- - -	1/10	BE (80)	- - -	- - -
ECHE	2/16	SPECHE, RECHE (100)	1/16	SPECHE (88)	- - -	Cf. III
EDDE	1/8	BEDDE (100)	2/10	BEDDE, SHREDDE (80)	2/8	BEDDE, SCHREDDE (100)
EIDE	1/10	SEIDE (80)	- - -	- - -	1/12	SEYDE (100)
ELLE	2/12	TELLE, FELLE (66)	2/12	TELLE (/spelle), felle (84)	2/10	FELLE, TEELE (100)
EN	6/6	∅	- - -	- - -	- - -	- - -

54

Rhyme Element	MS. C SG/11.	MS. C VOCAB.	MS. L SG/11.	MS. L VOCAB.	MS. O SG/11.	MS. O VOCAB.
ENCHE	2/10	BENCHE, ADRENCHE (100)	2/10	BENCHE, adrench (100)	2/10	BENCHE, DRENCHE (100)
ENDE	3/16	WENDE, ende, sende (100)	3/18	WENDE, SENDE, hende (100)		Cf. III
ENE	4/18	KENE, bene, quene, isene (100)	3/16	KENE, quene/bene (88)		Cf. III
ENNE	1/10	SUDDENNE (100)	2/16	KENNE, SUDENNE (100)	2/16	SODENNE, MENNE (100)
ENTE	2/14	WENTE, SENTE (100)	---	---	2/10	WENTE, SENTE (80)
ERDE	1/10	HERDE (60)	5/8	YHERDE, ONSUERDE, SUERDE (100)	1/8	HERDE (75)
EREN	---	---	---	---	1/8	FEREN (75)
ERIE	---	---	2/6	WERIE, DERYE (100)	---	---
ERNE	1/6	ƷERNE (100)	1/8	WERNE (100)		Cf. III
ERTE	2/6	HERTE/SMERTE (100)	---	---	---	---
ERVE	1/6	SERUE (100)	---	---	---	---
ESSE	2/18	WESTERNESSE, blesse (100)		Cf. III	2/14	WESTNESSE, estnesse (85)
ETE	2/10	SWETE, LETE (80)	3/12	LETE, SUETE, mete (100)	2/12	LETE, SWETE (83)

55

Rhyme Element	MS. C SG/11.	VOCAB.	MS. L SG/11.	VOCAB.	MS. O SG/11.	VOCAB.
ETTE	2/10	SETTE, grette (100)	2/12	SETTE, GRETTE (100)	3/10	SETTE, GRETTE, FLETTE, (100)
EVE	2/8	BILEUE, LEUE (100)	3/6	BILEUE, LEUE, EUE (100)	1/8	LEUE (100)
EWE	4/18	TREWE, fewe, schewe, newe (100)	2/14	TREWE, knewe (71)	3/18	TREWE, hewe, rewe (88)
EƷE	---	---	6/6	Ø	---	---
ICHE	1/6	ILICHE (100)	1/8	YLICHE (100)	1/8	YLICHE (100)
IE	12/12	Ø	---	---	---	---
IGGE	---	---	---	---	2/10	LEGGE, BRIGGE (80)
IƷE	2/8	ISIƷE, IƷE (100)	---	---	---	---
IƷTE	---	---	---	---	4/18	NIƷTE, KNYƷTE FYƷTE, ryƷte (100)
IHT	---	---	2/8	KNYHT, NYHT (100)	---	---
IKE	1/6	LIKE (100)	---	---	---	---
ILD	---	cf. III	1/16	CHILD (75)	---	---
ILDE	---	---	---	---	1/6	CHILDE (67)
ILE	2/10	WHILE, MILE (100)	2/10	WHILE,GYLE (100)	2/10	GILE, WILE (100)
ILLE	2/18	WILLE, STILLE (100)	2/18	WILLE, STILLE (100)	2/18	WILLE, STILLE (89)

Rhyme Element	MS. C SG/11	MS. C VOCAB.	MS. L SG/11	MS. L VOCAB.	MS. O SG/11	MS. O VOCAB.
IME	2/8	TIME, RIME (100)	2/8	TIME, RYME (100)	2/6	RIME, TYME (100)
IN	6/6	Ø	---	---	---	---
INE	1/12	ÐINE (67)	2/12	PYNE, ÐYNE (67)	1/6	PYNE (67)
INKE	1/8	DRINKE (100)	1/8	DRYNKE (100)	2/6	DRINKE/ÐINKE (100)
INNE	2/14	INNE, WINNE (100)	2/16	WYNNE, INNE (100)	1/6	Cf. III
IS	1/6	YWIS (67)	---	---	1/6	YWIS (100)
ISE	2/10	WISE, arise (100)	2/8	WYSE, ARYSE (100)	2/6	WISE, RYSE (100)
ISSE	1/10	WISSE (100)	1/10	WISSE (100)	2/12	WISSE, BLISSE (83)
ISTE	1/10	WISTE (100)	2/10	WISTE, LISTE (100)	2/8	LYSTE, WISTE (100)
IÞE	2/18	BLIÞE, SWIÞE (89)	2/18	BLIÞE, SWYÞE (100)	2/18	BLIÞE, SWIÞE (100)
ITTE	1/8	SITTE (75)	---		---	---
O	3/16	WO, ÐO, do (88)	---	Cf. III	4/16	WO, ÐO, go, do (100)
ODE	2/16	GODE, blode (87)	2/16	GODE, blode (100)	2/16	GODE, blode (100)
OF	2/6	ÐEOF/LEOF (67)	---	---	---	---
OFTE	2/6	OFTE, SOFTE (100)	2/6	OFTE, SOFTE (100)	---	---
OHTE		Cf. OЗTE III	3/12	ÐOHTE, wrohte, sohte (100)	---	---

Rhyme Element	MS. C SG/11	MS. C VOCAB.	MS. L SG/11	MS. L VOCAB.	MS. O SG/11	MS. O VOCAB.
OKE	2/8	LOKE, TOKE (100)	1/6	TOKE (loke) (100)	1/6	LOKE (/toke) (100)
OLDE	3/18	WOLDE, holde, golde (100)	4/18	HOLDE, GOLDE, WOLDE, sholde (100)		cf. III
OME	---	---	1/6	COME (100)	---	---
ON	---	---	2/18	GON, ON (89)	3/12	GON, ON, SLON (100)
OND	---	---	1/12	LOND (83)	---	---
ONNE	---	---	1/6	SONNE (100)	1/6	SONNE (100)
ORDE	1/8	BORDE (100)	2/8	BORDE, WORDE (100)	1/6	BORDE (100)
ORE	3/14	MORE, SORE, lore (100)	3/16	SORE, MORE, lore (88)	3/16	MORE, SORE, lore (75)
ORN	1/16	HORN (88)	1/8	HORN (100)	1/12	HORN (83)
ORWE	---	---	---	---	2/6	SORWE/AMORWE (100)
ODE	3/8	CLODE, LODE, WRODE (100)	3/10	ODE, LODE, WRODE (100)	3/10	BODE, CLODE, WRODE (100)
ODER	1/10	ODER (100)	1/10	ODER (100)	1/8	ODER (100)
OUNDE		Cf. III		Cf. III	1/12	STOUNDE (83)
OUNE		Cf. UNE II	2/12	TOUNE, doune (100)	1/8	TOUNE (75)
OURE		Cf. III	1/16	BOURE (100)		Cf. III
OUTE	1/6	ABUTE (100)	1/8	ABOUTE (100)	2/18	ABOUTE, BOUTE (100)

Rhyme Element	MS. C SG/11.	MS. C VOCAB.	MS. L SG/11.	MS. L VOCAB.	MS. O SG/11.	MS. O VOCAB.
OUTER	---	---	---	---	1/6	DOUTER (100)
OWEN	---	---	2/6	FLOWEN/ROWEN (100)	---	---
OWTE	---	---	---	---	1/6	BROWTE (100)
UGGE	---	---	6/6	Ø	---	---
ULLE	1/6	SCHULLE (67)	---	---	---	---
UNDE	---	---	---	---	1/8	GRUNDE (100)
UNDER	1/6	WUNDER (100)	---	---	---	---
UNE	2/10	CRUNE, DUNE (100)		Cf. OUNE II		Cf. OUNE II
UNNE	2/8	SUNNE, CUNNE (100)	---	---	---	---
URNE	1/8	TURNE (75)	1/6	TURNE (67)	---	---
URSTE	1/6	FURSTE (100)	---	---	1/6	furste (100)
USTE	2/6	CUSTE, LUSTE (100)	---	---	2/6	KUSTE, LUSTE (100)

59

Category III

Rhyme Element	SG/11.	MS. C VOCAB.	SG/11.	MS. L VOCAB.	SG/11.	MS. O VOCAB.
ALLE	3/26	HALLE, ALLE, bifalle (100)	2/28	HALLE, ALLE (100)	3/28	HALLE, ALLE, FALLE (93)
ECHE		Cf. II		Cf. II	4/20	SPECHE, TECHE, seche, reche (100)
EDE	4/34	LEDE, REDE, STEDE, SPEDE (77)	7/24	STEDE, REDE, SPEDE, lede, dede, nede, mede (92)	6/32	LEDE, REDE, STEDE, MAKEDE, mede, bede (100)
EIE	5/26	TWEIE, PLEIE, DEIE, weie, preie (100)	5/22	TUEYE, WEYE, PLEYE, preye, leye (100)	3/24	TWEYE, deye, seye (83)
ELDE	4/22	FELDE, HELDE, SCHELDE, welde (100)	4/20	FELDE, SHELDE, welde, helde (100)	3/22	FELDE, SCHELDE, HELDE (100)
ENDE		Cf. II		Cf. II	3/37	WENDE, HENDE, kende (94)
ENE		Cf. II		Cf. II	5/20	KENE, BENE, QUENE, schene, tene (100)
ERE	9/76	WERE, BERE, FERE, DERE, here, here, stere, swere, mestere (93)	9/72	WERE, FERE, BERE, dere, here, here, suere, chere, mestere (93)	9/69	BERE, WERE, DERE, HERE, FERE, here, swere, bere, mestere (95)

60

Rhyme Element	MS. C SG/11.	MS. C VOCAB.	MS. L SG/11.	MS. L VOCAB.	MS. O SG/11.	MS. O VOCAB.
ERNE		Cf. II		Cf. II	3/20	WERNE, ƷERNE, STERNE (100)
ESSE		Cf. II	2/20	WESTNESSE, blesse (100)		Cf. II
ESTE	4/30	BESTE, FESTE, WESTE, leste (100)	5/36	BESTE, WESTE, leste, reste, feste (/geste) (100)	3/32	BESTE, FESTE, reste (94)
ICTE	5/56	KNIƷTE, RIƷTE, NIƷTE, fiƷte, liƷte (100)	8/42	MIHTE, KNYHTE, RYHTE, nyhte, fyhte, bryhte, syhte, plyhte (100)	4/26	KNICTE, BRICTE (/ricte), micte, wihte (100)
IDE	4/30	RIDE, SIDE, TIDE, abide (100)	4/34	SIDE, RIDE, tide, abide (100)	4/34	SIDE, RIDE, tide, abide (100)
ILD	3/24	CHILD, wild, fikenhild (92)		Cf. II	3/20	CHILD, wild, fokenyld (90)
ING	---	---	---	---	5/42	KING, dobbing, ring, derling, rysyng (95)
ING(E)	9/86	KINGE, springe, ringe, Rymenhilde singe, bringe, dubbing, derling, þing (100)	9/96	KINGE, Ʒynge, springe, ringe, bringe, singe, bobbyng, derlyng, fysshyng (100)	---	---

Rhyme Element	MS. C		MS. L		MS. O	
	SG/11.	VOCAB.	SG/11.	VOCAB.	SG/11.	VOCAB.
INGE	---	---	---	---	5/46	KINGE, SPRINGE, BRINGE, SINGE, YENGE (96)
INNE	4/30	Cf. II		---	2/20	INNE, WINNE (90)
IVE	4/30	LIUE, ARIUE, wyue, driue (100)	4/34	LYUE, RYUE, DRYUE, WYUE (100)	4/32	LIUE, ARIUE, WIUE, driue (100)
O		Cf. II	6/22	WO, SO, DO, GO, do, to (100)	---	Cf. II
O3TE	4/20	BRO3TE, BO3TE, do3ter, wro3te (100)		Cf. OHTE II	---	---
OLDE		Cf. II		Cf. II	3/20	WOLDE, HOLDE, GOLDE (100)
ONDE	4/64	LONDE, HONDE, fonde, husebonde (100)	5/60	LONDE, HONDE, stonde, strorde, hosebonde (100)	4/63	LONDE, HONDE, stonde, stronde (100)
ONE	6/40	ONE, SONE, done, gon/anon, sone (95)	2/28	ONE, SONE (86)	2/20	SONE, ALONE (100)
ONGE	3/24	FONGE, 3ONGE, LONGE, (100)	4/20	FONGE, LONGE, SONGE, 3onge, (100)	4/32	FONGE, LONGE, SONGE, YONGE (100)

62

Rhyme Element	MS. C SG/11	MS. C VOCAB.	MS. L SG/11	MS. L VOCAB.	MS. O SG/11	MS. O VOCAB
(O)UNDE	5/28	GRUNDE, STUNDE, funde, bunde, cunde (100)	3/26	GROUNDE, STOUNDE, FOUNDE (92)		Cf. II
(O)URE	3/26	BURE, ture, ure (93)		Cf. II	3/20	BOURE, toure, houre (100)
OWE	9/48	KNOWE, INOƷE, FLOWE/ROWE, OƷE, PROWE, isoƷe, woƷe, lowe (100)	7/36	YNOWE, DROWE, KNOWE, OWE, BROWE, YSWOWE, lowe (94)	7/40	YNOWE, OWE, ROWE, KNOWE, LOWE, WOWE, howe (100)

63

In the previous chapter, we proposed--in theory--
that for each recurrent rhyme sound in King Horn its
jongleur may have possessed a small number of readily
recalled rhyme words (a subgroup for each cluster) with
which he could maintain the aural form of his extended
narrative (its couplets) during a live performance. We
may now note that all three of the surviving manuscripts
of King Horn--in fact--provide evidence for the workings
of such an improvisational system. Furthermore the
systematic rhyming vocabulary used in all three manu-
scripts seems to be much the same. Of the 116 rhyme
elements listed above, only six give no indication of
such systematic end-rhyme. These "exceptions" are the
AGE, EN, E3E, IE, IN and UGGE clusters. In a comment
following the appropriate appendix entry for each of
these exceptions, we have attempted to provide some
logical explanation (or excuse) for the fact that no
subgroup seems to function as an improvisational aid in
these six clusters. All such explanations proved to be
fundamentally the same; certain rhyme sounds may have
been, by their very nature (i.e., as common suffixes,
participial or gerundive endings, etc.), so readily
available in Middle English that the jongleur did not
also require an improvisational system for their im-
promptu recall.[7] And it might be noted that, of these
six exceptions, only the AGE cluster is common to all
three manuscripts. Nevertheless, we have not excluded
any of these exceptions from our inductive analysis,
since these six clusters do seem to represent evidence
that might contradict our theory (unlike the Category I
entries which simply provide no evidence at all).

In addition to designating what a jongleur's
systematic vocabulary of rhyme words may have been dur-
ing the performance of King Horn, Table II makes it
possible to specify some numerical values for the work-
ing of our theory. From the above listings, we can now
determine some meaningful averages: the average size of
a cluster within each category, the average size of
each of these categories' respective subgroups, and--
most significantly--the average percentage of couplets
in each cluster that may be considered systematic.
Since we have had no a priori figures for determining
whether a given cluster's end-rhymes should be con-
sidered more or less improvised, these inductive
statistics would at least provide a method for deter-
mining (in retrospect) each cluster's deviation from
King Horn's norm. They also provide, however, a far
more specific indication of the extent to which a
jongleur's oral performance may have affected the final
form of the three written versions that survive of this

romance.

For each manuscript of <u>King Horn</u>, the average size
of a cluster in each of the three categories may be
easily determined simply by dividing the total number
of lines in that category by its total number of rhyme
elements:

TABLE III

MS.	Category	Total # of lines	Total # of Clusters	Average Size of Cluster	
				Lines	Couplets
C	I	212	87	2.44	1
	II	628	62	10.13	5
	III	690	18	38.33	19
L	I	320	121	2.64	1
	II	606	56	10.82	5
	III	620	17	36.47	18
O	I	314	122	2.57	1
	II	536	54	9.93	5
	III	719	23	31.26	16

Similarly, the average size of a subgroup in Categories
II and III of each manuscript may be discerned by divid-
ing the total number of words employed in all their
respective subgroups by the number of these subgroups
themselves:

TABLE IV

MS.	Category	Percent of MS.	Average Size of Subgroup Number of Words
C	II	41%	2.15
	III	45%	4.89
	Composite[8]	86%	2.76
L	II	39%	2.09
	III	40%	5.06
	Composite	79%	2.78
O	II	34%	1.80
	III	46%	4.00
	Composite	80%	2.45

Of course, the actual number of words employed in any subgroup must be a positive integer. And it seems sufficiently accurate to observe that a jongleur's subgroup for any recurrent rhyme sound in King Horn would average from two to five words--a readily recalled system of repetitive end-rhymes.

In themselves, these averages may seem merely curious--if not completely tedious. These averages do, however, provide a far more accurate indication of King Horn's repetitiveness in the use of end-rhyme than did the "overall averages" with which we began this chapter. We believe, furthermore, that only an analysis of these averages of Horn's clusters and subgroups according to category will demonstrate conclusively that the three primary requirements of our theory about a medieval jongleur's systematic use of end-rhyme have been satisfied:

-First, that the subgroups themselves are sufficiently small, relative to the total size of their respective clusters, to be considered an improvisationally useful system.

-Second, that the subgroups themselves account for a sufficiently large number of couplets within their respective clusters.

-And, finally, that these clusters, in turn,
account for a sufficiently large percentage of
each manuscript in its entirety.

In order to discover what percentage of King
Horn's couplets may actually be considered improvised
according to our proposed theory, we need to discern
from our data how many couplets in each manuscript do
indeed employ the systematic rhyme words which comprise
each cluster's subgroup. We can determine what per-
centage of Categories II and III are so improvised sim-
ply by dividing the sum of the percentages given
parenthetically in Table II under "VOCAB" by the total
number of clusters listed in each category:

TABLE V

MS.	Category	Avg. % of Couplets that use systematic rhyme words
C	II	88%
	III	97%
L	II	88%
	III	97%
O	II	92%
	III	97%

Table V indicates the jongleurs' extraordinarily con-
sistent use of a systematic rhyming vocabulary to im-
provise King Horn's couplets--but only for those rhyme
sounds that recur in three or more couplets of each
manuscript. Composite percentages of the total number
of these couplets in each manuscript that employ re-
current rhyme sounds may be obtained by averaging Cate-
gories II and III together; we might argue, therefore,
that a jongleur actually improvised 93% of these coup-
lets in manuscripts C and L, and 94% of them in manu-
script O. It is worthwhile to note the statistical
similiarity of this evidence for improvised performance
among the three manuscripts--whatever their textual
differences, they seem to have been performed with
exactly the same improvisational method. But the fact

67

that the evidence for systematic rhyme word repetition
increases with rhyme sound recurrence should also be
noted.

In order to determine what percentage of each en-
tire manuscript of King Horn should be considered
demonstrably improvised according to our proposed theory,
we must refigure the Category I entries into our sta-
tistics. The composite percentages that we extracted
from Table V to indicate the pervasiveness of a jong-
leur's improvisation must be adjusted to account for the
whole of each version of the romance. This adjustment
can be easily made by multiplying the composite percen-
tages of couplets that use systematic rhyme in Categor-
ies II and III by the percentage of each manuscript's
total number of lines contained in these two categories
(listed in Table IV). Thus, we conclude that 80% of
manuscript C in its entirety is demonstrably systematic
in its use of end-rhymes for the sake of oral improvi-
sation, as is 73% of manuscript L, as is 75% of manu-
script O.

It seems appropriate that manuscript C, apparently
the oldest record of King Horn (itself probably the
oldest extant Middle English romance), might also prove
to be the most faithful transcription of a jongleur's
actual performance. But we consider our statistics
sufficient to support our initial hypothesis that all
three manuscripts of this romance represent as many
written records of oral improvisation.

We hesitate to assert that many of the discrepan-
cies noted among the three manuscripts of King Horn
should not still be attributed to scribal error rather
than to the effects of oral improvisation. Nor, how-
ever, do we believe that a jongleur improvised only
80% of his performance. We simply concede that, at
most, only 80% of King Horn's text is demonstrably
improvised. We reiterate that the evidence for
systematic rhyme word repetitions improves with rhyme
sound recurrence, and that there is merely insufficient
data to induce the operability of this same improvisa-
tional method among the couplets that comprise King
Horn's Category I entries.

ii. By our statistical analyses, we hope to have pro-
ven empirically the validity of our basic theory--that
a medieval jongleur used systematic end-rhyme with
remarkable consistency to improvise his performance of
a romance's couplets. But we do not believe that a
jongleur's performance depended on this system exclu-

68

sively. Novel rhyme-links might be recalled or invented
during his performance; and a jongleur's non-systematic
end-rhymes were probably appreciated as part of his
skill as well. Variety, after all, was not distasteful
--just extremely difficult and rare. Furthermore, the
systematic rhyming vocabulary which we have proposed as
a jongleur's primary improvisational device was, no
doubt, supplemented by the recurrent use of easily re-
collected phrases. Nevertheless, these recurrent
phrases did not in themselves provide the jongleur with
an adequate improvisational method for the oral per-
formance of King Horn. Their statistical inadequacy
as oral formulae has already been argued by numerous
scholars; furthermore, Laura Hibbard Loomis has shown
that they are not necessarily "oral." In the preceding
section of this chapter, we rejected the formulaic
nature of King Horn's "tag-lines" on theoretical grounds.
But we will conclude this chapter with a reconsideration
of the romance's repetitive phrasing in order to demon-
strate that these recurrent lines were a by-product
of the jongleur's systematic end-rhymes and not--as
A. C. Baugh suggested--vice versa.

For the sake of simplicity, we will focus on only
the most "oral" version of King Horn--MS. C. We have
already argued that a "tag-line" would not in itself
complete King Horn's formal unit, the indivisable coup-
let, except in so far as the line provides an improvised
match for the conjoining end-rhyme. If these lines re-
cur, their end-rhymes repeat, and all such "tag-lines"
have already been absorbed into our system as a rela-
tively small subset of the systematic rhymes themselves.
Such individual "tag-lines" merely alleviate a jong-
leur's difficulty in recalling or improvising the phras-
ing that leads to his end-rhymes; they do not provide
a substantially different method of oral improvisation,
since the end-rhyme itself remains the key connective
in such couplets.

But there are numerous instances in King Horn
of the fact that its jongleur apparently enhanced his
primary improvisational system by recurrently conjoin-
ing "tag-lines" with one another. A modification of
A. C. Baugh's original questions about the extent to
which such recurrent phrasing may be considered formu-
laic remains valid in terms of these "tag-couplets."
Even according to our theory, these recurrently con-
joined lines do, after all, provide a repetitive pattern
of fixed phrases that satisfy in themselves the formal
demands of a jongleur's oral performance--the couplets.
Such "tag-couplets" also seem to support a straight-

69

forward analogy between a jongleur's improvisation of a
medieval romance and the formulaic model of Old English
or Homeric verse.

In order to demonstrate that a jongleur's system of
repetitive end-rhymes may have generated a supplementary
improvisational system—that is, the recurrent linking
certain repetitive phrases--we have attempted to extract
all such recurrent "tag-couplets" from MS. C of King
Horn. In TABLE VI below, we have listed the line num-
bers of such recurrent couplets. But in the overwhelm-
ing majority of these couplets, we discovered that one,
if not both, of the rhyme words used is also what we
have designated a systematic rhyme-word, a member of its
cluster's subgroup. We have arranged the "tag-couplets"
of MS. C in TABLE VI alphabetically according to the
rhyme elements of their respective rhyme words. We have
underlined those words that belong to each cluster's
subgroup as listed in TABLE II above:

TABLE VI

hadde/ladde: 19-20; 1045-6

halle/alle: 71-2; 223-4; 255-6; 625-6; 893-4

halle/falle: 779-80; 1221-2

halle/walle: 1041-2; 1383-4

ȝare/ifare: 467-8; 1355-6

þare/Aylmare: 505-6; 1493-4

draȝe/felaȝes: 1289-90; 1419-20

day/may: 29-30; 727-28

bischee/speche: 453-4; 579-80

bedde/wedde: 299-300; 949-501

shelde/felde: 53-4; 513-4; 557-8; 1301-2

Suddenne/kenne: 143-4; 175-6; 985-6; 1517-8

hende/wende: 371-2; 1117-8

wende/ende: 911-2; 1211-2

70

wende/shende: 679-80; 1401-2

sente/wente: 525-6; 919-20; 1337-8

þere/ȝere: 523-4; 731-2; 917-8; 1139-40

were/þere: 297-8; 765-6; 1167-8; 1245-6; 1353-4

ȝerne/werne: 915-6; 1085-6; 1403-4

herte/smerte: 875-6; 1389-90; 1481-2

serve/sterve: 775-6; 909-10

feste/geste: 477-8; 521-2; 1217-8

pleie/tweie: 23-4; 345-6

tweie/deie: 887-8; 1345-6

side/ride: 32-3; 135-6

iliche/riche: 313-4; 339-40

iȝe/ isiȝe: 755-6; 975-6

child/mild: 79-80; 159-60

child/wild: 251-2; 295-6

stille/wille: 287-8; 541-2; 999-1000

wille/telle: 365-6; 943-4

pine/þine: 635-6; 539-40

ringe/rymenhilde: 613-4; 873-4; 1483-4

springe/kinge: 211-2; 495-6; 1427-8

drinke/think: 971-2; 1055-6; 1151-2

winne/inne: 603-4; 1071-2; 1357-8

wise/servise: 237-8; 989-90

wisse/misse: 121-2; 1457-8

kniȝte/ miȝte: 435-6; 935-6

niȝte/ miȝte: 123-4; 1199-1200
71

kniȝte/niȝte: 447-8; 491-2

bliþe/siþe: 355-6; 1347-8

swiþe/bliþe: 273-4; 791-2; 1225-6

sitte/witte: 651-2; 1083-4

live/wive: 559-60; 693-4

flode/gode: 139-40; 1183-4

soȝte/broȝte: 39-40; 465-6; 599-600

toke/loke: 1099-1100; 1141-2

wolde/golde: 1037-8; 1163-4

anon/gon: 45-6; 285-6; 1231-2; 1351-2

stronde/londe: 35-6; 125-6

sonde/londe: 809-10; 933-4; 1179-80

honde/londe: 59-60; 81-2; 215-16; 1109-10; 1299-
           1300; 1327-8; 1413-4

honde/stronde: 111-2; 1137-8; 1499-1500

fonge/longe: 719-20; 737-8

borde/worde: 113-4; 253-4; 827-8

sore/more: 69-70; 1193-4

Horn/born: 9-10; 137-8; 509-10

Horn/unorn: 329-30; 1525-6

hote/bote: 201-2; 767-8

oþer/broþer: 283-4; 577-8; 821-2; 1291-2

funde/grunde: 103-4; 133-4

stunde/grunde: 333-4; 739-40; 1159-60

cuppe/þeruppe: 449-50; 1125-6

bure/aventure: 325-6; 649-50; 709-10

turne/murne: 703-4; 963-4

furste/burste: 661-2; 1191-2

Athelbrus/hus: 225-6; 1501-2

It should be noted that the recurrent pairs of syntact-
ically and semantically similar phrases listed above are
not completely interchangeable. Each phrase may occur
in either line of a couplet, but an -adde phrase cannot,
of course, conjoin with an -us line and make a satis-
factory couplet.[9] Nevertheless, these recurrent lines
of King Horn (though restricted by end-rhyme rather than
alliteration) do seem analogous to the half-lines of
Beowulf. And we concede that King Horn's "tag-couplets"
may be formulaic in the broadest possible sense, but
they can hardly be considered formulae proper because,
all together, the above couplets account for only some
348 lines--a mere 22.5% of MS. C's total length.

These "tag-couplets" of King Horn (like Havelok's
conventional rhymes) may be quite common, but they
hardly appear to recur with the regularity that has
normally been attributed to oral composition. Nor do
they seem to provide the jongleur with an improvisational
method that has the same range and dependability of the
end-rhyme system which we have proposed. For example,
the narrative appropriateness of many of these "tag-
couplets" seems far more restricted by their semantic
content than does the remarkably flexible vocabulary
which a jongleur used in his subgroups. But, most
significantly, these "tag-couplets" account for less
than a fourth of MS. C's couplets, whereas improvisa-
tion by means of systematic end-rhyme accounts for more
than three fourths of this romance's total performance.

We have not rejected wholesale A. C. Baugh's theory
that the repetitive phrasing of medieval romance may be
considered an improvisational feature--but it is not
necessarily so. We have reduced such phrasing to secon-
dary status; it seems to have been a supplementary fea-
ture of oral improvisation, but was not the primary
improvisational method itself. Nevertheless, many of
Baugh's ideas about the improvisational functions of
repetitive phrasing during the performance of medieval
romance remain valid. The jongleur used such "tag-
lines" for familiar transitions, conventional epithets,
aphorisms, and sometimes, it seems, just for filler; in
general, they apparently provided the performer with

intermittent opportunities to relax his memory. We concede, however, that the writers of later medieval romances seem to have "relaxed" just as often as the true jongleurs.

In short, A. C. Baugh argued that many of both the formal peculiarities within and the textual variants among medieval romances should be attributed to the effects of oral performance and transmission. Baugh's fundamental insight was challenged because his specific analysis of the jongleur's improvisational method proved to be neither statistically adequate nor necessarily "oral." We conclude, however, that a jongleur's systematic use of end-rhyme is demonstrably both in all three versions of King Horn. In the next chapter, therefore, we will investigate the possible effects of oral improvisation on the transmission of this romance. And we hope, thereby, to revalidate many of the critical implications of Baugh's original theory.

Notes to Chapter V

[1]MS. C seems most "primitive" of the three both pro-
sodically and in Hall's sense that "C seems to have
best preserved the original readings." Joseph Hall,
ed., King Horn (Oxford: Clarendon Univ. Press, 1901),
p. xii.

[2]This "overall average" is attained simply by dividing
the noted total number of rhyme sounds counted for each
MS. into its total number of lines.

[3]We will, however, count the end-rhymes of Category I
in our final estimations of the total number of each
version's lines that seem to be demonstrably improvised.

[4]In the next chapter--which investigates the corres-
pondences that do or do not exist among King Horn's three
MSS.--we will distinguish the peculiar systematic rhymes
of each from their common subgroups. But here we are
discussing only rhyme sounds, not yet rhyme words.

[5]Precisely how "small" will have to be induced empiric-
ally. We will, however, distinguish two different points
of reference for determining the relative size of each
subgroup: both the actual vocab. (the total number of
different rhyme words that are, in fact, recorded in
the clusters of each MS.) and the max. vocab. (the
hypothetical number of different rhyme words that might
have been used in a given number of couplets for the
sake of maximum variety = 2 X # of couplets). When the
size of a subgroup approximates the size of its clus-
ter's actual vocab., we suspect conventional rather
than systematic end-rhyme--as seems to be the case in
Havelok the Dane. Cf. Appendix D.

[6]"VOCAB," thus, represents the jongleur's actual im-
provisational system, according to our theory. These
are the words that fulfill a performer's formal needs
in presenting King Horn from memory, rather than Baugh's
formulaic phrases.

[7]Of particular interest, however, is the fact that the
Category III -ing clusters did not prove to be excep-
tional despite the fact that the participial ending
would seem to provide a very "easy" end-rhyme.

[8] Since the initial distinction between Categories II and III was essentially organizational, we here offer these "composite" statistics in order to suggest the pervasiveness of the system in King Horn as a whole, Again we note that Category I entries will also be accounted for in our final statistics--the persuasiveness of which will thus be slightly diminished--although we still consider these Category I items "irrelevant" to our statistical analysis.

[9] Cf. "Methodlogy." "Near-rhymes" proved to be most problematic in our efforts to sort the rhyme clusters of King Horn. Likewise, if "off-rhymes" are mistakes in terms of a jongleur's performance, their placement in one of two clusters becomes somewhat arbitrary.

CHAPTER VI

ORAL TRANSMISSION: INTERTEXTUAL ANALYSES

i.   In the preceding chapter, we focused on the repetition of end-rhymes within each manuscript of King Horn--considered separately. Although the three extant texts of this romance were studied concurrently, they were not analyzed in terms of one another. Rather, each manuscript of King Horn was considered as a discrete example of the jongleur's improvisational system.

The purpose of this chapter, however, is to analyze both the similarities and the differences among King Horn's three manuscripts as evidence for the theory that they were actually transmitted orally--that is, by means of improvised performance. We do not hope to establish thereby any textual priorities among the three extant manuscripts of King Horn (as editors traditionally have sought to do). On the contrary, we question the entire premise that one manuscript must somehow be a scribal copy of some other written text. We suggest, simply, that certain copies of certain medieval romances--as the more or less accurate records of oral performances--may represent the end-results of such oral transmission. A given manuscript of a romance may, in other words, record a jongleur's actual performance, and the textual variants that exist among a number of such manuscripts may be attributed to the effects of his oral improvisation.

ii. We have already listed (in Table II above) the specific vocabulary used in each manuscript of King Horn for systematic end-rhymes. We considered these subgroups indicative of each manuscript's oral performance. We would now like to highlight the parallels that seem to exist among the three manuscripts' subgroups for each of their common rhyme elements. We will consider the recurrence of such common systematic rhymes indicative of a romance's oral transmission. Our theory has supposed that a jongleur would have memorized such subgroups prior to his actual performance of the romance; he could tap them at need to complete his couplets. We may now attempt to discern what may have been the jongleur's prototypical subgroups for such systematic end-rhyme by extracting those words which have proven common to at least two of the extant records of such performance. This procedure will, of course, tend to simplify the actual complexity and uniqueness of each performance. We will ignore, for example, the distinction between Categories II and III. It must remain highly conjectural that the various performers of King Horn all used one and the same improvisational system of end-rhyme; it is clear that they did not use exactly the same rhyme-words on which that system is demonstrably based in each performance. We can assert with confidence, however, that all three manuscripts of King Horn do share the following subgroups of systematic end-rhymes:

TABLE VII

Recurrent Rhyme Elements Common to Two or More Manuscripts	End-Rhyme Vocabulary Common to Two or More Subgroups of Said Rhyme Elements
ADDE	hadde
AKE	take, sake
ALLE	halle, alle, falle
ASTE	caste
AWE	drawe, felawe
AY	day, may, lay
ECHE	speche, reche
EDDE	bedde, shredde
EDE	lede, rede, stede, spede, mede
EIDE	seide
EIE	tweie, pleie, deie, weie, preie
ELDE	felde, helde, schelde, welde
ELLE	telle, felle
ENCHE	benche, drenche
ENDE	wende, sende, hende

78

ENE	kene, bene, quene
ENNE	Suddenne
ENTE	wente, sente
ERDE	herde
ERE	were, þere, fere, dere, here, here, swere, mestere
ERNE	werne, ȝerne
ESSE	West(er)nesse, blesse
ESTE	beste, feste, weste, leste
ETE	swete, lete
ETTE	sette, grette
EVE	bileue, leue
EWE	trewe
ICHE	iliche
IȜTE	kniȝte, riȝte, lyhte, niȝte, fiȝte, mihte
IDE	ride, side, tide, abide
ILD	child, wild, fikenhild
ILE	wile, gile
ILLE	wille, stille
IME	time, rime
INE	þine, pyne
INGE	kinge, springe, ringe, singe, bringe, dubbing, derling, ȝynge
INKE	drinke
INNE	inne, winne

79

IS	ywis
ISE	wise, rise
ISSE	wisse
ISTE	wiste, liste
IÐE	bliþe, siþe
IVE	liue, ariue, wyue, driue
O	wo, þo, do, go
ODE	gode, blode
OFTE	ofte, softe
OHTE	þoȝte, wrohte
OKE	loke, toke
OLDE	wolde, holde, golde
ON	gon, on
ONDE	londe, honde, stronde, stonde, husebonde
ONE	one, sone
ONGE	fonge, longe, songe, ȝonge
ONNE	sonne
ORDE	borde
ORE	more, sore, lore
ORN	horn
OÐE	cloþe, wroþe, loþe
OÐER	oþer
(O)UNDE	grounde, stounde, founde
(O)UNE	toune, dune

(O)URE	boure, toure, houre
OUTE	aboute
OWE	knowe, inoʒe, lowe, wowe, owe, rowe
URNE	turne
URSTE	furste
USTE	custe, luste

TABLE VII above, thus, offers a hypothetical re-
construction of the rhyme words around which any of
King Horn's various jongleurs might have improvized
his couplets; it, thus, represents what may have been
the jongleur's selections for the systematic rhyming
vocabulary to be used in King Horn--a vocabulary
selected by him prior to his actual performance of the
romance. The minor differences among the three manu-
scripts' actual subgroups, which have been noted in
Table II of the preceding chapter, may be attributed
either to a particular jongleur's own systematic
modifications of this "basic" system or to the im-
promptu modifications of this a priori system that he
spontaneously made during an actual performance.
Nevertheless, we may still theorize that essentially
the same predetermined system of repetitive end-rhymes
assisted any jongleur during every improvised perform-
ance of all three extant versions of King Horn.

Since the dates of King Horn's three manuscripts
range over some fifty years, and since their dialects
differ so markedly, it remains highly unlikely that
they could represent three performances of the romance
by one and the same jongleur. But the basic impro-
visational system of this romance might itself be
transferred--as such--from one jongleur's memory to
another's; the system could be learned not just as
readily, but much more so than the text of the poem
itself. In fact, the more easily remembered subgroups
largely alleviate the jongleur's difficulty in re-
calling his "text" per se.

It is the consistency of certain textual changes
that such oral improvisation should have on the final
transcriptions of King Horn--and not just a scribe's
random modifications--which we will now attempt to
discern. It may be the accuracy of a jongleur's

81

memory--and not of a scribe's eyesight--which best
explains the remarkable similarity of the narrative
contents in King Horn's three manuscripts; the
jongleurs did attempt to recollect the poem itself,
as faithfully as possible. But it may also be the
improvisational leeway permitted to a jongleur (so
that he could complete his specific couplets by means
of the systematic insertion of prefabricated end-
rhymes) which best explains the marked textual dif-
ferences among them.

The numerous variant readings of King Horn's
three manuscripts have already been analyzed exhaust-
ively as scribal modifications by Joseph Hall. In
1901, Hall argued that all three extant copies of King
Horn could be traced independently to a common, original
text "A". He charted their respective textual histories
from this common source as follows:[1]

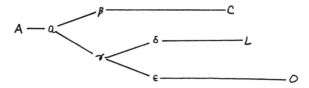

At the time, Hall was specifically attempting to refute
the views of Theodore Wissmann who "thinking that in
certain places L preserves the original against the
consensus of OC, and O likewise against LC, . . . fell
back on a theory of oral transmission which gets no
support from what we know of the history of all other
Middle-English romance texts."[2]

Since the turn of the century, A.C. Baugh, among
others, has provided much supporting evidence for the
theory of a romance's oral transmissions. Neverthe-
less, prior to publication of the major theories about
formulaic composition from which Baugh drew his
analogy for medieval romance, Wissmann could attribute
what seemed textual contaminations among King Horn's
manuscripts to little more than a transmitter's random
lapses of memory. Hall counterargued that it was "The
scribes" who "handled their texts with great freedom
whenever they thought they could improve on the sense
or metre of their original." They frequently failed;
yet, "Using a common stock of tags and conventional
phrases, it is no wonder if two of them now and then

independently hit on similar expressions."[3] We agree,
rather, with Wissmann to the extent that there may be
some wonder as regards these "independent" coinci-
dences--and with Baugh, that there may be some method
among the textual variants fostered by oral trans-
mission.

In the following pages, we will reopen a very old
impasse. As stated, however, we have little interest
in establishing the relative proximity of King Horn's
extant manuscripts to some, lost "original" version of
the romance. According to our theory, such fidelity
might be better discussed as an indication of the
precision of a jongleur's memory during a specific per-
formance. We would like, however, to review Joseph
Hall's evidence for his theory that King Horn's dif-
fering manuscripts represent only various stages in
its scribal transmission from a single written source.

iii. Hall discussed several, different types of
variant passages which may be discovered among the
three manuscripts of King Horn. Hall divided these
discrepancies into the following sorts of categories:

> -"peculiar" lines or couplets that have no
> corresponding statements in one or both of
> the other two manuscripts;
>
> -corresponding lines that have little in
> common;
>
> -parallel passages where the same idea is
> expressed quite differently;
>
> and -corresponding passages that express the same
> idea with only slight variations of phrasing.

Hall considered all of these textual differences at-
tributable to the asystematic modifications of overween-
ing scribes. We, however, suggest that each of these
types of discrepancies among King Horn's three manu-
scripts may be interpreted (at least in part) as
symptomatic of the romance's systematically improvised
oral transmission.

The most common variations noted by Hall and
Wissmann among King Horn's manuscripts--their minor
phrasal differences in expressing the same idea--are,
in fact, too numerous to cite; a thorough review of
such differences would require nothing less than a

detailed comparison of every corresponding line in
each version of the romance.[4] In chapter four,
we attempted such a comparison, but only for the
opening lines of each manuscript; yet, these minor
phrasal differences among parallel ideas in each ver-
sion of King Horn pervade the entire romance. Although
L and C have correspondences not shared by O, as do O
and C when contrasted to L, Joseph Hall argued that
"in the great majority of cases L and O exhibit the
closer resemblance," a fact which implies that "LO
form a manuscript group representing a single MS.γ"
and that the phrasal similarities they share with C
rather than with one another "may often be casual
coincidences."[5]

    We have already argued, however, that such minor
phrasal differences among King Horn's three manu-
scripts may also (if not more probably) have resulted
from the fact that a jongleur did not necessarily
perform fixed lines as such; rather, he improvised
the specific phrasing of his narration while main-
taining his couplets with systematic end-rhymes. Hall
himself acknowledged (and attempted to refute[6]) the
main weakness in his own argument (i.e., that the
minor phrasal discrepancies among King Horn's manu-
scripts should be attributed exclusively to scribal
error). If L and O have a common written source (γ)
different from C's source (β), and if C is closer to
the "original" (A) text of King Horn than any other
extant copy, it seems irrational both that L or O
should have correspondences with C rather than with
each other, and that L or O might preserve an "original"
reading rather than C. Yet, there is evidence for
both of these and apparent non-sequitur's among the
three extant manuscripts of King Horn.

    If we add, however, at least one stage of oral
transmission to Hall's model for the textual trans-
mission of King Horn, many of the seemingly "illogical"
correspondences or divergencies among Horn's three
manuscripts cease to be so problematic. For example,
the jongleurs who performed manuscripts C and O could
have naturally remembered (or reimprovised) an "original"
statement--independently of the jongleur who may have
forgotten (or modified) the same idea in manuscript L.
We do not reject the fundamental validity of Joseph
Hall's textual analyses; there remains a textual tree
to be traced, and manuscripts L and O do indeed seem
"closer" to one another than either does to manuscript
C. But we do not accept Hall's implicit insistance

that <u>every</u> step in the transmission of <u>King Horn</u> must involve a scribal copy of another text without <u>any</u> intermediate oral stages.

Hall seems to have considered his own theory and that of Wissmann (who interpreted some textual variants as a performer's "lapses of memory") to be mutually exclusive concepts. We do not know why. But, in so far as "the burden of proof" rested with Wissmann for his (at the time) novel hypothesis, Hall did succeed in demonstrating that Wissmann's evidence--which argued for <u>King Horn</u>'s oral transmission because L or O occasionally preserved the "original" reading against C--was not compelling. Hall disproved Wissmann's analysis, but he did not thereby truly prove the exclusive validity of his own. We consider these minor textual variants among <u>King Horn</u>'s manuscripts, which Wissmann attributed to a <u>jongleur</u>'s forgetfulness, to be indicative primarily of the same <u>jongleur</u>'s active improvisation. But we cannot—with phrasal variants alone—directly prove our own hypothesis against Hall's evidence either--precisely because the phrasal evidence alone is itself so asystematic.

The fundamental problem in finding a theoretical explanation for these minor phrasal differences is precisely that they are in themselves so completely unpredictable--and, therefore, aesthetically inexplicable. They are more than just misspellings or the garbles normally caused by scribal error. These variants often do seem to have been deliberate "editorial" choices. Nevertheless, there seems to have been no consistent effort on the part of whoever introduced these textual variants towards improving the romance's narrative or meter or, for that matter, its syntax. Phrasal changes simply occur that occasionally improve, frequently deteriorate, but (most often) gratuitously alter what seems to have been an "original" reading. Hall blamed "bad" (i.e., sloppy) scribes. Wissmann blamed "bad" (i.e., forgetful) transmitters. We intend to applaud "good" (i.e., improvising) <u>jongleurs</u>. But, without further evidence, we could argue <u>forever</u> about who bears the burden of proof, or blame.

Further evidence will be sought by a reconsideration of the more substantive variations which Hall noted among <u>King Horn</u>'s three manuscripts; some of these substitutions, insertions, or omissions may prove to be <u>systematic</u> (and as such would be

85

theoretically predictable). If so, the alternative
theories for explaining these more significant
variants among King Horn's manuscripts should prove
to be empirically testable. Both Hall's and Wissmann's
theories predict random substitutions from a stock of
conventional phrases effected by scribes acting as non-
chalant editors. We would also predict some very
specific types of substitutions that would be intro-
duced systematically by the jongleurs as improvising
performers.

In order to demonstrate the (partial) validity of
our own theory about the oral transmission of King
Horn, we will temporarily ignore the scribes' real
significance as textual revisers. In point of fact,
however, we believe that (at separate stages in a
romance's transmission) both oral and written emenda-
tions may have affected each manuscript's final form.
We also concede that the final transcriptions of King
Horn may have been collaborative efforts on the part
of both jongleur and scribe. Furthermore, the two
roles of performer and copyist may have been fulfilled
at times by a single individual. Nevertheless, we
believe we can demonstrate that many of the substantive
textual variants among King Horn's three manuscripts
were generated by the jongleurs' improvisational
system, and that these signs of oral performance
necessarily imply oral transmission at some stage
in the romance's publication.

In addition to the minor phrasal differences which
our theory anticipated and which are everywhere evident
in the three versions of King Horn, transmission of the
romance by means of oral improvisation should also in-
troduce two major sorts of substantive textual variants
when the jongleur's memory failed. The first sort of
significant emendation entails the jongleur's sub-
stitution of one (i.e., systematic) rhyme word for
another, but his preservation of the same couplet-
defining rhyme element; the jongleur would then have
to improvise (i.e., modify) the idea expressed in the
individual line containing the substitute rhyme--
improvisations which often lead to asystematic phrasal
substitutions. The other major type of textual emenda-
tion—which our theory predicts would also be caused by
oral improvisation—entails the insertion, omission, or
substitution of entire couplets.

Our primary interest will be with the jongleur's
systematic substitution of one rhyme word for another

because our system makes the vocabulary of such sub-
stitutions predictable, though we will also consider
what seems to be simple insertions or omissions. We
reiterate Wissmann's opinion that the insertion or
omission of entire passages or the substitution of one
element for another in King Horn might equally well
indicate the quirks of a jongleur's memory as the blinks
of a scribe's eye. But, if King Horn was in fact
orally reproduced at some stage in its transmission,
the jongleurs' substitutions of one rhyme word for
another should also reflect the patterns of sound-
recurrence and of word-recurrence which we designated
in Table VII to have been the "common" improvisational
system of all three performances. The effects of such
systematic improvisation should be discernable as such
in King Horn's three manuscripts, and should indicate
that the jongleur did not merely "carry" the text from
one place to another--either in memory or in hand--he
"reproduced" it.[7] Systematic substitutions argue
against the idea that the scribe alone is to be
"blamed" for all the textual variants among King Horn's
three manuscripts. If a "scribe" should improvise the
final form of a romance systematically, he becomes--by
definition--its "jongleur." In short, there could
still be some validity to the claim that a Middle
English romance might have been orally transmitted
even if the "jongleur" and "scribe" were one and the
same person.

    We are looking, therefore, for the common signs
of a single improvisational system that all three
manuscripts of King Horn might have shared (Table VII)
rather than the more detailed systems peculiar to
each performance (Table II). We have pre-supposed
from the start of this study that at least one written
text of the Middle English romance predates its in-
dividual oral performances. And we hope to have
demonstrated in the preceding chapter that during the
oral performance of King Horn a jongleur's improvisa-
tion affected the final transcription of each version
of this romance--considered separately. At the moment,
however, we may hypothetically diagram the hybrid
(i.e., written/oral) textual history of each of King
Horn's manuscripts only as follows:

DIAGRAM 1

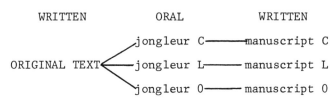

WRITTEN	ORAL	WRITTEN

ORIGINAL TEXT jongleur C——manuscript C
jongleur L——manuscript L
jongleur 0——manuscript 0

Even if fundamentally valid, such a diagram would, of
course, have to be recognized as extremely over-
simplified; multiple stages of both oral and written
transmission probably intervened between the "original"
text and each manuscript. But this diagram might prove
false in a far more significant sense because it gives
no indication of the possibility that oral improvisation
might somehow regenerate an "original" reading as well
as simply distort the text. Diagram I seems to indicate
that oral performance could only diminish the fidelity
of each manuscript (considered separately as an in-
dependent transcription) to the "original" text. The
concept implied by such fidelity remains, therefore,
nothing more than the idea of accuracy (a copyist's
skill) which we have traditionally ascribed to the
scribe himself, and which Wissmann merely attempted
to transfer--however flawed--to the jongleur's memory.
But the theory that several jongleurs using a similar
system improvised each performance of a romance might
also require a radical reappraisal of this concept of
fidelity itself. The performer of a romance might
remain "faithful" to his improvisational system (i.e.,
his predetermined subgroups of rhyme words) even when
his memory of the "text itself" failed. And, to a
certain extent, the multiple choices among the
jongleur's subgroups may have been considered "the
text itself" by the jongleur himself. In other words,
the "text" of a medieval romance, though not so
ephemeral as that associated with oral poetry proper,
may not be so fixed as that associated with a written
(i.e., printed or "edited") composition either. It
may be necessary to acknowledge more than one "original"
reading. Again, we must anticipate the essentially
mixed nature of King Horn's transmission--rather than
just the "transitional" nature of its composition. And
only with this idea of mixed transmission may we review
Joseph Hall's analysis of King Horn's transmission in
terms of its partially "oral" nature.

For example, Hall noted that any two of King Horn's manuscripts might contain correspondent passages omitted by the third. Hall noted that manuscripts L and O have thirty-two passages in common for which there are no parallel statements in manuscript C. If L and O do form a textual group as Hall argued, the pattern of correspondences between them (to the exclusion of C) is indeed thoroughly logical. But Hall was then hard pressed to explain--on the basis of scribal error alone--why manuscripts L and C should have twenty-eight passages in common which are not to be found in O, while manuscripts O and C share twenty-three passages not found in L. So as not to distort or diminish the real-- if partial--validity of Joseph Hall's explanation of these apparently "alogical" correspondences, we give his analysis in full:

There is at first sight no great numerical majority in favour of the combination LO. But the last two results are greatly modified by taking into account the conditions of trans- mission of the manuscripts. O or ϵ is the work of an extremely careless copyist; he leaves out with reason lines corresponding to L 501, L 682, and passages as at L 1247-1250, displaces couplets (comp. L 1109, 1110 with O 383, 384; L 1243, 1244 with O 1048, 1049), repeats words out of preceding lines, as at L 241, O 244, and where the repeated word is initial remodels the passage as at O 473. On the other hand, L often fails to agree with O because it or its predecessor has been carefully edited by a man who aimed at pure rhymes, smooth rhythm, delicacy of expression and consistency of sense. Passages in OC which are corrupt or difficult, like O 268; O 666, O 1311, 1312; O 1362, 1363, are simply omitted by him; defective rhymes are avoided in the same way at O 413, 414; O 553, 554, or by compression of four lines into two, as at O 407-410; O 623-626; considerations of taste dictate the omission of O 225, 226; O 952-955; and having once admitted the couplet L 17, 18, he consistently leaves out the original represented by C 95, 96, which is altered in O 101, 102. Though some deduction must be made from the list of agreements of LO, as at L 405; L 407-410; L 411, 412, where C is manifestly defective, the net result places the combination LO far ahead of the other two in point of numbers. Still more conclusive is a qualitative examination of the passages themselves. The great majority

possessed in common by LC and by OC are beyond
doubt original, that is, descended from α, and
there is not one of them which may not be so,
while a large proportion of those in which LO
agree are plainly later addition. Thus L 17, 18;
L 864; L 1041, 1042; L 1389, 1390; L 1526 are
mere tags; L 75, 76; L 147, 148; L 663, 664;
L 889, 890; L 1143, 1144; L 1183, 1184; L 1305,
1306 are expansions of preceding lines; L 715,
716 is a reminiscence of L 585, 586; L 1313,
1314 is suggested by L 1321. Now it is clear
that while any two of the MSS. may agree in
exhibiting lines derived from the original MS.,
if two or them coincide in a considerable number
of subsequent additions they must have a common
source in some intermediate MS.[8]

In short, if the scribe of 0 omits a passage in LC,
scribal "carelessness" is to blame, but if the scribe
of L omits a passage in OC, Hall attributes this ed-
itorial decision to "taste." Two different scribes
follow two different principles.

    The clear advantage of Wissmann's theory, as a
theory, is that it offered one explanation for these
apparently contradictory types of emendations--forget-
fulness. It is an explanation that our modified theory
of oral improvisation would restate slightly because
some of these variants may have been deliberate emenda-
tions as well as accidental omissions. In either case,
such phrases might have been passed over by the
jongleur rather than by the scribe. And the jongleur's
intent may not have been to improve the "text," nor,
of course, intentionally to corrupt it--but simply to
maintain his oral performance of it. He skipped them
rather than falter.

    In a manner similar to the above reconsideration
of the omissions in each manuscript of King Horn, we
may reevaluate those lines or couplets which are
peculiar to one manuscript and entirely unrepresented
in the romance's other extant versions--these we shall
designate insertions.[9] Hall noted that manuscript L
has only one couplet peculiar to itself and considered
it a scribal correction, "an attempt by the writer
. . . to bring it into better syntactical relation to
the preceding lines."[10] This insertion reads:

            L 267   wiþ horn þat wes so feir & fre
               268   þo hue ne myhte wiþ him be
                        90

Although -E is a recurrent rhyme element (Category II) in manuscript L with "be" as the only entry in its own subgroup of systematic end-rhymes (Table II), and although the improvised nature of this couplet thus indicates its oral performance, we have no further indication from our common stock of predetermined subgroups (Table VII) that this insertion in manuscript L should also be considered indicative of oral transmission. This insertion may have, in other words, been "peculiar" to a single performance of King Horn in much the same way that Hall considered it "peculiar" to a single copyist's transcription of the romance.

But in manuscripts C and O, Hall cites twenty-two other examples of "peculiar" lines or couplets, of which more than half (specifically, twelve) do tap what seems to have been the jongleurs' common improvisational system. In the following quotations, we will underline the systematic rhyme words used in these (improvised) insertions--data which we consider to be indicative of King Horn's oral transmission as well as of each manuscript's oral performance.

Hall listed eleven couplets and one line as peculiar to manuscript O.[11] He considered the following examples to be "lines repeated out of their proper context":

O 123   And all his feren
    124   þat ware him lef and dere*
               (*indicates "off-rhymes")

O 241   To riden wel wit shelde

O 383   And after mete stale
    384   Boþe win and ale

Hall also noted "repetitions in another shape of ideas already expressed":

O 425   Leste me þis sorwe
    426   Lyue hy mawt to morwe

O 1076   From honder chyrche wowe
   1077   þe gan louerd owe

Finally, Hall attributed some of these peculiar insertions in manuscript O to "phrases which form the common stock of romance writers":

    O 491   And sette him on kneuling
      492   And grette wel þe king

The following couplets peculiar to O are cited by Hall without further comment:

    O 373   He wende forþ to horne
      374   Ne wolde sche him werne*

    O 521   And sette on his fotes
      522   Boþe spores and botes

    O 613   Of art londiesse manne
      614   Of sarazine kenne*

    O 724   To boure he gan ȝerne
      725   Burst hym noman werne

    O 1282   And þe king mody
      1283   Hym he made blody

    O 1296   Of horn þat was so hende
      1297   And of reymyld þe ȝonge*

Hall considered none of the above insertions in manuscript O--with the possible exception of lines 425-6--to have been "original." But we would note that, by our theory, at least seven of these twelve "insertions" are not truly "exceptional" either; rather they seem to be "faithful" implementations of the jongleurs' common improvisational method. An additional two couplets (ll. 425-6, 613-4) employ manuscript O's own system of end-rhymes (cf. ENNE, Category II, and ORNE, Category II; Table II). In fact, only two of Hall's examples above need be considered asystematic and, as such either a jongleur's impromptu innovations or a scribe's--with much the same results (for better or for worse).

We will not haggle again with Hall's rationale for the idea that the romance writers might have "a common stock of phrases." Such a debate would only lead once more to A.C. Baugh's theory about formulaic lines. But we would like to highlight two distinct phenomena among these "insertions" in manuscript O, both of which seem more probably to have resulted from oral transmission than from scribal emendation.

92

It should first be noted that four of these
alleged scribal insertions in manuscript O are off-
rhymes; feren/dere; horne/werne; manne/kenne; hende/
ʒonge. It remains quite difficult to understand why
a scribe would insert such mistakes; negligence of
end-rhymes (i.e., their omission) is one thing, but
such prosodic vandalism on the scribe's part seems
quite another. It should also be noted, however, that
each of these couplets entails at least one systematic
end-rhyme. We consider it at least as plausible to
imagine the performaing jongleur--at times struggling
for a particular rhyme sound--to have borrowed a
systematic rhyme word from another rhyme element "near"
to the one he needed (cf. Methodology). By definition,
these unusual combinations would be "insertions" and
indeed "mistakes"--but plausible, as such, during a
live performance; the jongleur "cheated" his rhyme.
These off-rhyme insertions, if generated by a jongleur,
seem the lesser of two evils, mistakes which prevented
a far greater mistake--hesitation during performance.
As Hall himself said, if a scribe, who had the ability
to revise such mistakes, made them anyway, he would
indeed seem "not very intelligent."[12]

We would also like to reconsider what seems to be
manuscript O's unique insertion (rather than omission)
of a single line, "Of wode and of felde." In context,
line 241 reads:

> Stiward haue þou here
> Horn chil fort lere
> Of þine mestere
> Of wode and of felde   241
> To riden wel with shelde
> Tech hime of þe harpe
> Wit his nayles sharpe
> Biforn me forto harpen
> And of þe cuppe seruen
>
> (11. 237-245).

Lire 241 might more properly be considered manuscript O's
expression of an idea paralleled in the other two manu-
scripts, but phrased quite differently (a type of
variant to be considered below)--the distinctions among
Hall's types of variants are sometimes vague. But Hall
is quite correct in observing that the precise state-
ment of line 241 is lacking in the other two versions
of King Horn:

MS. C (ll. 227-232)	MS. L (ll. 232-238)
Stiward, take nu here	stiward tac þou here
Mi fundlyng for to lere	my fundling forto lere
Of þine mestere,	of þine mestere
Of ude & of riuere;	of wode & of ryuere
& tech him to harpe	ant toggen oþ harpe
Wiþ his nayles scharpe,	wiþ is nayles sharpe

Indeed, the additional statement in manuscript O about
Horn's riding well with shield is "not very intelligent."
In context, the King is telling Athelbrus to instruct
Horn in certain domestic (i.e., non-combative) skills,
including music and carving (at table, that is, not
other knights). Mysterium, in fact, could have
particularly "bourgeois," or guild-oriented connota-
tions. Nevertheless, manuscript O would have Child
Horn pricking o'er the plain. But in addition to
manuscript O's insertion of a gratuitous (if not
tonally alogical) idea, we would like to consider
the significance the end-rhyme substitution which
precedes this insertion--that is, manuscript O's
"felde" instead of "rivere" as found in the other two
manuscripts.

Since manuscript O's "felde" seems to be an
"original" reading, we would like to note that it is
both a systematic and common substitution; as is the
insertion, shelde (cf. ELDE, Table II); Ryvere, how-
ever, is not, though mestere is. Similarly, in the
preceding couplet, here is systematic and common, but
lere is not (cf. ERE, Table II). In other words, the
variant reading "felde" in manuscript O might as
readily have been effected by a jongleur's improvisa-
tion as by a scribe's revision. We can imagine that
the performer of manuscript O, having completed the
here/lere couplets, attempted to recall the next
couplet. He concluded his first line with mestere,
a systematic rhyme word from the same cluster of the
preceding couplet. But then the jongleur (perhaps
having already begun the next line) forgot the non-
systematic rhyme word rivere. So he abandoned the
-ere "triplet," considered his "wode-and- ? " (tag-)
phrase, added the conventional "of felde," was forced
to improvise the (alogical) verb, "to riden," and
systematically completed the couplet with shelde.
In other words, the here/lere/mestere sequence in manu-
script O might have been its jongleur's failure to
perform a double couplet (which is completed

successfully in the other two manuscripts), rather
than a scribe's deliberate reduction of the sequence
to a triplet.[13] It should also be noted that, as a
result of this rhyme substitution in manuscript O, the
prepositional phrases seem no longer to modify the
"mestere" of the preceding couplet, but to have become
adverbial, modifying "To riden" in their own couplet.
The "of felde" and "wit shelde" phrases, thus, seem to
have been conjoined syntactically as well as phonically
as if the rhymes themselves were indeed chosen together.
In short, we consider line 241 in manuscript O to be an
example of an oral performer's systematic substitution
rather than of a scribe's random insertion. The very
fact that this "change" in manuscript O is none too
logical seems to indicate a forced improvisation rather
than a (curiously sloppy) revision. The question be-
comes how often do such systematic substitutions recur
in King Horn's manuscripts.

Before considering other examples of such system-
atic substitutions in King Horn (the recurrence of
which we consider to be clearly indicative of the
romance's oral transmission), we may quickly review
the lines and couplets (i.e., the "insertions") that
are peculiar to manuscript C. Hall records nine such
couplets and one line. Again, we have underlined the
end-rhymes among them that are both systematic and com-
mon. Again, more than half of these variants (five,
or 56%) may thereby be explained as having been im-
provised systematically during oral transmission.

Hall considers only one of the couplets and a
single line, which are peculiar to manuscript C, to
preserve the "original" reading of King Horn:

C 379   Horn in herte leide
  380   Al þat he hime seide

C [875   He smot him þurey þe herte,]
  876   þat sore him gan to smerte;

Rather than "original," our theory would suggest that
seide is both common and systematic. Smerte is not.
We might note, however, that the other two manuscripts
pair smerte with an off-rhyme, "furste," instead of
with manuscript C's peculiar though exact herte. If
we consult Table II in the preceding chapter, we may
note that the herte/smerte link seems to be systematic,
but only in the performance of manuscript C. Since the
performers of manuscripts L and O do not seem to have

95

had this "matched pair" at their disposal, the
"original" couplet did not transmit as such. Instead,
the jongleurs of L and O apparently substituted the
off-rhyme furste which is both systematic and common
to manuscripts L and O (though not shared by C). Again,
we suggest that line 876 in manuscript C--which seems
at first an insertion and which Hall considered
"original" (and, as such, a scribal omission in the
other two manuscripts)--may just as readily be inter-
preted as a jongleur's systematic substitution-- a
"substitution" effected not in C, but in L and O.

Hall also noted that the following couplets
peculiar to manuscript C were--whether "later additions"
or "doubtful"--not to be considered "original":

C 879	Horn & his compaynge
880	Gunne after hem wel swiþe hiʒe
C 1065	He maded him vn bicomelich,
1066	Hes he nas neuremore ilich.
C 1113	Bute horn alone
1114	Nadde þerof no mone.
C 1265	Ine seie hit for no blame,
1266	Horn is mi name.
C 1439	Rymenhild litel weneþ heo
1440	þat horn þanne aliue beo.
C 361	To wude for to pleie:
362	Nis non þat him biwreie.
C 1103	'Ine may no leng hure kepe,
1104	For foreʒe nu y wepe.
C 1435	Er þane horn hit wiste,
1436	Tofore þe sunne vpriste,

We would note, however, that at least four of these
"doubtful" insertions may be considered both systematic
and common substitutions by a jongleur. And, as such,
they seem completely "original"in terms of oral trans-
mission, though they do not preserve the specific
reading of a first copy or even of a prior transcrip-
tion of another oral performance. Of the remaining
four insertions, three employ Category I rhyme elements
of manuscript C. As a result of their insufficient
recurrence, it is impossible to deduce whether they

96

too might be systematic repetitions of rhyme words according to our established criteria. But the -AME, -EO, -EPE entries in Appendix A Category I do suggest a jongleur's potentially systematic insertions of the couplets using name, beo and wepe above. If so, they would be improvisations peculiar to a specific performer, rather than apparently common substitutions (like the four examples above) in King Horn's performance. But it remains arguable that seven of the eight insertions in manuscript C, which Hall considered "doubtful," may be attributed to a jongleur's doing.

Only the compaynye/hiʒe insertion in manuscript C seems completely asystematic and, therefore, somewhat inexplicable as a jongleur's improvised modification. But, as noted in the IʒE entry of Appendix A (Category II), this cluster is itself quite asystematic, or "exceptional," in manuscript C--most probably because the strong assonances which comprise this "rhyme" cluster are themselves so readily available in English. We anticipated that such "exceptions" might in fact be a deliberate part of the jongleur's performance--an impromptu "loop-hole," as it were. It is at least possible, therefore, for even this completely (and uniquely) asystematic insertion in manuscript C to be attributable to a jongleur's improvisation.[14]

These reinterpretations of the insertions, omissions and pervasive (though minor) phrasal differences that are peculiar to each manuscript of King Horn have been intended only to offer an alternative (not contradictory) analysis of Joseph Hall's own evidence. If we acknowledge impromptu as well as systematic substitutions as part of the performer's skill, any one of the above examples may be attributed to a jongleur's improvisation at least as readily as to a scribe's emendation--but not conclusively. The alternative explanations of the source of King Horn's textual variants considered so far, both seem equally valid; we do not, like Hall, consider them mutually exclusive.

But Joseph Hall also noted several variants among King Horn's three manuscripts that have not yet been reinterpreted as a jongleur's improvisation. These consist either of statements in one version that have little in common with corresponding lines in the other two, or of parallel passages among the three manuscripts in which essentially the same idea is very differently expressed. Our theory will consider these two types of textual variants as twin manifestations of one and the same phenomenon--systematic substitution. But we will maintain Hall's distinction. It is the very consistency with which these systematic substitutions are made that we consider most indicative of the probability that King Horn was reproduced orally at some stage in its transmission.

We are, in fact, inverting the priorities that Hall gave his own data. Hall argued that these substantive divergences "throw no light on the relationship of the MSS., unless so far as their number and importance make it improbable that any one of them is the direct source of any other. More instructive is the class of passages where the same idea occurs in all three MSS., but with small variations in the turn of the expression."[15] Indeed, Hall used not these minor phrasal differences themselves, but concurrences within them to demonstrate the textual cohesiveness of manuscripts L and O as distinct from C. From that same cohesiveness, Hall inferred a common written source; and from that source, he inferred King Horn's scribal transmission. Hall, however, neglects to attribute the differences themselves-- as differences--to anything but arbitrary scribal mistakes. In general, Hall argued that the existence of corresponding lines which have little in common "are due to an attempt to emend a corrupt or defective original."[16] We would note, however, three of those variants seem to have been caused by the substitution of rhyme elements (i.e., of entire couplets). Again, all systematic end-rhymes will be underlined:

1) L 449   Nou horn to soþe
   450   yleue þe by þyn oþe

   O 465   And seyde wel ricte
   466   þou art so fayr and briycte

   C 445   'Horn,' quaþ heo, 'vel sone
   446   þat schal beon idone:

2) L 571   deþ underfonge
   572   ne buer yslaye wiþ wronge

   O 587   Of none doute fayle
   588   þer þou biginnes batayle

   C 573   Of none duntes beon of drad,
   574   Ne on bataille beon amad,

98

```
3)  L 1377    we shule þe houndes kecche
     1378    & To þe deʒe vecche

    O 1406    þis lond we scollen winne
     1407    And sle al þat ben inne

    C 1369    All we hem schulle sle
     1370    & al quic hem fle.'
```

Hall considered none of these nine couplets to
have been "original"; rather, they are all independent
efforts by (at least) three different scribes to cor-
rect a flawed "original" text. As such, they seem
more akin to concurrent "insertions" than to actual
substitutions for one another. Hall considered the
third grouping above--that is, L 1377-8, O 1406-7,
and C 1369-70--to have been composed as "reminiscences,"
or scribal reduplications of lines L 1227-8, O 619-20,
and C 86-7 (sic) respectively:

```
    L 1227    to day ychulle huem cacche
     1228    nou ichulle huem vacche

    O 619     Dis lond we wile winne
     620     And slen all þat þer ben hinne

    C 85      Payne him wolde slen
     86      Oþer al quic flen
```

First, the minor phrasal differences (symptomatic in
themselves of oral improvisation) between the lines
within each manuscript should be noted. But more
significantly, the correspondence of the ideas (i.e.,
the "kill everyone" concept of which the key verb is
slay) expressed by C and O, but not mentioned in L
should be noted. We agree with Hall's suggestion
that the scribe recalled a substitute couplet applies
best, in this case, to manuscript L's reading; there
is a gap of only about 150 lines between the couplet's
first use and its "reminiscence." But this explana-
tion's plausibility, we would argue, diminishes
greatly as that gap increases; the alleged "reminis-
cence" occurs after almost 800 lines in manuscript O,
and after almost the entire length of the romance in
manuscript C. Let us assume, rather, as Hall normally
does, that manuscript C preserves the "original" idea
to be expressed at this point in the performance of
King Horn. The slen/flen combination, however, is
neither a systematic nor a common rhyme link.[17] The
jongleur of manuscript O, therefore, might easily

forget the exact phrasing of the couplet, but recalled the "kill" concept; he substituted the winne/inne rhymes--which are both systematic and common. The jongleur of manuscript L--in this single instance--did not improvise so well and merely repeated a tag-couplet. Such a hypothesis regarding these "corresponding lines that have little in common" seems at least as plausible as Joseph Hall's analysis, but has the advantage of explaining how O might agree with C rather than with L--in other words, how a later performance might regenerate a more "original" reading.

The nature of each of the other two examples of corresponding couplets listed above should be analyzed separately, and without further evidence the "source" or "cause" of this type of discrepancy among King Horn's manuscripts must remain hypothetical. But we offer the following possible explanations precisely as equally plausible possibilities.

Again, the ideas expressed by C 573-4 and by O 587-8 do correspond to one another, but not to L 571-2. The correspondence we attribute to O jongleur's memory of the "original" concept; the difference in phrasing to the fact that the of drad/amad link in C is neither systematic nor common. Therefore, the fayle substitution in manuscript O is a predictable substitution because it is systematic rhyme word for O's jongleur; but it is not common and did not "transmit" to (or from) manuscript L. The performer of manuscript L avoided both the idea and the rhyme of the "original reading" by improvising around the systematic and common--i.e., "original" in terms of his improvisational method--end-rhyme, "underfonge."

Likewise, the L 449-50, O 465-6 and C 445-6 variants may also be considered equally explicable as their respective jongleurs' improvisations. In this case, however, none of these couplets express corresponding concepts. All three end-rhyme conjunctions, however, seem improvised; two couplets use rhyme words that are both systematic and common (ricte in O and sone in C), while the ope substitution, though improvised, seems peculiar to the performer of L. In other words, in all three instances, the jongleurs may have sacrificed their memory of a fixed narrative content (or lack thereof) to their improvised oral form.

100

Finally, the fourth such variant which Hall
cites seems merely to have been a rhyme word sub-
stitution:

L 552   oþer wyþ wymmon forewart make

O 570   þer fore ne haue ich þe forsake

C 554   For þi me stondeþ þe more rape*

Again, let us assume that the C manuscript preserves
the "original" reading, rape. But rape is neither a
systematic nor a common rhyme word in King Horn. A
jongleur might recall rape in another performance; he
would not, however, reimprovise a couplet with it.
Furthermore, rape, although "original," generates an
off-rhyme (i.e., an audible mistake). All three cor-
responding passages listed above are preceded by
lines that convey the same idea and whose final rhyme
word is both systematic and common--take.

L 551   er ne he eny wyf take

O 569   Her ich eny wif take

C 553   Or He eny wif take

The ready availability of take might itself explain
the correspondence of these lines. The end-rhyme
element of the succeeding line has thus been
established, but not necessarily its specific rhyme-
word or the content of its phrasing. We can imagine
the jongleur of manuscript L (as readily as its scribe)
rejecting or failing to recall the rape off-rhyme, and
replacing it with the exact and systematic end-rhyme,
make (cf. Table II). But since make is not common,
another jongleur would probably not reproduce it
(except by accident); he could, however, replace it
with a systematic rhyme word either from the romance's
common subgroups or from a subgroup peculiar to his own
performance. The forsake substitution in manuscript
0 is both systematic and common--and, therefore,
theoretically predictable as a result of oral trans-
mission. Such substitutions as these (unlike the many
minor phrasal changes discussed earlier) clearly can-
not also be the sort of changes made by a copyist
simply as copyist. If a scribe introduced these sub-
stantive changes he did so consciously--as a deliberate
(if not a particularly skilled) reviser of the poem.
If he did so systematically--as we hope to have already

101

suggested--he did so as a <u>jongleur</u>.

The last type of variants which Hall noted (and which we consider most important) consists of ten sets of parallel passages among <u>King Horn</u>'s three manuscripts in which the same idea is very differently expressed. Such phrases may be considered true substitutions for one another. Hall himself considered these variants attributable "mostly to the avoidance of rhymes which are impossible in the scribe's dialect."18 In all fifteen of the following couplets--half of the examples cited by Hall--the substitutions may be considered the predictable results of a <u>jongleur</u>'s <u>systematic</u> improvisation.

We have underlined those rhyme words that are both <u>systematic</u> and <u>common</u> (cf. Table VII). In each of the following couplets, at least one of the endrhymes (and only one is mandatory to consider the entire couplet as improvised) proved to be such:

1) L 371   Athelbrous goþ wiþ <u>alle</u>
       372   horn he fond in <u>halle</u>

    O 379   Aylbrous fram boure <u>wende</u>
       380   Horn in halle he <u>fonde</u>

    C 367   Aylbrus wende hire fro
       368   Horn in halle fond he <u>þo</u>

2) L 483   Ich þe rede mid al my <u>myht</u>
       484   þat þou make horn <u>knyht</u>

    O 499   Ich þe wolde rede ate <u>lest</u>
       500   þat þou horn knict <u>madedest</u>

    C 479   Hit nere noʒt for loren
       480   For to kniʒte child <u>horn</u>*

3) L 1353   he louede horn wiþ <u>mihte</u>
       1354   & he him wiþ <u>rhyte</u>

    O 1382   He louede horn wel <u>derne</u>
       1383   And horn hym also<u>ʒerne</u>

    C 1343   He luueþ him so <u>dere</u>
       1344   & is him so <u>stere</u>.

4) L 1483   knyhtes of þe beste
    1484   þat he euer hede of weste

    O 1510   Knyʒtes swyþe felle
    1511   And schurde him in pelle

    C 1463   Of kniʒtes swiþe snelle
    1464   Ðat schrudde him at wille.*

5) L 1543   In trewe loue hue lyueden ay
    1544   ant wel hue loueden godes lay

    O 1566   All folc hyt knewe
    1567   þat he hem louede trewe

    C 1521   Al folk hem miʒte rewe
    1522   þat loueden hem so trewe

Hall also cites three sets of single line-substitutions:

1) L 1273   he seyde kyng of londe

    O 1306   He seyde kynd so longe*

    C 1263   'King,' he sede, 'þu luste*

2) L 1294   & lerne kynges roune

    O 1329   And wite of kynges owne

    C 1286   & bere kinges crune.

3) L 1222   worþi men & lyhte

    O 1257   Hyrische men so wyʒte

    C 1214   Redi to fiʒte

In the first of these single-line substitutions--the
londe/longe/luste sequence--each end-rhyme is both
systematic and common. In manuscript L, londe
rhymes exactly with understonde. Understonde also
follows longe[19] in manuscript O, and the "rhyme,"
though "off," remains both systematic and common--
the sort of "mistake" (or compelled substitution of
a "near" rhyme element) that an improvising jongleur,
not a revising scribe, might most plausibly make.
Similarly, in manuscript C luste combines with beste
to express the same idea as in the other two

103

manuscripts (but notably, in direct rather than in-
direct discourse); again, the rhyme word substitutions
seem to be predictable oral improvisations, though
"off."

As for Hall's other two examples of single-line
substitutions, it might be noted that lyhte and fiȝte
are also systematic and common. But of far more sig-
nificance is the fact that manuscript L's lyhte, manu-
script O's (non-systematic) wyȝte, and manuscript C's
fiȝte all rhyme with some form of kniȝte(s). Likewise,
manuscripts L's roune, manuscript O's owne, and manu-
script C's crune (none of which is common or systema-
tic), all rhyme with some form of toun. It is toun
and knighte that are both systematic and common. And
it is the very availability of each of these two
rhyme words themselves that permits the transmitting
jongleur to improvise three other rhyme word substitu-
tions in the various conjoining lines of King Horn's
three manuscripts.

Of Hall's ten examples of variant readings among
King Horn's three manuscripts, in which the same idea
is very differently expressed, only two sets of coup-
lets remain to be reconsidered as the result of jong-
leur transmission. They are:

        1)   L 299   Athelbrus & Athulf bo
                  300   to hire boure beþ ygo

              O 304   Aylbrous and Ayol him myde
                  305   Boþe he to boure ȝede

              C 293   Aþelbrus gan Aþulf lede
                  294   & in to bure wiþ him ȝede

        2)   L 1057   þer worþ a dole reuly
                  1058   þe brude wepeþ bitterly

              O 1092   þer worþ a relich dole*
                  1093   þer þe bryd wepeþ sore

              C 1049   Ðe bride wepeþ sore,
                  1050   & þat is muche deole.'*

Even among the six couplets that comprise these two
examples, four substitutions of end-rhymes are both
systematic and common (i.e., ygo and lede; terminal
sore and preliminary sore). These four, therefore,

may be directly attributed to both jongleur improvisation and oral transmission.

Only two couplets seem to be "exceptional" in the above list: the myde/ȝede and the reuly/bitterly combinations are neither common nor systematic. They are, however, predictable "exceptions"--that is, they are quite possible within the parameters of oral improvisation. The -ly rhymes of manuscript L are made by means of the common adverbial suffix--the availability of which reduces any need for the systematic recall of a specific rhyme word. Thus, the reuly/bitterly combination in manuscript L may be considered successfully "novel." The myde/ȝede link in manuscript O, however, seems not. It is not common, nor systematic, and either an extraordinarily weak rhyme ([ɪdə]/[də]) or an off-rhyme ([ɪd·ə]/[éd·ə]). In other words, the myde/ȝede combination may be considered a "predictable" "exception" in this manuscript in so far as "mistakes" are to be expected during any improvised performance.

In summary, of the thirty instances cited by Joseph Hall—his parallel passages among King Horn's three manuscripts in which the same idea is very differently expressed—twenty-eight (or 90%) may clearly be attributed directly to oral transmission. And the remaining two examples of this type of variant are at least equally possible as the results of this same mode of transmission as of scribal emendation. We do not mean to assert that any one of these couplets is definitely the work of an improvising jongleur rather than of a revising scribe. We merely wish to highlight the consistency with which systematic (i.e., improvised) substitutions are made in this type of variant. It is precisely in terms of this overall consistency--rather than from any one instance above--that we argue the superior plausibility of our own theory regarding the source of such variants.

vi. The primary intent of the above survey was to demonstrate that neither Hall's nor Wissmann's theory is adequate alone. And, yet, the two theories are not easily combined into a single explanation. For example, if we simply add an "oral stage" to Hall's chart of King Horn's textual history, we might try to insert jongleur performances where he posited lost scribal copies:

DIAGRAM II

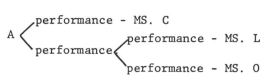

performance - MS. C

A performance

performance - MS. L

performance - MS. O

Though this diagram does reflect Hall's claim that manu-
script C frequently preserves an "original" against the
consensus of L and O, one would be hard pressed to ex-
plain how manuscripts LO form any sort of "group"-though
Hall did prove this fact and attributed it to their
common written source. If, however, each oral perform-
ance by means of a jongleur's improvisation simply
distorts the "original" (as the above diagram suggests),
manuscripts L and O should have less (not more) in com-
mon with one another than with manuscript C.

In order to combine these divergent theories about
the oral and written transmission of medieval romance
with any sort of validity, we must recognize from the
start the constant potential for any combination of
these modes of reproduction. Each manuscript of King
Horn may represent both oral and written transmission
at the same time. This principle permits us to explain
the textual cohesiveness, that Hall noted among manu-
scripts L and O, as a sign of written transmission. For
example, Hall's original chart may be modified as
follows:

DIAGRAM III

performance - MS. C

A

performance - MS.T

MS. L

MS. O

Though all of these diagrams must remain speculative
and simplified, it does seem clear that L and O share
a common written source not shared by C. But again
Diagram III presents certain difficulties in explaining
how L or O would preserve an "original" reading against
C, or how a reading in L or O might correspond to C
rather than to one another. We must postulate, instead,
some process of transmission analogous to the following
schemae:

106

DIAGRAM IV

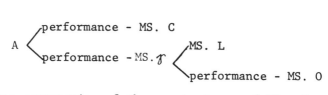

performance - MS. C

A

performance - MS. L - performance - MS. O

or, more probably,

DIAGRAM V

performance - MS. C

A

MS. L

performance - MS. Ƴ

performance - MS. O

A precise enumeration of the exact stages of King Horn's mixed transmission remains impossible. But it is mandatory to acknowledge that manuscripts L and O seem to share at least one written source not shared by C, and that at least one improvised performance seems to separate manuscript O from manuscript L. It is the former, written mode of transmission which explains the basic cohesiveness of manuscripts L and O as a textual group. But it is the latter, oral mode of improvised transmission (rather than mere serendipity) which best explains the occasional cohesiveness of these later manuscripts with an "original" reading preserved by C, rather than with each other. In addition to the question of a scribe's fidelity to the source of King Horn, we must consider another sort of "fidelity"--the jongleur's-- which consists of both his ability to remember the "original" text (traditionally defined) and his skill in employing the romance's "original," or common, improvisational system.

Notes to Chapter VI

[1]Joseph Hall, ed., <u>King</u> <u>Horn</u> (Oxford: Clarendon
Press, 1901), p. xi.

[2]Hall, p. xiv. Theodor Wissmann had suggested only
that oral transmission might <u>also</u> explain certain textual
variants among <u>King</u> <u>Horn</u>'s manuscripts--changes, it
seems, that were, nevertheless, introduced <u>during</u> <u>the</u>
<u>copying</u> <u>process</u>. He did not truly address <u>himself</u> <u>to</u>
<u>the</u> <u>systematically</u> improvised modifications which we
consider most indicative of a <u>jongleur</u>'s actual perfor-
mance. Wissmann argued:
  Ich vermuthe daher, dass die mundlich Fort-
pflanzung des Gedichts auf die Gestaltung der Handschriften
von wesentlichem Einflusse gewesen ist, ja ich erblicke
in unsern Handschriften oder vielmehr ihren Vorlagen
Textbucher verschiedener Spielleute, welche sich in ihrem
Vortrage keineswegs streng an die ursprungliche Fassung*
banden und einander ihre Lieder durchweg mundlich
uberlieferten.
  Auf diese Weise erklaren sich die zahlreichen
Varianten, welche weder aus einem Schreibe- oder Lesefeh-
ler, noch aus der Thatigkeit schritstellernder Bearbeiter
entsprungen sein konnen, so erklart sich auch der Umstand,
dass O and H, welche sich zeitlich naher stehen, haufiger
untereinander ubereinstimmen, auch dort, wo ihre Lesart,
ohne an sich schlecht zu sein, keineswegs die Merkmale
derder Ursprunglichkeit hat.
  (I suppose therefore that the oral transmission of
the poem into the form of the manuscripts has been the
important influence; indeed I perceive in our manuscripts,
or rather their models, the textbook itself of different
musicians who were by no means bound to the original form
in bringing forth their recitations and always orally
transmitted their songs to each other.
  In this way, the numerous variations are explained
which either from one slip of the pen or reading error
or from the writing of the author/revisor came to be;
this also explains the circumstance that O and H [Hall's
L MS.] which stand nearer in time, more frequently agree
with each other, also that their author without being
inferior himself by no means has the feature of origin-
ality.)
<u>Studien</u> <u>Zu</u> <u>King</u> <u>Horn</u> (Strassburg & London: Trubner,
1876), p. 6; rpt. verbatim in <u>King</u> <u>Horn</u>: <u>Untersuchengen</u>
<u>zur</u> <u>Mitlelenglischen</u> <u>Sprach-</u> <u>und</u> <u>Litteraturgeschichte</u>,
<u>der</u> <u>Germanischen</u> <u>Volker</u>, XVI (Strassburg & Lond:
Trubner, 1876), p. 6.

Notes to Chapter VI

[3]Hall, p. xii.

[4]For the sake of just such a comparison, Hall had the three texts of King Horn printed in parallel columns.

[5]Hall, pp. xii-xiii.

[6]Hall, pp. xiv-xv.

[7]In other words, the variants introduced by scribal emendation or by a performer's lapses of memory may not be empirically distinguishable from one another. But a jongleur's systematic improvisation may be distinguished from both by virtue of its very consistency.

[8]Hall, p. xiii.

[9]The designations insertion and omission become somewhat artibrary in our own study. Whereas Hall presupposed an original text in terms of which such lines might be legitimately so labelled, we do not. We largely maintain Hall's categories, but note that a line or couplet which appears in any two manuscripts of Horn, yet not in the third, may often as readily be considered a double insertion as a single omission.

[10]Hall, p. xi.

[11]Hall, p. xi.

[12]Hall, p. xi.

[13]We do not mean to imply that the shelde rhyme of line 242 (which is both systematic and common) is a formal mistake. On the contrary, it satisfactorily completes its own couplet and resolves what may have been an aurally perceptible flaw introduced by the substitution of felde for rivere. The resulting triplet that precedes this couplet in MS O may not have seemed an aurally perceptible "flaw" either, though the four line -ere sequence of MSS C and L seems a more artistic improvisation.

[14]Such a "loop-hole" would prove desirable to a jongleur in so far as it provided rhyme-word variety without diminishing the exactness of his rhyme-sounds.

[15]Hall, p. xii.

[16]Hall, p. xii.

[17]Cf. Table II, Category II. -EN does recur with
sufficient frequency in MS C to be considered a statisti-
cally significant rhyme element, but generates no
apparent subgroup. (Cf. "Comment" to its Appendix A
entry.) Compare the -ENE clusters of all three manu-
scripts.

[18]Hall, p. xii.

[19]MS. 0, 1. 1307: "My tale þou honder stonde."

CHAPTER VII
SOME FURTHER STYLISTIC CONTRASTS BETWEEN
THE RHYME-CRAFTS OF HAVELOK THE DANE
AND KING HORN, MANUSCRIPT C

In Appendix D, we attempt to clarify and verify the distinction that we have made between the system-atic end-rhymes of King Horn and the conventional end-rhymes of Havelok the Dane. We have already attempted to demonstrate that the repetitiousness of a certain rhyming vocabulary in King Horn does indeed function as an improvisational aid to the jongleur's perform-ance (and that this system best explains both the parallels and discrepancies among its three manu-scripts). The rhymes of Havelok's manuscript do not.

In this chapter, however, we would like to high-light briefly certain other stylistic features that may distinguish the rhyme-craft employed in King Horn from that of Havelok. These features may be considered supplemental evidence in so far as they indicate the "orally" improvised nature of King Horn as opposed to the essentially "written" and, therefore, revisable composition of Havelok. For the sake of simplicity, we will contrast only the C manuscript of King Horn (which Hall considered the most "original," and which our own analysis discovered to be the most improvised) to Havelok.

Despite its frequent use of "tag-lines," all the evidence from our analysis of Havelok's end-rhymes seems to refute any notion that its manuscript could be the accurate transcription of an improvised oral per-formance. Though the end-rhymes of Havelok the Dane are indeed repetitive, we found no consistent evidence for the existence of proportionately small subgroups of words within its clusters (i.e., systematic end-rhymes around which the romance's couplets may have been im-provised). The repetition of conventional rhymes in Havelok can be occasionally demonstrated, but nothing more "formulaic" than this. Rather, one need simply consider the following passage from Havelok in order to perceive that the crafting of its end-rhymes differs significantly from the performance of King Horn:[1]

He was the best knight at nede
That evere mighte riden on stede
Or wepne wagge or folk ut lede;
Of knight ne havede he nevere drede
That he no sprong forth so sparke of glede,
And lete him knawe of his hand-dede--
Hu he couthe with wepne spede;
And other he refte him hors or wede,
Or made him sone handes sprede
And "Loverd, merci!" loude grede.
He was large and no wight gnede.

Havede he non so good brede
Ne on his bord non so good shrede,
That he ne wolde thorwith fede
Povre that on fote yede--
Forto haven of Him the mede
That for us wolde on rode blede,
Christ that all can wisse and rede
That evere woneth in any thede.

(11. 87-105)

There are nineteen, consecutive and exact end-rhymes in
the above tirade from Havelok, and not one verbal re-
petition--a remarkable tour de force in English. This
run of end-rhymes may have been memorized by its in-
tended performer, but would be numerically impossible
for a jongleur to improvise according to our proposed
system (i.e., around a subgroup of only two to five
rhyme words per cluster).

In the above excerpt from Havelok, we are not
primarily concerned with the length of the run of its
end-rhymes, though their number is indeed extraordinary.
Consecutive couplets that rhyme together appear quite
regularly in this romance; such consecutively rhyming
couplets seem deliberately to exploit "near-rhyme" as
well as exact runs. Nor are such linked couplets en-
tirely absent from Horn (cf. MS. C, lines 43-6, 227-30,
and 291-4 for exact runs; lines 115-8, 127-30, and 236-
8 for "near" runs). In Havelok such runs of end-rhymes
frequently reach six lines without verbal repetition
(cf. 11. 240-5, 326-31, 402-7, 673-8, 825-30, 1684-9,
1740-5, 2904-9). But in manuscript C of Horn such runs
(with the dubious exception of the kniȝte/briȝte/whit/
ilik/wiȝt/kniȝt sequence in lines 499-504) never exceed
two couplets. Such consecutive couplets remain rare in
Horn, whereas in Havelok they seem to appear on the
average of once every fifty lines. At least one uses
macaronic rhyme (1. 20). Furthermore, there seems to

112

be some evidence in Havelok for the poet's careful
placement of intermittent couplets so that they form
intentional patterns--such as the slo/fro-(bour/tour)-
go/wo-(bitween/wene)-wowe/lowe) sequence of lines 2070-
9. In general, the end-rhymes of Havelok seem far
more consciously crafted--or revised--or "written"--
than those of King Horn.

It seems more important to note, however, that such
runs of consecutive rhyme in King Horn are almost al-
ways divisible by two,² whereas the above excerpt of
nineteen lines from Havelok, as well as its bothe/rode
blod sequence (11. 430-2), possibly the faste/unwraste/
fnaste rhymes (11. 547-9),³ and perhaps such consec-
utive couplets as the (sawe)/lowe/slowe/flowe run
(11. 2430-3) are not. Since regular tetrameter meter
also provides Havelok with an audibly conspicuous form,
its author seems no longer so doggedly concerned with
maintaining the phonically exact couplet as his basic,
indivisable formal unit. But this is an entirely
relative assessment of Havelok's rhyme features in
terms of Horn's.

The end-rhymes of Havelok may be more "studied". On
the other hand, they also seem to have been reduced to
a supplementary function, as ornamentation of its pre-
established form--the tetrameter line. In so far as
Havelok's couplets were meant to be aurally appreciated,
the function of their end-rhymes remains much the same
as those of King Horn. But they do not seem to have
been orally improvised; they do not recur with the same
systematic repetitiveness; and, therefore, they do not
suggest that the manuscript preserves a jongleur's actu-
al performance.

Syntax provides one more general indication of the
difference between the formal priorities of an impro-
vised text like Horn's manuscripts and a more polished
composition like Havelok's. All of King Horn's couplets
and most of its lines are significantly end-stopped.
This phenomenon might suggest that its improvised lines
could, thus, be readily annexed to one another, but it
also occurs in mere hack-work. Its absence, however,
might always be taken to indicate a more skillful
composition (that is, a revised text).

The first twenty-six lines of Havelok seem to be
more or less discrete phrasal units; they form the
traditional "come hither" of a minstrel ("Herkneth to
me, gode men,"). But the very first narrative sentence

113

of this romance runs over two couplets:

It was a king by are dawes,
That in his time were gode lawes
He dede maken and full well holden;
Him lovede yung, him lovede olde, (11. 27-30).

And random enjambment is not very difficult to find in
Havelok; for example, "Thanne mighte chapmen fare/Thur-
hut Englond . . ." (11. 52-2). Yet, in reading Horn,
one constantly senses that it is only the end-rhymes
which tie two consecutive lines together. Again, this
is an entirely relative assessment of the two romances.

We have already noted that Donald Sands considered
it unfortunate that Horn and Havelok should be "dis-
cussed together, often as though they were of equal
literary value . . . because the latter is really a bet-
ter piece all around."4 Applying one set of critical
principles by which the art of end-rhyme may be evalua-
ted inevitably reaches this same conclusion about the
relative merits of these two romances. Yet, if King
Horn's text is the record of a jongleur's performance
while Havelok's text records a tale intended for oral
performance, their respective manuscripts present the
critic with two substantially different commodities.

For example, the "tag-lines" in Havelok are largely
a compositional short-cut; they are prefabricated con-
ventions, as Baugh suggested, but they do not seem to
have been improvised during an oral performance. Such
"tag-lines" may be justifiable when they signal a tran-
sition or give the audience some familiar point of
reference. But they may also be nothing more than
trite. And, in general, the Havelok poet did relatively
well in avoiding such cliched phrasing. The authors of
later Middle English romances often used these conven-
tional "tag-lines," but by the very act of writing, they
did not necessarily perform the same improvisational
skill which had first generated these lines. These
lines may represent the vestiges of a fading craft, but
not the craft itself. And, as Ruth Crosby first noted,
we occasionally find even "In Chaucer the line or half
line added for no apparent purpose but the rhyme. Such
superfluous phrases as these, however, are not common."5

The phrasing and end-rhymes of such romances might
still imitate (albeit, to a lesser extent), the effects
of certain improvisational conventions associated with
oral performance--but without the same formal skills of

a jongleur's actual performance. The romance composer, as writer--by the very fact that he can pause--need not have confined himself to the repetitiveness of a jongleur's improvisational system, and often did not. Some would argue, therefore, that the later romance writers should not have settled for a certain lack of "originality" in composition which seems to have been mandated by the jongleur's craft. We will consider this and other critical implications of our theory more thoroughly in our final chapter.

But for now we would simply like to recall that the actual distinction between jongleur and original poet is not so absolute in determining the final form of a medieval romance. Just as often as the jongleur performed for the poet, the poet wrote for the performer. And we do not now wish to replace one either/or fallacy (that of "written" vs. "oral") with another (that of "improvised" vs. "revised").

In summary, we believe that we have discovered and explained the medieval jongleur's improvisational (if not truly formulaic) system; the system is based primarily on a recurrent end-rhyme vocabulary, not on recurrent phrases, as evidenced in King Horn; it is a system peculiar to the formal needs of a jongleur during his oral performance of the romance. We have made no claim that all extant medieval romances which used regular end-rhyme will reveal this same system so well as Horn. On the contrary, we acknowledge the unlikely possibility that the three manuscripts of King Horn--the oldest Middle English romance--may represent uniquely faithful records of such oral performances. We also acknowledge that systematic end-rhyme may not prove to have been a jongleur's only improvisational device. But, once, an improvisational system clearly did exist, and its effects are evident in the three final transcriptions of King Horn. Furthermore, the effects of a tradition of this oral improvisation (if not the improvisation itself) may be evident in numerous, later and clearly written texts--like Havelok the Dane or the Auchinlek romances.

It is the empirically discernible difference between the systematic end-rhymes of Horn and the conventional end-rhymes of Havelok which should provide the first basis for any future comparisons of their respective verse-crafts. And all relative assessments of their various formal features should be made only in terms of this basic distinction. More studied effects seem more probable (and, therefore, more aesthetically necessary) in a more revisable composition--such as Havelok. But, by this general concession, we hope not to have diminished a specific jongleur's real skill at achieving his real craft--improvisation, which includes such features as rhyme-word variety, sound patterning, narrative compression, and clever (if not always novel) rhyme links, but which is limited by the overriding formal demands of uninterrupted live performance.

Notes to Chapter VII

[1]All citations of Havelok the Dane come from Donald
Sands, ed., Middle English Verse Romances (New York:
Holt, Rinehart and Winston, 1966), pp. 55-129.

[2]We might have said "always"--without qualifica-
tion--in reference to manuscript C. But "odd lines,"
particularly those of manuscript O (Horn's most "writ-
ten," or least "oral" version), present certain
difficulties. Detailed analysis of Horn's triplets
indicates, however, that they normally seem to be al-
tered double couplets. In Havelok, however, extending
a series of end-rhymes beyond the basic couplet--regard-
less of the odd or even number of lines that result in
such tirades--seems desirable in its own right. Lines
87 to 105 remain the best example of this "newer," more
revised rhyme-craft that distinguishes Havelok's style
from Horn's.

[3]Sands, p. 72 n. 547. This line has traditionally
been borrowed from the "Cambridge Fragment" of Havelok
and added to the reading of the Laud Misc. MS.

[4]Sands, p. 55.

[5]Ruth Crosby, "Chaucer and the Custom of Oral Deliv-
ery," Speculum, 13 (1938), 423.

CHAPTER VIII

IMPLICATIONS TEXTUAL AND CRITICAL

There are simply too many kinds of oral poetry and too great a variety of compostional features within each kind for any one rigidly definable style to be designated both uniquely and universally oral. As Ruth Finnegan has written; "The hope for a precise generalization about the nature of oral style of the kind that Magoun, Parry and others have envisaged is, in my opinion, bound to be disappointed."[1] It remains true that repetition offers the least common denominator for the analysis of all oral poetries, but--as Finnegan also argues--this same repetition (most broadly defined to accommodate the full range of oral styles) also provides a formal basis for the study of all written styles of poetry as well.

We make no claim that our statistical analyses of King Horn's end rhymes have revealed the true nature of all oral poetry. We are quite willing to admit that there is no one, true, holy and universal style for all oral poetry. But we do believe, confident that Finnegan would not totally disagree, that stylistic analysis may still help to distinguish one type of oral poetry from another, one type of written poetry from another, and even one type of oral poetry from one type of written poetry. Although there may be no general truths, there are specific facts (e.g., the statistical frequency of repetitions) to help us make specific stylistic distinctions. Acknowledging the complexity of a problem does not solve it, nor preclude attempting to.

We admit that the specific conclusions to be drawn from our inductive analysis of a jongleur's end-rhymes apply exclusively to King Horn. Nevertheless, certain speculations may be tentatively suggested in so far as Horn can be considered typical of an entire, albeit hypothetical, class of medieval literature--the improvised romance. We have demonstrated that Horn's three surviving manuscripts represent as many written records of oral transmission. Such transmissions imply oral performance, and such performance requires some sort of improvisational system. The readily recalled sub-groups of end-rhyme words for each rhyme element provided this system and generated a supplemental type of readily recalled lines. These stylistic phenomena justify and limit the designation "oral" in reference to a medieval romance, King Horn.

119

If King Horn is (and this earliest English romance may well be) a unique record, a sole survival of the jongleur's actual craft in England, the direct transfer of our conclusions to other romances--like Havelok or even "The Knight's Tale"--would prove most foolhardy. But certain implications can be drawn with caution. Further study will obviously be required.

First, we believe we have discovered a methodology for establishing--on the basis of internal evidence alone--whether an extended, medieval narrative poem that employs end-rhyme as its fundamental formal feature (i.e., in which stress patterns are flexible enough to permit phrasal improvisation) can be distinguished as either a written record of an actual oral performance (like Horn) or a fundamentally written composition (like Havelok). Though rhyme words certainly recur in a work such as Havelok, they do so with a far greater uniformity among the entire vocabulary of a given cluster or, conversely, with far less frequent recurrence of a readily recalled subgroup (cf. Appendix D). Such a statistical distinction may be considered analogous to the substantial difference between the occurence rates of formulae proper in a truly oral composition and their frequency in a clearly studied work. For quite a different purpose, C.S. Lewis once distinguished a primary epic from a secondary.[2] If we extend his terminology to a consideration of their respective uses of formulae, we might note that the perseverence of "formulaic" phrases in a secondary epic (such as The Aeneid) may imitate the stately diction, the formal vocabulary, and traditional texture--in short the style of a primary epic (such as The Iliad), but they do not fulfill the same compositional functions, and they simply do not recur so often. By analogy, we might consider the end-rhymes of King Horn as actual manifestations of the jongleur's craft, while Havelok's couplets represent a modified imitation of that traditional romance style. The resulting editorial and critical implications seem manifold, and we can here hope to indicate only a few.

One of the first effects that our theory might have will be its implications for the future editing of med-ieval romances. Most recent editors of King Horn,[3] in addition to regularizing spellings, have attempted to regenerate a "true" sense of the romance primarily by selecting "original" lines from each of the extant manu-scripts. Our theory might imply that such a procedure should be seriously reconsidered if we wish to convey a faithful record of a jongleur's actual artistry.

Joseph Hall published the three extant manuscripts of _King Horn_ in parallel columns; this policy remains the most accurate (if not the most economical) procedure for printed records. Of course, if we wish to appreciate the aural appeal of a romance more fully, phonographs or tapes might provide a more faithful representation--records that would include the dramatic quality of such performances. But an ideal recreation of the _jongleur_'s actual skills (not "the text") can be attained only by finding (or imagining) an actual improviser who could perform the work without text in hand--in short, a live _jongleur_. If such a _jongleur_ would employ systematic end-rhymes and improvised lines, rather than just brute memory, a record of his new performance would duplicate none of the extant manuscripts exactly, but it would recreate the dynamic process, the performing skills, that actually generated them some 600 years ago.

Dennis Tedlock has described the fundamental challenge confronting modern (i.e., thoroughly literate) editors of the extant written copies of all literature that was once truly oral:

> A restoration of the oral sense of. . . written literatures cannot be limited to the discovery of formulas or measured verse, but requires comparison with poetry that can still be listened to, and that poetry must be listened to with an ear that is not bent solely on alphabetic reduction to familiar written form. Further, restoration requires participation.[4]

Two specific challenges seem to confront future editors of the extant manuscripts of Middle English romances, therefore. First, the editor of such a romance must establish whether his manuscript represents a primarily written compostion (be it original or redacted) or an accurate recording of an improvised performance. This distinction, we believe, may be made statistically as regards a Middle English romance by determining whether the manuscript records oral/_systematic_ end-rhymes or written/_conventional_ couplets (cf. Appendix D). If the manuscript represents a fundamentally written record, standard editorial policies should apply. But if the manuscript represents a _jongleur_'s actual performance, the modern editor is confronted with his second, more complex challenge.

As suggested earlier, the editor of a romance like _King Horn_ must strive not simply to establish the original text, but also to define the entire concept of "originality" as it applies to a specific systematic

improvisation. Fidelity is easy enough to define when
there exists only one point of reference. But multiple
renderings of specific statements in King Horn, as we
have seen, might be considered equally original (i.e.,
systematically improvised), though no one of them faith-
fully preserves what Hall designated the romance's A
text (i.e., an exact memory or a rigorous copy of the
poet's first composition). If we could imagine a vari-
orum edition that does not, however, necessarily estab-
lish textual priorities among versions, we might see the
"original" text of King Horn--in potency. But we would
fail to hear its production--in act.

    As a final note regarding such textual problems, we
might anticipate certain manuscripts of medieval romance
which combine both oral and written recording processes.
For example, one and the same manuscript may be partial-
ly transcribed and partially dictated--an accurate record
of an oral performance, but only in parts. We may also
anticipate migraines for the editors of such texts.

    These still unresolved textual complications, of
course, also pose certain, correspondent challenges for
critics of Middle English romance. The critical proce-
dures for analyzing such written romances like Havelok
may differ not at all from the methods applied to other
narrative poems like Paradise Lost or the Faerie Queen
except in their respective findings. But if an impro-
vised romance, like Horn, belongs, as it were, to a
separate genre, the critical principles applied to it
should vary accordingly. Again, Dennis Tedlock states
the basic challenge:

        Just as the critical act in oral poetry begins where
        a performance begins, rather than waiting until it
        is over, so the critical act in an oral poetics be-
        gins with the establishment of a critical text . . .
        The critical texts of an oral poetics must be de-
        tailed librettos . . .[5]

We hope, however, that Horn will not simply be designa-
ted oral and, thereby, evaluated in terms of The Iliad.
We hope not for Horn's sake.

    We concede that any "oral theory" for the critique
of medieval poetry, not to mention poetry in general,
has become so amorphous a matter that the theory itself
might seem more or less useless to practical critics.
To recapitulate, the first studies of formulaic phrasing
in the narrative poetry of medieval England (by Crosby,

Baugh, et al) showed great promise in the fifties and sixties, but scholars of the seventies responded with far more scepticism regarding the truly compositional nature of such "formulaic" repetitions. The analogy between the actually oral productions of a scop and these far later performances of a jongleur proved unsatisfactory as a straightforward equation.

But we are not, therefore, satisfied that the theoretical distinction between strictly "oral" and strictly "written" poetry should remain forever vague, nor that students of medieval literature need be confined to the mutually exclusive concepts of a work being either an "oral" or a "written" composition. Rather than simply blurring the distinction between these two theoretically and historically valid modes of composition (as many theorists recently have done), we suggest that they might be considered not alternatives, but options among many other modes of composition, performance and appreciation. Rather than ignoring (throughout all the Middle Ages) a clear demarcation between the oral nature of one poem (such as Horn) and the written nature of another (such as Havelok), and rather than conflating the various critical principles that pertain specifically to each, we prepose (at least) the following range of possibilities for describing the complex of composition, performance and audience-appreciation circumstances that may surround the production of any poem:

FORMULAIC: A poem is formulaically composed simultaneous to its public performance; there exists no real distinction in this mode between the author and the performer. By definition, these works cannot exist in written form. The manuscripts of even The Iliad or Beowulf are, at most, the written (often highly edited) records of one such performance; the "fixed" texts are preserved after the oral composition (and, in so far as they may have been subsequently, non-formulaically revised, they do not accurately reflect the mode).

MEMORY ABSOLUTE: The non-literate equivalent of PUBLIC READING below; the composed (though perhaps not written) text is fixed prior to public performance, and is intended to be reproduced exactly as composed by its subsequent public performer (who may have been its author as well). This seems to have been the traditional craft of the rigorously trained Welsh

123

bards, and requires such institutions as the Eistedfodd to preserve the rigorously traditional readings.

MEMORY SUPPLEMENTED BY SYSTEMATIC IMPROVISATION: The public performer approximates fidelity to a poetic composition that exists prior to his performance, but improvises locally to maintain his form when his memory of that text fails. (Such phrasal alterations, by contrast, would probably be considered artistic failures if attempted by a Welsh bard.) Two subgroups need to be made within this mode:
1) the preexistent composition was aurally committed to memory by its future oral, performers. From our intertextural analyses (Chapter VI), we induce that the King Horn manuscripts may have been so reproduced at some stage during their transmission. The jongleur is implicitly illiterate in such cases.
2) the preexistent composition was visually committed to memory by its future performer. The text of Havelok the Dane may have been intended for this purpose. Its jongleur would implicitly be literate and was probably expected to approximate MEMORY ABSOLUTE by its author, if not by his future audience. Studied revision becomes possible in composition, but not during performance.

MEMORY SUPPLEMENTED BY FREE IMPROVISATION: Essentially, this process would offer a literary analogue to jazz.[6] Theodor Wissmann more or less described Horn in such terms. The performer improvises (when his memory fails) in no systematic and, therefore, no predictable manner. This process may accurately describe how textual variants came to be introduced into many shorter performances--such as the ballads-- but the process itself seems far too unreliable to sustain the formal demands of such extended performances as the Middle English romances.

PUBLIC READING: This mode offers an amateur substitute for earlier, professional performance; it is made possible by the mass production of manu-

124

scripts and then by printing--both promoted by
a popular increase in literacy. A clear dis-
tinction still exists, however, between the
roles of author, performer and an audience.
The public reader maintains absolute (i.e.,
visual) fidelity to the fixed text in his
hands. If the members of this listening audi-
ence are also literate, they may individually
eliminate the intermediary role of such a per-
former (cf. PRIVATE READING below). But the
author of such poetry still intended that his
craft should be appreciated publicly and aur-
ally as well. (Such counter-intentions on the
part of poet and audience have led to much
discussion of the "inner ear" which we would
designate a dual mode of appreciation.)
PUBLIC READING is still a viable mode of en-
tertainment and may not be dismissed as just
a historically temporary transition from
"oral" to "written" modes.

PRIVATE READING: This has clearly become the most com-
mon mode for appreciating English literature.
From the artist's perspective, it is frequent-
ly designated as WRITTEN or LITERATE. Our
label, PRIVATE, designates the intended mode
of appreciation. Like its theoretical anti-
pode, ORAL, it seems to be an extreme on the
critical spectrum between the eye and the ear
for the intended appreciation of poetic skill.
The main distinction between "skillful" com-
position and mere "hack-work" in this mode
seems to be the result of an artist's studied
revisions--which subsequently may be appre-
ciated as such. Eric A. Havelock has observed
that "When a citizen reads something 'to him-
self,' as we say, and by himself, and does so
habitually, he has become a member of a soci-
ety which has divorced itself, or begun to
divorce itself, from the audience situation."7
The social implications of this transition
from the communal to the individual apprecia-
tion of literature are manifold. But they are
not the primary concern of this study, nor are
they necessarily identical in all cultures.
We are solely concerned here with the stylis-
tic and textual implications of one such
transition that occurred in England from 1200-
1500. The printing press was merely the
efficient cause, the tool, of this transition

125

that eliminated jongleurs. But the transi-
tion itself often entailed (and entails) a
blurring in the author's mind of the theore-
tical distinction between "performer" and
"audience" since the solitary "reader"
actually assumes both identities. With the
aid of their "new" ability to revise, authors
made (and still make) stylistic adjustments
in order to accomodate their new market.
These adjustments are intended to satisfy a
two-fold change in that market. On the one
hand, as audience, these new readers have
(and will use) the ability to review their
texts and make critical judgments according-
ly. On the other hand, as performers, these
private readers have no special skills
(compositional, improvisational, or mnemonic)
other than literacy itself--and, more im-
portantly, their authors anticipate none.
Rather than for a few professionals (the
jongleurs), the English poet now writes for
innumerable, albeit more critical, amateurs
(the entire reading public).

ELECTRO-AURAL: The popularization of the term is pri-
marily McLuhan's. The concept has been
called both prophecy and fantasy. As a trans-
ition in the composition, performance, and/or
appreciation of "literature," it is more news
than history, and some scholars consider it
mere gossip. Other scholars, however, per-
ceive or anticipate in various ways the re-
oralization of literature. This perception
has led to discussion of the decline of
literacy in the West and of SAT scores, to
philippics against TV and to courses in
Critical Theory. As medievalists, however,
we claim our scholars' privilege to be totally
ignorant of all such relevant matters.

We consider the above listing of categorical des-
criptions neither definitive nor exhaustive. Other
labels will, no doubt, have to be coined to describe
both past and present literatures outside of our exper-
ience, and future literatures that may be composed,
performed, and appreciated in completely unexpected
manners. Nor is our roughly chronological listings of
these modes intended to indicate a linear progression
from one to another. We see no real transition from
one mode to another. Each seems to be the discrete
response of individual authors recognizing specific

conditions for the performance and appreciation of their work. And to consider the given historical development of these modes as some sort of "evolutionary process" in the development of English prosody would be a gross oversimplification. Furthermore, a single poet, like Chaucer or Tennyson or Olsen, might write with a fusion of such modes in mind.

The general trend from "oral" to "written" phases in English literature should, therefore, be considered only a series of discrete prosodic (i.e., technological) inventions. Just as the lightbulb did not "evolve" from the candle (and both still have their merits), so too what may be one of the now less common modes of versecraft, like MEMORY ABSOLUTE, SUPPLEMENTED MEMORY, or even PUBLIC READING, were once invented to meet the formal demands of their historic audiences and to exploit whatever skills that their intended mode of performance provided towards their aesthetic end. In so far as the historical conditions of a poem's own composition, performance, and appreciation can be re-created, all these various modes still remain valid aesthetic experiences. Furthermore, many of these modes have been, are, and will be simultaneously viable. It is, however, the unique conditions for the viable appreciation of each of these modes that determines its own, proper principles of criticism.

At present, therefore, we also reject all notions that any one of these modes of composition, performance and appreciation offers an aesthetic "improvement" over any other. We doubt that any critical benefit is to be gained by an a priori assessment of one mode as inherently superior to the others. For example, the Aeneid is obviously different from The Iliad; there may also be some critical validity to designating the Aeneid as the more sophisticated epic of the two. But, if anything, this observation precludes a direct comparison of the two quite, distinct types of epic. There seems no need for and little truth in the assertion that one type of epic is itself superior to the other.

Much the same might now be said about King Horn and Havelok the Dane--but seldom has been. We would argue, therefore, that any poem from whatever era must be assessed solely according to the principles determined by its own intended mode of composition, performance, and appreciation. First, of course, this mode itself must be recalled or rediscovered; then, this determination may function (much as the designation of a poem's genre once did) to establish principles for a subsequent

127

evaluation of the poem's formal merits--we make no
claims about its poetic content. We confine our dis-
cussion to skill and not ART.

As an example of the critical implications derived
from determining a poem's own intended mode of appre-
ciation, we may recall the frequent comparisons that
have been made regarding the respective artistry of
Havelok and Horn--comparisons, we may note, that norm-
ally favor the craftsmanship of the former as more
"polished" or "varied" in its prosody. First, we would
assert that the straightforward comparison itself should
be considered fundamentally invalid since Havelok and
Horn employ two quite distinct verse-crafts. But in so
far as formal comparisons may be made between such
"types," the following might be said regarding the res-
pective repetitiousness of each.

Variety is freqently considered to be the hallmark
of a master rhymer. If Havelok and Horn are both eval-
uated according to a single criterion of variety (i.e.,
"the more the better"), then Horn necessarily falls far
short of the achievement of Havelok (just as Havelok
itself falls far short of, for example, the Rape of the
Lock). But if we recognize that the very concept,
"variety," may be defined only according to the context
of composition and performance--and that there are
multiple definitions available for multiple contexts--
we come to the heretofore implausible conclusion that
Horn might have actually achieved more artistic "variety"
within the parameters established by its own mode of
composition than Havelok did within its. We have no in-
tention here of defending such an outré critical state-
ment to the death (of it or of us), but we offer it
merely as an example of the way in which critical opin-
ion may alter with a recognition of aesthetic principle
as peculiar to various modes of composition. Whereas
rhyme word repetitiousness seems to have served a valid
artistic function for the improvising jongleur of King
Horn (i.e., aural exactness), the rhyming vocabulary
of the Havelok poet, as writer, could have been revised
for the sake of more variety--and was--and should have
been.

Having implicitly awakened this dragon of the
historicity of such aesthetic principles, we will now
run away with only a handful of treasure--Ða se wyrm
onwoc.

We assert only that a manuscript record of a
jongleur's actual performance of a romance may be

128

recognized as such on the basis of its rhyme recurrence, and that the improvisational system employed to achieve these end-rhymes offers the most plausible explanation for substantive variants which occur among manuscripts when more than one written record survives of more than one oral transmission. We hope that the basic methodology which we have established for such a study will apply equally well to other medieval romances (perhaps those performed on the continent as well as in England in so far as they had to satisfy the same or similar formal requirements as those confronted by the jongleurs of King Horn). We do not believe that all the rhymes of every manuscript of each romance need to be sorted. Rather, a sampling of five to ten significant clusters should prove statistically sufficient.

What we do not know--and what we cannot tell from the evidence gathered for this study--is whether the same system may have been used in not just two versions of one romance, but in two quite distinct romances. But negative discoveries (i.e., that a given romance does not employ systematic end-rhyme and may not, therefore, be considered the record of an actual oral performance) would prove just as significant as positive findings for improvisation by jongleurs. The corpus of medieval romances could, thus, be distinguished according to their proper modes of composition and then appreciated accordingly. We do not truly consider that such criticism would then be relativistic so much as categorical. But since this chapter offers only ruminations on the implications of a theory, we will speculate no further.

Notes to Chapter VIII

[1]Ruth Finnegan, Oral Poetry: Its Nature, Significance and Social Context (London: Cambridge Univ. Press, 1977), p. 130.

[2]C. S. Lewis, Preface to Paradise Lost (1942; rpt. New York: Oxford Univ. Press, 1969), p. 13.

[3]Donald Sands, for example, bases his text primarily on the C MS., but inserts ten additional lines from the other two MSS. in Middle English Verse Romances (New York: Holt, Rinehart and Winston, 1966), pp. 15-54. Similarly, Charles W. Dunn and Edward I. Byrnes base their edition of King Horn primarily on the Harley Miscellany 2253 (MS. L), but insert two lines from the Laud Miscellany (MS. O) in Middle English Literature (New York: Harcourt Brace Jovanovich, 1973), pp. 114-149.

[4]Dennis Tedlock, "Towards an Oral Poetics," New Literary History, 8, No. 3 (Spring, 1977), 516. This entire issue of NLH is dedicated to far-ranging discussions of "Oral Cultures and Oral Performances."

[5]Tedlock, pp. 516-517.

[6]Marshall McLuhan has provided the jazz metaphor in The Gutenberg Galaxy (London: Routledge and Kegan Paul, 1962), p. 3.

[7]Eric A. Havelock, "The Preliteracy of the Greeks," New Literary History, 8, No. 3 (Spring, 1977), 387.

APPENDICES

METHODOLOGY

The purpose of the appendices that follow is quite
simple, and at first we believed the task itself, though
extraordinarily tedious, would be equally straightfor-
ward. We intended only to sort the various rhymes-
sounds employed in all three manuscripts of King Horn
so that the recurrence patterns of a specific rhyming
vocabulary for each sound might be observed within each
manuscript. Numerous reasons (mostly financial) made
it impossible to employ a computer for the processing
of this raw data. Certain considerations, such as the
ability to distinguish homonyms from one another, may
have been benefitted by our "personal touch." But we
are quite well aware that each stage of our handling the
material introduces a new opportunity for new errors.
We present these appendices not merely to confirm our
own analyses, but to provide the means for a reduplica-
tion of the experiment. And we invite all corrigenda.

We have taken as our text of King Horn Joseph
Hall's extraordinarily rigorous, 1901 edition of the
three surviving manuscripts.[1] We have made no editorial
decisions of our own, and, thus, we have sought to avoid
any deliberate tampering with the evidence. All deci-
sions about the proper reading of a rhyme-word had been
made over three-fourths of a century ago. But we have
found it necessary to invent a somewhat technical jar-
gon in order that these rhyme words might be consistently
sorted.

First, the definition of end-rhyme itself might be
clarified. William Rickert has recently discussed the
remarkable variety (and resultant confusion) of terms
which critic-scholars have accumulated in order to
describe rhyme.[2] Our concerns in the analysis of the
jongleur's craft are solely with his end-rhyme; indeed,
other manifestations of rhyme in medieval romances are
most rare. The placement of such rhyme in King Horn
seems to present no real difficulty; it appears at the
end of each line in a couplet. It might be noted again,
however, that rhythmic irregularity, particularly that
of the C MS. of King Horn, seems to invert our conven-
tional understanding of the relationship between a line
and its end-rhyme. Rather than the fixed length of a
line determining the location of its final rhyme, it
seems that the jongleur's placement of his rhyme word
established the termination of his line. Rhyme and line
length are, at least, simultaneously determined phenomena

131

in King Horn, and no formal priority may be given to
one over the other.

A rigorous and functional definition of rhyme
itself has proven to be somewhat more elusive. If
the exact reduplication of verbal sounds--normally,
V-C(-V)--offers the simplest conception of rhyme, then
the Middle English jongleur seems to have generally
required such simplicity, or aural exactness. We have
attempted, therefore, to let each manuscript of King
Horn define its own principles of exactness.

In order to avoid any gratuitous controversy about
the specific pronunciation of individual words in King
Horn--a controversy compounded by questions of an in-
dividual jongleur's own debatable dialect and of a
copyist's subsequent emendation--we have not attempted
to represent all rhymes phonetically. We will, on
occasion, analyze a particular question (e.g. -IE vs. -Y)
by means of the IPA, but normally we maintain manuscript
orthography in so far as our own typography permits.
We have separated the rhyming vocabulary of each manu-
script of King Horn into clusters according to their
rhyme elements.

A glance at the designation of each item in the
following appendices should clarify our term, rhyme
element. Most simply and most often, a rhyme element
is nothing more than the final syllable(s) of words
conjoined by adequate phonetic harmony. To arrange
such rhyme elements in our appendices we have adopted
a standardized spelling,[3] but in recording each rhyme
word, we have striven to preserve the actual spellings
in each manuscript so far as typography permits; thus,
IȝTE in C may parallel IGHTE in L, which in turn may
parallel ICTE in O, but we make no claim that these
respective rhymes are themselves identical between
manuscripts. We are far more concerned with deter-
mining the concept of exactness for each rhyme element
within each text.

Our normal conception of "near-rhymes" proved to
be far more problematic than that of "off-rhymes."
"Eye-rhymes," of course, are irrelevant to a considera-
tion of oral performance, and any end-rhymes that might
be so labelled elsewhere, we would consider to be "off-
rhymes" in King Horn. "Off-rhymes" as such should be
considered nothing more than mistakes; for example,
such a pairing as /douter/ofte/ seems to fail, by all
standards, to designate the aurally recognizable end-
rhymes of a couplet. At such moments, the jongleur

has simply not satisfied the formal requirements of his performance, and boos by his audience may not have been unjustified.

But "near-rhymes" introduce the puzzling possibility of rhyme elements that are "exact enough." For example, should EDE /ēdə/ be considered sufficiently "near" to EDDE /ɛdə/ so that they might be paired by the jongleur as equivalents? Then, what about ETE /etə/ or ETTE /ɛtə/ or ED /ɛd/ or ADE /ādə/ or . . .? It is for precisely this reason that we have attempted to let each manuscript define its own parameters for equivalent rhyme elements. Rather than imposing our own taste in the matter on the jongleur's principles, we have (through much trial and error) sought to observe empirically what might and might not have been considered "exact enough" end-rhymes by King Horn's original audiences.

Likewise, the phonological distinction between open and closed long vowels (e.g., open and closed long e /ɛ:/ and /e:/, and open and closed long o /ɔ:/ and /o:/) pertains to the Middle English dialects north of the Thames. Since, however, the dialect of King Horn seems predominantly Southern mixed with Midland forms, this distinction should not apply to its end-rhymes. And, indeed, open and closed long vowels that might elsewhere be differentiated rhyme exactly in this romance. For example, in the EDE cluster of MS. C (Category III), two of the four most recurrent rhyme words are words with closed e--rede and spede; spede forms two couplets with words having open e's--fairhede and lede (ll. 797-8 and 1393-4); and rede forms a couplet with the open e in lede (ll. 183-4). The other two words, stede and lede, have open e's; in addition to the two couplets just mentioned, lede rhymes with the closed e in bede (ll. 907-8), and stede is the first element in two couplets with the open e words drede and nede (ll. 25-6 and 47-8).

It soon became clear that the jongleur's concept of rhyme was once, more or less, binary--a rhyme conjunction was either "exact" or "off." Either the long vowel of EDE equalled the short vowel of EDDE and the jongleur could conjoin them regularly, or (as proved to be the case) they were considered aurally distinguishable and matched most infrequently, if at all. There are numerous examples--particularly in the C MS. of King Horn--of rhyme elements that, though we were first inclined to consider them equivalent, were apparently kept quite distinct by the jongleur. We might suggest two major types of such rhyme proximity. First,

133

as with the potential equivalents for ETE noted above,
numerous rhyme elements may be considered "near" only
in so far as the various vowels that precede their com-
mon rhyme consonant(s) may also be designated "near."
Short and long pronunciations of the same vowel may
be considered "nearest" by this concept (e.g., ETE,
ETTE), and such rhymes indeed posed the most common
dilemma in our sorting of rhyme elements. In line with
one of our fundamental hypotheses about the thirteenth
century jongleur--i.e., that his rhyme was more or less
a binary system in which the links were either "exact"
or "off"--we always attempted to sort such near rhymes
as ETE & ETTE or EDE & EDDE (not to mention ETE & EDE)
into separate clusters. If the experiment failed--
that is, if such near rhymes commonly conjoined with
one another--the rhyming words were re-conjoined into
a single cluster (cf. IE). We found, however, that such
near rhyme elements normally were not used as equiva-
lents. On the contrary, their distinctness was far more
rigorous than we initially anticipated, and they almost
always employed different systems of word recurrence.
Any exceptions to this rule have been cross-referenced
and commented upon within the appendices themselves.

   The second major type of rhyme proximity to be con-
sidered in King Horn involved vowels that follow the
rhyme consonant(s)--particularly final e. This type of
"near" rhyme differs from that discussed above in that
the phonetic variant is often something more, rather
than something else. Again, we empirically resolved
the dilemma by letting each manuscript define its own
principles of exactness. For example, ING /ī̄ŋ/ never
rhymes with INGE /ī̄ŋgǝ/ in the C MS. of King Horn, but
does so frequently in the O MS. Thus, we present ING
and INGE as separate clusters in the C MS., but conjoin
them into an ING(E) cluster for O. In the L MS. /ī̄ŋ/
links with /ī̄ŋgǝ/ only once (ll. 579/580). Though this
couplet might have been considered an exception (i.e.,
a scribal omission), the /ī̄ŋ/ / /ī̄ŋgǝ/ conjunction seems
hardly an "off-rhyme" as such; so, we present ING(E)
as a single cluster in the L MS. as well as the O. In
attempting empirically to determine just what rhymes
and what does not in the various manuscripts of King
Horn, we have always opted for such hyperprecision.
Our intent with each such decision has been to preserve
general consistency, rather than to establish specific
rigor; we can be no more accurate in the recording of
a jongeur's rhyme principles than was the scribe of
each manuscript. We hope to have been no less. But
we have indeed posited that each manuscript may, in
fact, record a unique oral performance and that the

rhyme principles of performance C may not be identical
to those of performances L or O.

So the fundamental question of whether sound a
rhymes with sound b has always been answered within
the hypothetical context of each oral performance.
Thus, each appendix represents each manuscript sep-
arately. Within each appendix, the rhyme elements
are divided into three major categories--solely for
organizational purposes. Category I represents rhyme
elements that occur in less than three couplets of
each romance. As such, they can provide no adequate
indication of rhyme recurrence; Category I, thus, may
be considered a gathering of negligible entries.
Category III, however, represents rhyme elements
that occur in ten or more couplets of each romance
and, as such, provides the strongest evidence for rhyme
recurrence in King Horn. Category II, quite simply,
is "in between" and consists of rhyme elements that
occur in three to nine couplets of each manuscript;
the evidence for rhyme recurrence extracted from Cate-
gory II is more convincing than that from Category I,
but far more ambivalent than that of Category III.
Within each category of each appendix, the rhyme
elements are headnoted and entered alphabetically
according to standardized spelling of the element it-
self (as mentioned earlier) so that parallel entries
for each manuscript might be more readily compared.

With this firm understanding that the designation
of each rhyme element in the appendices that follow
has been an inductive decision, we may look at a sample
entry in order more fully to explain the format and
procedures involved in our analysis of the rhyme clus-
ters of King Horn and of its systematic end-rhyme.

If we again take the cluster of rhyme words in the
C MS. which use the rhyme element EDDE as our model
(cf. Chapter IV), its entry in Appendix C Category II
would appear as follows:

MS. C   (1) Rhyme Element: __EDDE__

(2) Preliminary		(2) Terminal	
bedde	299, 839, 1195	bedde	950
wedde	949	hudde	1196 *
		schredde	840
		wedde	300

(3) Total: 4

(4) Word	(4) Recurrence	(5) #	(6) %
bedde	4	4	100
wedde	2	0	Ø

(8)   (7)   (9)

(12.5) SUBGROUP: bedde (100%)

(10) Comment: The bedde/hudde couplet (ll. 1195/1196)
               may be considered excludable as an
               "off-rhyme."

136

This format is the norm in Categories II and III of the appendices, and its various entries may be defined as follows:

(1) EDDE--the rhyme element, indicates the common rhyme sound that makes this grouping of words a cluster in MS. C, and that we have determined inductively may be considered distinct from any other cluster in the same manuscript.

(2) PRELIMINARY & TERMINAL--merely designate whether the various rhyme words used in this cluster appear in the first or second line of a couplet respectively. Within each column, each specific word is then listed in alphabetical order once; it is accompanied, however, by line references to all its occurrences. Variant spellings are preserved, but bracketed and considered a single rhyme word. Similarly, compounds are entered into the alphabetical order under their root word (e.g., "featherbed" would appear under "bed"), bracketed and considered an occurrence of the root word itself. Since, however, our analysis focuses on rhyme words as semantic as well as phonetic entities, we have striven to distinguish homonyms from one another and have provided glosses parenthetically when necessary to avoid confusion. "Off-rhymes," that is, words which do not reproduce the rhyme element of the cluster exactly, are asterisked.

(3) TOTAL--merely indicates the number of couplets that this cluster contains.

Thus, the first task of each appendix entry is merely to record data; nothing more is possible in Category I. But it is the four additional columns (i.e., "Word," "Recurrence," "#," and "%"), which follow this listing process in Categories II and III, that actually attempt to discern a system in the jongleur's use of end-rhymes.

(4) WORD & RECURRENCE--are best explained at once. All words that recur two or more times in a cluster are listed under "Word"--not alphabetically, but according to the frequency of their use which is noted under "Recurrence." No distinction is made under "Recurrence" between whether a word is used in a Preliminary or a Terminal position. Only when two or more words do recur the same number of times within a cluster are they then entered alphabetically. This somewhat arbitrary decision about priority in the order of listing should be noted since it effects both # and %.

137

(5) #--indicates the number of couplets that may
be "accounted for" by a given rhyme word. "Accounted
for" implies the entire concept of systematic rhyme
that we are attempting to discern. A word "accounts
for" its couplet (defined as a pairing of end-rhymes)
when it provides a readily available means by which
the jongleur could complete his aurally perceptible
form--the couplet. It is this implicit notion of
relative recallability which explains why Recurrence
and # are not one and the same column. We do not con-
sider a recurrent word to "account for" a couplet that
has already been "accounted for" by a more readily avail-
able rhyme word. (Again, priority among rhyme words is
determined first by rate of recurrence and then by alpha-
betical order when the recurrence rate of several words
is the same). It is most common, therefore, for the
figure given under "Recurrence" and under "#" to be
identical only for the first listing in each cluster;
in fact, only rare instances of word duplication in a
single couplet (e.g., "were" and "nere," or "ne were")
will alter this equation. But the discrepancies between
Recurrence and # soon become apparent with the second
and third entries in each column. Whereas Recurrence
represents in a very real sense the total number of
couplets that each word may "account for" potentially
(if considered absolutely), # indicates the number of
new couplets that each word "accounts for" in actuality.
Thus Recurrence provides an isolated consideration of
each word's relative usefulness to an improvising
jongleur, and this third column must be read as a
vertical series.

(6) %--represents the number of couplets "accounted
for" by each word divided by the total number of coup-
lets in its cluster (#÷TOTAL). It suggests what portion
of the entire cluster may be considered "accounted for"
by an individual rhyme word. It, like #, also repre-
sents a vertical series.

It is under the heading SUBGROUP (7) that we actually
extract the evidence for our theory. The words that
we have determined (from their respective # and %
columns) to have actually provided the jongleur with
a system of readily recalled rhymes are listed here.
So, the SUBGROUP for each rhyme element theoretically
reconstructs the actual words around which a jongleur
would improvize his lines. On occasion, particularly
with Category III entries, we have found it useful to
subdivide the SUBGROUP into Major and Minor items; this
distinction (like that among the Categories themselves)

138

is strictly organizational. The division is rather arbitrarily made when the recurrence rate of the most recurrent word in a cluster first equals or exceeds double the recurrence rate of another word in the same subgroup. The purpose of this divison is merely to help our subsequent evaluation of the relative significance of these words in a jongleur's system.

The heading, SUBGROUP is always preceded by a parenthetical percentage (8); this figure represents the ratio of the total number of words in a subgroup to the total number of words that theoretically would be used in a cluster to achieve complete variety, its maximum vocabulary. Maximum vocabulary, of course, usually equals double the Total number of couplets (unless odd words are introduced by extraneous lines, as occurs three times in MS. O). Likewise, another percentage (9) is also given parenthetically following the actual listing of the words in the Subgroup; this figure represents the cumulative sum of the total percentage of couplets in a cluster "accounted for" by the Subgroup as a whole (or by its Major and Minor subdivisions); it is quite simply the sum of the total subgroups' individual percentages (6). These parenthetical percentage figures are given precisely to help evaluate the systematic nature of each rhyme cluster.

(10) COMMENT-- is the final, optional entry for each item in Categories II and III of the appendices. Under the heading Comment we note exceptions, cross reference clusters, discuss peculiar difficulties, and the like.

In summary, each entry in Categories II and III of the appendices should be considered a tripartite study. The function of the columns headed Preliminary and Terminal is simply observational; they merely present the words of each cluster as such. The four columns that follow this listing, however, establish a frame for analysis. Finally, the information represented as the Subgroup-- the words themselves and their percentages--record our conclusions extracted from this analysis; it is this information that forms the core of our theory. We hope, however, that our appendices do not create an impression of the jongleur as some sort of rhyming machine. As the Comments frequently indicate, there is still much room for interpretation of the data. For example, a not uncommon problem in our initial sorting of couplets was determining what to do with those "off-rhyme" pairs that might be put into one of two significant clusters. Should the

139

kinne/sodenne link (MS. O 11. 894/895) be placed in the INNE cluster (Category III) or the ENNE cluster (Category II)? All things being equal, we normally placed such couplets in the cluster of the Preliminary rhyme element, though we insist that the jongleur conceived of his couplet as a unit. If, however, the Terminal word of such a couplet proved to be a significant element of the subgroup in its own cluster, we might opt for this variant placement. Such a decision might be considered "tampering" with a fixed procedure. The specific placement of a particular couplet may be argued, and the actual statistics given may, therefore, vary slightly. Nevertheless, we believe the net result of such differences in the final analysis would prove slight if not moot--for while the rhyme recurrence in one cluster might diminish, it would normally increase in another.

NOTES TO <u>METHODOLOGY</u>

[1]Joseph Hall, ed., <u>King</u> <u>Horn</u> (Oxford: Clarendon Press, 1901).

[2]William Rickert, "Rhyme Terms," <u>Style</u>, 12, No. 1 (Winter, 1978), 35-46.

[3]Our standardized spelling is modelled on that of Donald Sands, ed., <u>Middle</u> <u>English</u> <u>Verse</u> <u>Romances</u> (New York: Holt, Rinehart and <u>Winston, 1966)</u>, pp. 15-54.

[4]MS. C, 11. 697-698; MS. L, 11. 609-700; MS. O, 11. 716-717.

APPENDIX A

THE END-RHYMES OF <u>KING</u> <u>HORN</u>, MS. C

<u>Category</u> <u>I</u>: Rhyme elements that occur in less than
three couplets of MS. C.

<u>Rhyme</u> Element	<u>Preliminary</u>	<u>Terminal</u>
ABLE	table 587	stable 588
ACE	grace 571 lace 717	place 572, 718
AD (Cf. ADDE (II)	ofdrad 573	amad 574
AGHTE	laȝte 243	taȝte 244
AILLE	assaille 637 bataille 855	assaille 856 faille 638
AIE (Cf. AY II)	bitraie 1251	laie 1252
A(L)D	Admirad 89	bald 90
ALE	sale 1107 tale 1031	ale 1108 brudale 1032
ALKE	halke 1087	walke 1088
AM (Cf. AME I)	nam 585	cam 586
AME (Cf. AM I, AN I)	blame 1265 name 197	game 198 name 1266
AN	þeran 575 man 787	lemman 576 cam 788*
ANG	sprang 493	lang 494
ANNE	wymmanne 67	þanne 68
APE	slape 1417	rape 1418
AR (Cf. ARE II)	þar 505	Aylmar 506
ARD	gateward 1067	hard 1068
ARME	arme 705	barme 706
ARNE	warne 689	berne 690*

142

Rhyme Element	Preliminary	Terminal
ARPE	harpe 231	scharpe 232
AS	was 13	glas 14
ASSE	Christesmasse 799	lasse 800
ATE	late 1473 ʒate 1043	gate 1474 late 1044
ATERE	watere 1019	latere 1020
ATTE	smatte 607	hatte 608
EGGE	legge 1057 ligge 1275*	rigge 1058* wiþ segge 1276
EL	grauel 1465	castel 1466
ELF	twelf 489	him self 490
ELTE	pelte 1415	hilte 1416*
EME	fleme 1271	reme 1272
EMEÐ	iquemeþ 485	bisemeþ 486
ENT (Cf. ENTE II)	adrent 977	isent 978
ENGÐE	strengþe 899	lengþe 900
EO	heo 1439 þre 815*	beo 816, 1440
EOSE	leose 663	cheose 664
EPE	kepe 1103 wepe 657	aslepe 658 wepe 1104
EPEST	kepest 1307	slepest 1308
ERIN	þerin 1241	ferin 1242
ERKE	derke 1431	werke 1432
EÐE	eþe 835	deþe 836
EUED	heued 621	bireued 622
EUENE	steuene 665	sweuene 666

Rhyme Element	Preliminary	Terminal
EURE	eure 1101	neure 1102
EWÐE	rewþe 409	trewþe 410
IBBE	libbe 63 ribbe 315	libbe 316 sibbe 64
ICH (Cf. ICHE II, IKE II, IT I)	un bicomelich 1065	ilich 1066
IF	strif 407	wif 408
IGGE	abugge 1075*	brigge 1076
IKKE	þikke 1239	nekke 1240*
IMME	swymme 189	brymme 190
INDE	binde 191	bihynde 192
IPE	gripe 51, 605	smite 52 wype 606
IPPE	scrippe 1061	lippe 1062
IRES	ires 959	tires 960
ISSE	fisse 1143	disse 1144
IT (Cf. ICH I, ICHE II, IKE II)	whit 501	ilik 502*
ITE	lite 1131 write 931	lite 932 white 1132
IX(T)E	sixe 391	nixte 392
LE	sle 1369	fle 1370
NE⎱ S MI⎰	Reynes 951	enemis 952
OD (Cf. ODE II)	stod 529 þralhod 439	god ("good") 530 kniȝthod 440
OLE	fole 589	cole 590
OME	nome 1173	come 1174

144

Rhyme Element	Preliminary	Terminal
ONG (Cf. ONGE III)	among 1527 strong 93	long 94 song 1528
OR(E)ȜE	amoreȝe 837	sorȝe 838
OR(S)TE	schorte 927	dorste 928
OTE	hote 767 ihote 201	hote 202, 768
OUE(D)	houe 1267	proued 1268
OȜ (Cf. OWE III)	sloȝ 871	droȝ 872
RIS/ERIS	heris 897	pris 898
ROS	aros 1313	gros 1314
RUNGE	sprunge 1015	irunge 1016
ÐE	þe 895	þe 896
UDE	crude 1293	lude 1294
UȜTEN	fuȝten 1375	uȝten 1376
UME(S)	gumes 161	icume 162
UN (Cf. UNE II)	adun ("down") 1121 galun 1123	brun 1122 glotoun 1124*
UND (Cf. UNDE II)	sund 1341	wund 1342
UNGE	tunge 1259	sunge 1260
UPPE	cuppe 449, 1125	þer uppe 450, 1126
URCHE	wurche 1379	chirche 1380*
(O)URS	harpurs 1471	gigours 1472
US	aþelbrus 225 Aþelbrus 1501	hus 226, 1502 (n.)
USE	spuse 993	huse 994 (v.)

Rhyme Element	Preliminary	Terminal
UÐE	cuþe 353 ruþe 673	Muþe 354 truþe 674
WARD	stuard 451	foreward 452
Y (Cf. IE I)	Murry 1335	hendy 1336

Category II: Rhyme elements
that occur in three to nine   Rhyme Element: ADDE
couplets of MS. C.

Preliminary	Terminal
hadde 19, 1045, 1165 nadde 863	dradde 1166 harde 864* ladde 20, 1046

Total: 4

Word	Recurrence	#	%
(ne)hadde	4	4	100
ladde	2	0	Ø

(12.5%)SUBGROUP: (ne)hadde (100%)

Comment: Cf. AD (I).

Rhyme Element: <u>AGE</u>

Preliminary	Terminal
heritage 1281	age 1324
homage 1497	baronage 1282
passage 1323	trewage 1498

Total: 3

Word	Recurrence	#	%
Ø	Ø	0	Ø

SUBGROUP: Ø

Comment: There is no apparent word recurrence for this
end-rhyme cluster. The common suffix -<u>age</u>
(indicating condition, residence or collec-
tivity) does, however, appear in all three
couplets.

Rhyme Element: <u>AKE</u>

Preliminary	Terminal
blake 1319	awake 1306
make 1409, 1453	forsake 1320
spake 535	gate 1078*
take 553, 1305	rape 554
tobrake 1077	sake 1454
	⎰take 536
	⎱itake 1410

Total: 7

Word	Recurrence	#	%
(i)take	4	4	57
(for)sake	2	2	29

(14%)<u>SUBGROUP</u>: take, sake (86%)

Comment: The <u>tobrake</u>/<u>gate</u> couplet seems a clear and
valid exception, but may be excludable as an
"off-rhyme"; cf. ARE (I).

MS. C   Rhyme Element: __ARE__

Preliminary	Terminal
Alymare 1243	Aylmare 1494
bare 891	ifare 468
fare 1355	kare 1244
þare 1493	ȝare 892, 1356
ȝare 467	

Total: 5

Word	Recurrence	#	%
ȝare	3	3	60
Aylmare	2	2	40
(i)fare	2	0	Ø

(20%)SUBGROUP: ȝare, Aylmare (100%)

Comment: Cf. AR (I).

MS. C   Rhyme Element: <u>ASTE</u>

Preliminary	Terminal
⎰caste 841	caste 1014
⎱icaste 659	faste 842
haste 615	⎰laste 616
maste 1013	⎱ilaste 660

Total: 4

Word	Recurrence	#	%
(i)caste	3	3	75
(i)laste	2	1	25

(25%) <u>SUBGROUP</u>:   (i)caste, (i)laste (100%)

151

Rhyme Element: __AWE__

Preliminary	Terminal
aslaʒe 1491	aslaʒe 860
draʒe 1289	draʒe 1420
felaʒe 1419	ſfelaʒe 996
haue 995*	⎸felaʒes 1290
withdraʒe 859	todraʒe 1492

Total: 5

Word	Recurrence	#	%
(-)draʒe	4	4	80
felaʒe(s)	3	1	20

(20%)<u>SUBGROUP</u>: draʒe, felaʒe (100%)

Comment: The <u>haue/felaʒe</u> couplet (ll. 995/996) may be
          considered excludable as an "off-rhyme."

MS. C   Rhyme Element: <u>AY</u>

Preliminary	Terminal
day 29, 727	may 30, 728
lay 1303, 1477	walalay 1478
	way 1304

Total: 4

Word	Recurrence	#	%
lay	2	2	50
day	2 }		
may	2	2	50

(38%) <u>SUBGROUP</u>: lay, day/may (100%)

Comment: Cf. AIE (I).

MS. C   Rhyme Element: <u>ECHE</u>

Preliminary	Terminal
biseche 453, 579	areche 1220
fecche 351	recche 352
efreche 1283	speche 170, 454, 580, 1368
seche 169	teche 388
speche 387	wreche 1284
teche 1219, 1367	

Total: 8

Word	Recurrence	#	%
speche	5	5	63
(-)reche	3	3	37
(-)seche	2	0	Ø
teche	2	0	Ø

(12.5%)<u>SUBGROUP</u>: speche, reche (100%)

MS. C   Rhyme Element: __EDDE__

Preliminary	Terminal
bedde 299, 839, 1195 wedde 949	bedde 950 hudde 1196* schredde 840 wedde 300

Total: 4

Word	Recurrence	#	%
bedde	4	4	100
wedde	2	0	Ø

(12.5%)<u>SUBGROUP</u>: bedde (100%)

Comment: The <u>bedde</u>/<u>hudde</u> couplet (ll. 1195/1196) may be
          considered excludable as an "off-rhyme."

MS. C   Rhyme Element: EIDE

Preliminary	Terminal
deide 1185	bitraide 1270
leide 379	leide 692
{ sede 691	maide 272
{ seide 271, 1269	preide 1186
	seide 380

Total: 5

Word	Recurrence	#	%
se(i)de	4	4	80

(10%) SUBGROUP: seide (80%)

Comment: The deide/preide (1185/1186) rhyme is a clear
           and valid exception to this cluster (20%).

MS. C   Rhyme Element: <u>ELLE</u>

Preliminary	Terminal
belle 1253	felle 62, 1254
pelle 401	fulle 402
quelle 61	quelle 618
snelle 1463	spelle 1030
telle 617, 1029	wille 1464

Total: 6

Word	Recurrence	#	%
telle	2	2	33
felle	2	2	33

(8%) <u>SUBGROUP</u>: telle, felle (66%)

Comment: The <u>pelle/fulle</u> (ll. 401/402) and <u>snelle/wille</u>
(ll. <u>1463/1464</u>) couplets may be considered
variants, or they may be considered excludable
from this cluster as "off-rhymes" (33%); cf.
ILLE (II) and ULLE (II).

MS. C   Rhyme Element: __EN__

Preliminary	Terminal
kyn 633*	ben 8
quen 7	flen 86
slen 85	Men 634

Total: 3

Word	Recurrence	#	%
Ø	Ø	0	Ø

SUBGROUP: Ø

Comment: Cf. ENE (II).

MS. C   Rhyme Element: <u>ENCHE</u>

Preliminary	Terminal
adrenche 105	adrenche 1412
benche 369, 1105, 1475	clenche 1476
blenche 1411	ofþinche 106
	schenche 370, 1106

Total: 5

Word	Recurrence	#	%
benche	3	3	60
adrenche	2	2	40

(20%)<u>SUBGROUP</u>: benche, adrenche (100%)

Rhyme Element: ENDE

Preliminary	Terminal
ende 733 hende 371, 1117 sende 1001 { wende 679, 911, 1401 { ywende 1211	ende 912, 1212 schende 680, 1402 sende 734 wende 372, 1118 yrlonde 1002*

Total: 8

Word	Recurrence	#	%
(y)wende	6	6	75
ende	3	1	13
sende	2	1	13
hende	2	0	Ø

(19%)SUBGROUP: Major: wende (75%)
             Minor: ende, sende (25%)

Comment: The sende/yrlonde (ll. 1001/1002) couplet may
          be considered excludable as an "off-rhyme";
          cf. ONDE (III).

MS. C   Rhyme Element: ENE

Preliminary	Terminal
fiftene 37	ʃbene 508
grene 851	ɭbeon 1520*
kene 91, 507	kene 38, 164, 852, 1128
quene 1519	quene 350
tene 349, 683	isene 92, 684
þrottene 163	
wene 1127	

Total: 9

Word	Recurrence	#	%
kene	6	6	67
be(o)n(e)	2	1	11
quene	2	1	11
isene	2	1	11
tene	2	0	Ø

(22%)SUBGROUP: Major: kene (67%)
                Minor: bene, quene, isene (33%)

Comment: Cf. EN (II).

MS. C   Rhyme Element: <u>ENNE</u>

Preliminary	Terminal
kenne 985	kenne 144, 176, 1518
Suddenne 143, 175, 1365	menne 1366
suddenne 1517	Suddenne 986

Total: 5

Word	Recurrence	#	%
suddenne	5	5	100
kenne	4	0	Ø

(10%)<u>SUBGROUP</u>:   suddenne (100%)

Comment: It seems to make more sense that the common
           verb <u>kenne</u> which recurs four times (80%),
           should be considered the primary element of
           this cluster as a predictable link to the
           "proper name" <u>Suddenne</u>. And it should be noted
           that <u>Suddenne</u> occurs primarily in the first
           lines of couplets that <u>kenne</u> then completes
           (60% of the total cluster).

MS. C   Rhyme Element: <u>ENTE</u>

Preliminary	Terminal
dunte 609*	rente 914
rente 725	schente 322
sente 525, 919, 1337	sente 726
⎧ wente 913	wente 526, 610, 920, 1338
⎩ biwente 321	

Total: 7

Word	Recurrence	#	%
(-)wente	6	6	86
sente	4	1	14

(14%)<u>SUBGROUP</u>:   wente, sente (100%)

Comment: Cf. ENT (I).

MS. C   Rhyme Element: <u>ERDE</u>

Preliminary	Terminal
answerde 199	answarede 42
ferde 751	ferde 938
herde 937	herde 200
ofherde 41	hurede 752*
swerde 623	orde 624*

Total: 5

Word	Recurrence	#	%
(of)herde (a)	3	3	60
answerde	2	0	Ø
ferde	2	0	Ø

(10%)<u>SUBGROUP</u>: herde (60%)

MS. C   Rhyme Element: __ERNE__

Preliminary	Terminal
ȝerne 915, 1085, 1403	werne 916, 1404
	wurne 1086*

Total: 3

Word	Recurrence	#	%
ȝerne	3	3	100
werne	2	0	Ø

(17%) <u>SUBGROUP</u>:   ȝerne (100%)

MS. C   Rhyme Element: __ERTE__

Preliminary	Terminal
herte 875, 1389, 1481	smerte 876, 1390, 1482

Total: 3

Word	Recurrence	#	%
herte smerte	3 ⎫ 3 ⎭	3	100

(33%)<u>SUBGROUP</u>: herte/smerte (100%)

MS. C   Rhyme Element: ERVE

Preliminary	Terminal
kerve 233	serue 234, 776
serue 909	sterue 910
sterue 775	

Total: 3

Word	Recurrence	#	%
serue	3	3	100
sterue	2	0	Ø

(16%) SUBGROUP: serue (100%)

MS. C   Rhyme Element: ESSE

Preliminary	Terminal
agesse 1181	blesse 584
blesse 555	blisse 158*
fairnesse 213	cusse 1208*
kesse 583	meeknesse 1496
posse 1011	pruesse 556
{ Westernesse 157, 921	sorinesse 922
{ westernesse 1207, 1495	{ Westernesse 214, 1012
	{ westernesse 1182

Total: 9

Word	Recurrence	#	%
westernesse	7	7	78
blesse	2	2	22

(11%) SUBGROUP: Major: westernesse (78%)
                  Minor: blesse (22%)

168

MS. C   Rhyme Element: __ETE__

Preliminary	Terminal
grete 889	ete 1258
schete 939	forlete 218
swete 217, 1407, 1257	lete 890
suete 1257	imete 940
	mete (dream) 1408

Total: 5

Word	Recurrence	#	%
swete	3	3	60
(-)lete	2	1	20

(20%)SUBGROUP: swete; lete (80%)

Comment: The schete/imete couplete (ll. 939/940) seems
          a clear and valid variant (20%).

MS. C   Rhyme Element: <u>ETTE</u>

Preliminary	Terminal
mette 1027	biflette 1396
sette 383, 757, 1201, ·1395	grette 384, 1028
	kepte 1202
	sette 758

Total: 5

Word	Recurrence	#	%
sette	5	4	80
grette	2	1	20

(20%)<u>SUBGROUP</u>: <u>Major</u>: sette (80%)
                <u>Minor</u>: grette (20%)

Comment: The <u>sette/sette</u> link (ll. 757/758) is one of
          the few examples of a couplet in <u>King Horn</u>
          that employs the reduplication of the same
          word to make its end-rhymes.

MS. C   Rhyme Element: <u>EVE</u>

Preliminary	Terminal
bileue 363, 1321	bileue 742
leue 463, 741	eue 364, 464
	reue 1322

Total: 4

Word	Recurrence	#	%
bileue	3	3	75
leue	2	1	25
eue	2	0	Ø

(25%)<u>SUBGROUP</u>: bileue, leue (100%)

MS. C   Rhyme Element: <u>EWE</u>

Preliminary	Terminal
fewe 55	fewe 1462
knewe 1441	to hewe 1312
rewe 1521	leue 562
schewe 1311, 1461	newe 746
trewe 377, 561, 745, 1171	nywe 1442
	rewe 378
	schrewe 56
	trewe 1522
	þrewe 1172

Total: 9

Word	Recurrence	#	%
trewe	5	5	56
fewe	2	2	22
schewe	2	1	11
(y)			
newe	2	1	11

(22%)SUBGROUP: Major: trewe (56%)
               Minor: fewe, schewe, newe (44%)

MS. C   Rhyme Element: <u>ICHE</u>

Preliminary	Terminal
kinge riche 17 iliche 313 riche 339	iliche 18, 340 riche 314

Total: 3

Word	Recurrence	#	%
iliche	3	3	100
riche	2	0	Ø

(17%)<u>SUBGROUP</u>: iliche¯(100%)

Comment: <u>Riche</u> occurs two times as a matched pair with
<u>iliche</u>. Cf. ICH (I) and IKE (II).

Preliminary	Terminal
brunie 591	denie 592
companye 879	derie 786
enuye 687	folye 688
lie 1451	hi e 880*
+serie 1385	merie 1386
werie 785	twyę 1452

+Hall (p. 223) considers
serie a scribal error for
ferie ("carry").

Total: 6

Word	Recurrence	#	%
0	0	0	Ø

SUBGROUP: Ø

Comment: There are no apparent systematic end-rhymes
in this "cluster." Rather, this grouping
demonstrates the greatest possible variety
in the composition of end-rhyme--six couplets
employ twelve different rhyme words. It
may be argued that the -ie ending provides
one of the more readily available end-rhymes
in the English language. But it should also
be noted that only three of the above coup-
lets employ "exact" rhymes: brunie/denie,
serie/merie and werie/derie; these three
links alone match identical consonants
followed by /i‑Jə/ or /ı·ə/. The remaining
four couplets are linked solely by assonance,
cf. Y (I) where the assonantal link between
Murry and hendy is reduced to /ı́/; and it
should be noted that /ı́/ is never considered
equivalent to /i·Jə/ or /i·ə/. Since none

Comment (cont.): of the "exact" rhymes in
this cluster recurs with sufficient frequency
to determine any formulaic elements, and
since none of the remaining couplets employs
"exact" rhyme, this entire "cluster" may be
broken up into several Category I items or
excluded from our consideration as "off-
rhymes."

MS. C   Rhyme Element: <u>IGHE</u>

Preliminary	Terminal
adriʒe 1035	isiʒe 756, 976
isiʒe 1157	iʒe 1036
iʒe 755, 975	liʒe 1158

Total: 4

Word	Recurrence	#	%
isiʒe	3	3	75
iʒe	3	1	25

(25%)<u>SUBGROUP</u>:   isiʒe, iʒe (100%)

176

MS. C   Rhyme Element: _IKE_

Preliminary	Terminal
biswike 667	biswike 290
ilike 289	mislike 668
mis lyke 425	sike 426

Total: 3

Word	Recurrence	#	%
(-)like	3	3	100
biswike	2	0	Ø

(17%)SUBGROUP: like (100%)

Comment: Biswike occurs two times as a matched pair with
          (-)like. Cf. ICHE (II) and IK (I).

MS. C   Rhyme Element: ILE

Preliminary	Terminal
(seint) gile 1175	⎰bigile 320
Mile 319	⎱bigiled 958*
while 595, 957, 1317	ille 1318
	Mile 1176
	myle 596

Total: 5

Word	Recurrence	#	%
while	3	3	60
mile	3	2	40
bigile(d)	2	0	∅

(20%)SUBGROUP: while, mile (100%)

Comment: The while/ille (11. 1317/1318) couplet may be
          considered excludable from this cluster as an
          "off-rhyme"; cf. ILLE (II).

MS. C   Rhyme Element: ___ILLE___

Preliminary	Terminal
ille 675 stille 287, 373, 541, ·999 wille 193, 365, 943, 1315	duelle 374* spille 194 stille 676 telle 366, 944* wille 288, 542, 1000 ylle 1316

Total: 9

Word	Recurrence	#	%
wille	7	7	78
stille	5	2	22
(y)			
ille	2	0	Ø
telle*	2	0	Ø

(11%)SUBGROUP: wille, stille (100%)

179

MS. C   Rhyme Element: <u>IME</u>

Preliminary	Terminal
paynyme 803	(bi)me 534*
rime 1363	pryme 966
⎰time 533	ryme 804
⎱bitime 965	time 1364

Total: 4

Word	Recurrence	#	%
(bi)time (y)	3	3	75
rime	2	1	25

(25%)<u>SUBGROUP</u>: time, rime (100%)

MS. C   Rhyme Element: <u>IN</u>

Preliminary	Terminal
Arnoldin 1443	cosin 1444
pin (door-bolt) 973	in 974
wyn 1153	pilegrym 1154*

Total: 3

Word	Recurrence	#	%
0	0	0	Ø

<u>SUBGROUP</u>: Ø

Comment: Cf. INE (II).

MS. C   Rhyme Element: <u>INE</u>

Preliminary	Terminal
birine 11	bischine 12
lyne 681	fine 262
myne 1053	⌠pine (n.) 540
⌠pine (n. "anguish") 261	⌡pine (v.) 682
⌡pine (v. "to torture") 635	sclauyne 1054
þine 539	þine 636

Total: 6

Word	Recurrence	#	%
pine	4	4	67
þine	2	0	Ø

(8%)<u>SUBGROUP</u>: pine (67%)

Comment: The <u>birine/bischine</u> (11/12) and <u>myne/sclauyne</u>
          (1053/1054) rhymes are valid exceptions (33%).
          Note that various possessive pronouns or adjec-
          tives (which may be considered "easy" rhymes)
          occur three times and account for one of the
          exceptions (17%).

Rhyme Element: <u>INKE</u>

Preliminary	Terminal
brinke 141	⎧drinke 1152
⎧drinke 1055	⎩nadrinke 142
⎨adrinke 971	efþinke 972, 1056
þinke 1151	

Total: 4

Word	Recurrence	#	%
(-)drinke	4	4	100
(ef)þinke	3	0	Ø

(12.5%) SUBGROUP: drinke (100%)

MS. C   Rhyme Element: __INNE__

Preliminary	Terminal
biginne 1277	ginne 1456
inne 1455	linne 992
lynne 311	⌠inne 604, 1358
winne 991, 1357	⎨her inne 312
wynne 603	⌡þerinne 1072
awynne 1071	winne 1278

Total: 7

Word	Recurrence	#	%
(-)inne	5	5	71
(y) (-)winne	5	2	29

(14%)SUBGROUP: inne, winne (100%)

184

MS. C   Rhyme Element: <u>IS</u>

Preliminary	Terminal
his 1255 ywis 517, 1233	blis 1234 is 518 palais 1256*

Total: 3

Word	Recurrence	#	%
ywis	2	2	67

(17%)<u>SUBGROUP</u>: ywis (67%)

Comment: This -IS cluster may be merely a subgrouping
of the -ISSE cluster in which (-)wisse is the
primary rhyme word; cf. ISSE (II) & ISE (II).

The his/palais couplet (oo. 1255/1256) is an
exception (33%) which may be considered ex-
cludable as an "off-rhyme."

185

MS. C   Rhyme Element: <u>ISE</u>

Preliminary	Terminal
agrise 867	arise 868
arise 359	deuise 930
wise 237, 929, 989	seruise 238, 990
	wise 360

Total: 5

Word	Recurrence	#	%
wise	4	4	80
arise	2	1	20
seruise	2	0	Ø

(20%)<u>SUBGROUP</u>:   Major:⁀ wise (80%)
                    Minor: arise (20%)

Comment: Cf. ISSE (II) & IS (II).

186

MS. C   Rhyme Element: ISSE

Preliminary	Terminal
kesse 431*	blisse 414, 1210
wisse 121, 413, 1457	misse 122, 1458
vwisse 1209	ywisse 432

Total: 5

Word	Recurrence	#	%
(y)wisse	5	5	100

(10%)SUBGROUP: wisse (100%)

Comment: Cf. IS (II) & ISE (II).

Rhyme Element: <u>ISTE</u>

Preliminary	Terminal
criste (Christ) 77 liste 235, 1459 miste 1361 wiste 1435	vpriste 1436 wiste 78, 236, 1362, 1460

Total: 5

Word	Recurrence	#	%
wiste	5	5	100
liste	2	0	Ø

(10%)<u>SUBGROUP</u>: wiste (100%)

MS. C   Rhyme Element: __IÞE__

Preliminary	Terminal
bliþe 1, 355, 967, 1225, 1347 swiþe 273, 471, 791 yþe 57	bliþe 274, 792 bliue 472, 968* diþe 58 lyþe 2 siþe 356, 1348 swiþe 1226

Total: 9

Word	Recurrence	#	%
bliþe	7	7	78
swiþe	4	1	11
bliue*	2	0	Ø
siþe	2	0	Ø

(11%)SUBGROUP: bliþe, swiþe (89%)

Comment: The yþe/diþe (57/58) rhyme is a clear and
          valid variant (11%); cf. IVE (III).

MS. C   Rhyme Element: <u>ITTE</u>

Preliminary	Terminal
flitte 711 sitte 627, 651, 1083 ·	anhitte 712 mitte 628 witte 652, 1084

Total: 4

Word	Recurrence	#	%
sitte	3	3	75
witte	2	0	Ø

(12.5%)<u>SUBGROUP</u>:   sitte (75%)

Comment: The <u>flitte/anhitte</u> (11. 711/712) rhyme seems
           a clear and valid exception (25%).

MS. C   Rhyme Element: ___O_____

Preliminary	Terminal
fro 367	also 98
go 97	do 268, 276
to 267	two 430
two 49	þo 50, 116, 264, 368
wo 115, 263, 275, 429	

Total: 8

Word	Recurrence	#	%
wo	4	4	50
þo	4	2	25
do	2	1	13
two	2	0	Ø

(19%)SUBGROUP: Major: wo, þo (75%)
                Minor: do (13%)

Comment: The go/also (ll. 97/98) rhyme seems a clear
          and valid exception (12%).

191

MS. C   Rhyme Element: <u>ODE</u>

Preliminary	Terminal
blode 177	blode 1406
flode 139, 1183	fode 1340
gode ("God") 75	forbode 76
gode ("good") 1339	gode 140, 146, 178, 282,
mode 281, 1405	1184
moder 145*	

Total: 8

Word	Recurrence	#	%
gode	6	6	75
blode	2	1	12
flode	2	0	Ø
mode	2	0	Ø

(13%)<u>SUBGROUP</u>: <u>Major</u>: gode (75%)
                 <u>Minor</u>: blode (12%)

Comment: The <u>gode/forbode</u> link (ll. 75/76) seems a
           clear and valid exception (13%). As usual,
           we have not considered homonyms to be single
           elements. But this instance may be prove
           to be an exception, since the "good/God"
           pun may have been considered an etymological
           identity by the medieval jonleur himself.
           (Cf. OD (I).

MS. C   Rhyme Element: <u>OF</u>

Preliminary	Terminal
drof 119	leof 324, 708
þeof 323, 707	þerof 120

Total: 3

Word	Recurrence	#	%
þeof leof	2 ⎱ 2 ⎰	2	67

(33%)<u>SUBGROUP</u>: þeof/leof (67%)

Comment: The <u>drof/þerof</u> (11. 119/120) rhyme seems a
          clear and valid exception in this minimal
          system (33%).

MS. C   Rhyme Element: <u>OFTE</u>

Preliminary	Terminal
doʒter 697*	briʒte 390*
softe 389, 1069	ofte 698, 1070

Total: 3

Word	Recurrence	#	%
ofte	2	2	67
softe	2	1	33

(33%)<u>SUBGROUP</u>: ofte, softe (100%)

Comment: If the <u>doʒter/ofte</u> (ll. 697/698) and <u>softe/</u>
          <u>briʒte</u> (ll. 389/390) rhymes were to be
          excluded from this cluster as examples of
          "off-rhyme," the cluster itself would divide
          into three Category I entries. Cf. ICTE (III).

MS. C   Rhyme Element: OKE

Preliminary	Terminal
asoke 65	loke 748, 1100
forsoke 747	toke 66, 1142
loke 1141	
toke 1099	

Total: 4

Word	Recurrence	#	%
loke	3	3	75
toke	3	1	25

(25%)SUBGROUP: loke, toke (100%)

Rhyme Element: <u>OLDE</u>

Preliminary	Terminal
bolde 375	golde 1038, 1164
golde 459	holde 376
holde 307, 1249	scholde 1250
Molde 317	⎧wolde 308, 318
scholde 395	⎩woldest 396, 644
⎧wolde 1163	iȝolde 460
⎩nolde 1037	
iȝolde 643	

Total: 9

Word	Recurrence	#	%
(-)wolde(st)	6	6	67
golde	3	1	11
holde	3	2	22
iȝolde	2	0	Ø
scholde	2	0	Ø

(17%)<u>SUBGROUP</u>: <u>Major</u>: wolde (67%)
                 <u>Minor</u>: holde, golde (33%)

MS. C   Rhyme Element: <u>ORDE</u>

Preliminary	Terminal
borde 113, 253, 827, 1485	orde 1486 { worde 114, 254 { wordes 828

Total: 4

Word	Recurrence	#	%
borde	4	4	100
worde(s)	3	0	Ø

(12.5%)<u>SUBGROUP</u>:   borde (100%)

Comment: <u>Worde(s)</u> occurs all three times as a matched
           pair with <u>borde</u>; <u>borde</u> is always <u>preliminary</u>,
           and <u>worde(s)</u> always <u>terminal</u> in these
           pairings.

MS. C   Rhyme Element: <u>ORE</u>

Preliminary	Terminal
{ more 95, 441, 1193 { namore 1193 { ore 1509 { þinore 655 sore 69, 1049	deole 1050* lore 442, 1510 more 70 sore 656, 1194 ȝere 96*

Total: 7

Word	Recurrence	#	%
(-)more	5	5	72
sore	4	1	14
lore	2	1	14
(-)ore	2	0	Ø

(21%)<u>SUBGROUP</u>: <u>Major</u>: more, sore (86%)
                    <u>Minor</u>: lore (14%)

Comment: Cf. ERE (III).

198

MS. C   Rhyme Element: ORN

Preliminary	Terminal
forloren 479*	biforn 532
horn ("Horn") 9, 137, 329,	born 10
509, 531,	iborn 138
1525	iboren 510*
horne (v. "to drink")	horn 480
1145*	i orn ("travelled") 1146
	unorn ("ugly") 330, 1526

Total: 8

Word	Recurrence	#	%
horn ("Horn")	7	7	88
(i)bor(e)n	3	0	Ø
unorn	2	0	Ø

(7%)SUBGROUP: horn (88%)

Comment: The horne ("to drink")/i orn (ll. 1145/1146)
rhyme seems a clear and valid exception (12%).
As usual, we have not counted homonyms as a
single rhyme work; nevertheless, the simi-
larity of the verb "to drink" and the pro-
tagonist's proper name may have provided the
jongleur himself with a particularly easy
substitution. Cf. the "good"-"God" comment
under ODE (II).

199

MS. C   Rhyme Element: <u>OþE</u>

Preliminary	Terminal

{ cloþe 1215
{ cloþes 1059*
  loþe 1197
  oþe 347
	boþe 1198
	loþe 1060
	wroþe 348, 1216

Total: 4

Word	Recurrence	#	%
cloþe(s)	2	2	50
loþe	2	1	25
wroþe	2	1	25

(37.5%)<u>SUBGROUP</u>:   cloþes, loþe, wroþe (100%)

Preliminary	Terminal

{ anoþer 283
{ oþer 187, 821
  broþer 577, 1291
	{ anoþer 578
	{ oþer 1292
	  broþer 284, 822
	  roþer 188

Total: 5

Word	Recurrence	#	%
(an)oþer	5	5	100
broþer	4	0	Ø

(10%)SUBGROUP: (an)oþer (100%)

Comment: All four times, broþer is linked with (an)-
                oþer; these matched pairs alone, thus, com-
                prise 80% of this cluster. Each rhyme word
                appears with equal regularity in both the
                preliminary and terminal positions.

MS. C   Rhyme Element: __OUTE__

Preliminary	Terminal
abute 343, 1081 vte 245	abute 246 dute 344 snute 1082

Total: 3

Word	Recurrence	#	%
abute	3	3	100

(17%)<u>SUBGROUP</u>: abute (100%)

MS. C   Rhyme Element: ULLE

Preliminary	Terminal
fulle 1155 schulle 207, 847	hulle 208 telle 1156* wulle 848

Total: 3

Word	Recurrence	#	%
schulle	2	2	67

(17%)SUBGROUP;   schulle (67%)

Comment: The fulle/telle (1155/1156) variant may be
           excluded from the system as an "off-rhyme;"
           cf. ELLE (II).
           Though apparently not exploited in King Horn,
           the phonemic similarity of the modal auxil-
           iaries in English provides one of its more
           readily available rhyme links.

MS. C   Rhyme Element: <u>UNDER</u>

Preliminary	Terminal
hundred 1329* vnder 1421 wunder 1247	tunge 1248* wunder 1330, 1422

Total: 3

Word	Recurrence	#	%
wunder	3	3	100

(17%) <u>SUBGROUP</u>:   wunder (100%)

MS. C   Rhyme Element: <u>UNE</u>

Preliminary	Terminal
crune 475, 1487	crune 1286
sune 209	{dune ("upland") 154, 210
{ Tune 153	{adune 1488
{ tune 1285	tune 476

Total: 5

Word	Recurrence	#	%
crune	3	3	60
(-)dune	3	2	40
tune	3	0	Ø

(20%)<u>SUBGROUP</u>: crune, dune (100%)

Comment: Cf. UN (I).
          The omission of <u>tune</u> from the subgroup of this
          cluster may seem completely arbitrary--an
          accident of the alphabet--since it recurs
          as often as does <u>crune</u> or <u>dune</u>. Its omission,
          however, does maintain the consistency of our
          approach. But it should also be noted that
          the OUNE clusters of MSS L and O (II) do re-
          veal <u>toune</u> (not <u>crune</u>) to be the primary rhyme
          word of their respective subgroups.

MS. C   Rhyme Element: __UNNE__

Preliminary	Terminal
bigunne 1433	birunne 654
kunne 865	cunne 568
⎰ sunne 567	Suddene 866*
⎱ sunne ("window-seat") 653	sunne 1434

Total: 4

Word	Recurrence	#	%
sunne	3	3	75
(k) cunne	2	1	25

(25%)<u>SUBGROUP</u>:   sunne, cunne (100%)

206

MS. C   Rhyme Element: URNE

Preliminary	Terminal
sturne 877 turne 703, 963, 1073	⎰Murne 704 ⎱murne 964 vnspurne 1074 vrne 878

Total: 4

Word	Recurrence	#	%
turne	3	3	75
murne	2	0	Ø

(12.5%)SUBGROUP: turne (.75%)

Comment: The sturne/vrne (ll. 877/878) rhyme seems a
clear and valid exception (25%).

MS. C   Rhyme Element: <u>URSTE</u>

Preliminary	Terminal
furste 661, 1119, 1191	berste 662, 1192* ofþurste 1120

Total: 3

Word	Recurrence	#	%
furste	3	3	100
berste	2	0	Ø

(17%)<u>SUBGROUP</u>: furste (100%)

MS. C   Rhyme Element: <u>USTE</u>

Preliminary	Terminal
custe 405, 1189 luste 1263	beste 1264* luste 406 reste 1190*

Total: 3

Word	Recurrence	#	%
custe	2	2	67
luste	2	1	33

(33%)<u>SUBGROUP</u>: custe, luste (100%)

Comment: The <u>custe/reste</u> (1189/1190) and <u>luste/beste</u>
(126<u>3/1264</u>) couplets may be excluded from
the cluster as "off-rhymes"; cf. ESTE (III).

Category III: Rhyme elements
that occur in ten or more
couplets of MS. C.

Rhyme Element: __ALLE__

Preliminary	Terminal
alle 171	alle 72, 100, 224, 256,
⌈bi falle 99	626, 894
⌊falle 455	⌈bifalle 420
halle 71, 223, 255, 625,	⌋biualle 172
779, 893, 1041, 1221,	⌊falle 780, 1222
1383	halle 456
þralle 419	walle 1042, 1384

Total: 13

Word	Recurrence	#	%
halle	10	10	77
alle	7	2	15
(u)			
bi(-)falle	3	1	8
falle	3	0	Ø
walle	2	0	Ø

(12%)SUBGROUP: Major: halle, alle (92%)
              Minor: bifalle (8%)

Comment: Bifalle and falle have not been conjoined as
a single semantic unit above because their
respective meanings had already become so
divergent. If, however, they were to be so
conjoined, the (-)alle compound's "recurrence"
would equal ten, and, having alphabetical
priority, it would exchange "#" and "%" fig-
ures with halle.

　　　　　　　　　Rhyme Element:　<u>EDE</u>

Preliminary	Terminal
bede 907	bede 462
dede (dead) 1523	dede 826
dedes 537	drede 258
fairhede 83, 797	lede 184, 908, 1524
lede 293, 1393	makede 84
makede 165	mede ("reward") 470
nede 469	misrede 292
ofdrede 291	nede 48
rede 183, 825, 1051	sedes (said) 538*
spede 461	spede 798, 1394
stede 47, 257, 715	sprede 716
	verade 166*
	wede 1052
	₃ede 294

Total:　17

Word	Recurrence	#	%
lede	5	5	29
(mis)rede	4	3	18
stede	3	3	18
spede	3	2	12
bede	2	0	Ø
dede(s)	2	1	Ø
(-)drede	2	0	Ø
fairhede	2	1	6
makede	2	1	6
nede	2	1	6

(22%)<u>SUBGROUP</u>:　<u>Major</u>:　lede, rede, stede, spede (77%)
　　　　　　　　　　<u>Minor</u>:　fairhede, makede, nede (18%)

Comment:　<u>Dedes/sedes</u> (ll. 537-8) may be excludable as
　　　　　its own Category I entry; so, <u>dede(s)</u> has
　　　　　not been included in this subgroup.

MS. C   Rhyme Element: EIE

Preliminary	Terminal
deie 109	abeie 110
galeie 185	biwreie 362
he 331*	deie 332, 888, 1346
pleie 23, 345, 361	Galeie 1008
preie 763, 1235	leie 302
{ tueie 1345	pleie 186
{ tweie 301, 887	seie 764
weie 759, 1007	tweie 24, 346, 760
	weie 1236

Total: 13

Word	Recurrence	#	%
(u)			
tweie	6	6	46
deie	4	2	15
pleie	4	2	15
weie	3	2	15
preie	2	1	7
galeie	2	0	Ø

(19%)SUBGROUP: Major: tweie, pleie, deie (77%)
                Minor: weie, preie (23%)

Rhyme Element: <u>ELDE</u>

Preliminary	Terminal
bihelde 601, 1147	belde 602
elde 1391	bihelde 846
felde ("field") 557, 845,	chelde 1148
987	⌠feld ("field") 514
⌠scheld 513	⌡felde 1302
⌡schelde 53, 1301	helde 902, 1392
welde 481, 901	quelde 988
	schelde 558
	yfelde ("slay") 54
	ȝelde 482

Total: 11

Word	Recurrence	#	%
felde	5	5	45
(-)helde	5	4	36
schelde	4	1	9
welde	2	1	9

(18%) <u>SUBGROUP</u>: <u>Major</u>: felde, helde, schelde (91%)
                      <u>Minor</u>: welde (9%)

Preliminary	Terminal
beggere 1133	banere 1374
chaere 1261*	ber ("beer") 1112*
chere 403, 1063	bere 570
damesele 1169*	dere 222, 1130, 1204
dere 433, 677, 789, 1343	{ ifere 102
fer ("whole") 149*	{ yfere 242
{ fere ("companion") 743,	fisser·1134*
941, 1349	her ("here") 150
{ ifere 221, 1129	{ here 790, 942, 1350
yfere 497	{ ihere 678, 1262
here ("here") 227	lere 228
{ here ("hear") 397	lupere 498
{ ihere 1469	manere 550
ire 309*	palmere 1170
lere 241	riuere 230
mestere 229, 549	stere 434, 1344
squier 1111*	swere 404, 744, 1064
stere 101, 1373	þere 298, 766, 1168, 1246
swere 1203	were 88, 310, 398, 1354,
{ þer 523*	1470
{ þere 731, 917, 1139, 1353	{ ꝫ er 524*
{ were 297, 569, 765, 1167,	{ ꝫ ere 732, 918, 1140
1245	
{ nere ("ne were") 87	

Total: 38

Word	Recurrence	#	%
(ne)were	11	10	26
þere	9	4	11
(y)fere	8	8	21
dere	7	5	13
here ("here")	5	2	5
(y)here ("hear")	4	1	3
stere	4	1	3
swere	4	2	5
ȝere	4	0	Ø
chere	2	0	Ø
lere	2	0	Ø
mestere	2	2	5

(12%)<u>SUBGROUP</u>:   <u>Major</u>: were, þere, (y)fere, dere (72%)
                 <u>Minor</u>:· here, (y)here,·stere, swere,
                          mestere (21%)

Comment: The linking of <u>beggere</u> and <u>fisser</u> (ll. 1133/
           1134) precludes the subdivision of an ER
           cluster from the ERE cluster in this MS.
           But the three other occurences of -<u>er</u> rhymes
           do not overlap with -<u>ere</u> words (i.e., ll.
           149/150, 523/4, 1111/2). There are a total
           of three exceptions (8%) in the above clus-
           ter, and two belong to this potentially
           distinct ER cluster--i.e., <u>beggere/fisser</u>
           (ll. 1133/4) and <u>squier/ber</u> (ll. 1111/2);
           the third exception, <u>damesele/palmere</u> (ll.
           1169/1170), may be considered excludable as
           an "off-rhyme." Two of these exceptions
           could also be interpreted as occurences of the
           readily available -<u>er</u> agent suffix which, if

it were itself taken as a rhyme element,
could account for 13% of the cluster. The
<u>nere/were</u> link (ll. 87/8) offers a rare in-
stance of "identical rhyme." The exclusive
pairing of <u>chere</u> with <u>swere</u> (2x) and of ʒ<u>ere</u>
with <u>þere</u> (4x) should also be noted.

Rhyme Element: <u>ESTE</u>

Preliminary	Terminal
beste 27, 977	beste 174, 474, 770, 824,
⌠(bi)este 1135	1178, 1326
⌡bieste 1325	feste 1136, 1218
faireste 173	⌠geste 478
feste 477, 521	⌡gestes 522*
geste 1217	⌠laste 6*
leste 473	⌡leste 862
reste 861	treweste 998
strengeste 823	werste 28*
⌠weste 1177	Westernesse 946*
⌡biweste 5, 769, 945	

Total: 15

Word	Recurrence	#	%
beste	8	8	53
feste	4	4	27
(bi)weste	4	2	13
(a)			
leste	3	1	6
geste(s)	3	0	Ø

(13%)<u>SUBGROUP</u>: <u>Major</u>: beste, feste, (bi)weste (93%)
                  <u>Minor</u>: leste (6%)

Comment: <u>Feste</u> occurs three times as a matched pair
with <u>geste</u>. The <u>beste/werste</u> (ll. 27/28)
rhyme may be considered as an "off-rhyme,"
as may the <u>biweste</u>/<u>Westernesse</u> (ll. 945/946)
couplet; cf. ESSE (II).

MS. C   Rhyme Element: <u>ICTE</u>

Preliminary	Terminal

<u>   Preliminary   Terminal</u>

briȝte 1429   briȝte 382, 500
fiȝte 811, 1331   Driȝte 1310
⎧kniȝt 447, 935   fiȝte 552, 830, 1004, 1214
⎨kniȝte 435, 491, 499,   fliȝte 1398
⎩   515, 551   ⎧kniȝt 504
⎩kniȝtes 885, 1213   ⎨kniȝte 458
⎧liȝt 519   ⎩kniȝtes 520, 812
⎩liȝte 1003, 1309, 1397   ⎧liȝt 124
⎧niȝt 123   ⎩liȝte 386
⎨niȝte 259, 1199   ⎧miȝt 700
⎩middelniȝte 1297   ⎩miȝte 260, 436, 936
 pliȝte 305   ⎧niȝt 448, 1200
 ariȝte 457   ⎨niȝte 492
⎧riȝt 699   ⎩biniȝte 1430
⎩riȝte 381, 829   pliȝte 672
 siȝte 385   riȝte 306, 516, 1298, 1332
⎧wiȝt 503   wiȝte 886
⎩wiȝte 671

Total: 28

Word	Recurrence	#	%
kniȝte	13	13	46
(-)niȝte	8	5	18
riȝte	8	6	21
fiȝte	6	3	11
liȝte	6	1	4

(9%)SUBGROUP: Major: kniȝte, riȝte, (-)niȝte (85%)
                 Minor: fiȝte, liȝte (15%)

Comment: The rhymes in lines. 519/520 and in lines
          935/936 indicate that elements -iȝt, -iȝte,
          and -iȝtes should all be considered as
          belonging in the same cluster.

Rhyme Element: __IDE__

Preliminary	Terminal
abide 1023	⎰abide 854, 1048
biside 853	⎱tabide 1446
bistride 749	biside 962, 1426
glide 1047	bridel 772*
⎰ride 771, 1511	ride 34, 136, 544, 750,
⎱Ride 1425	850
side 33, 135, 203	side 954, 1024
⎰tide 849, 1445	tide 204
⎱bitide 543, 961	wide 1512
wide 953	

Total: 15

Word	Recurrence	#	%
ride	8	8	53
(bi)side	8	5	35
(bi)tide	5	1	7
abide	4	1	7

(13%)SUBGROUP: Major: ride, side, (bi)tide (93%)
                Minor: abide (7%)

Rhyme Element: <u>ILD</u>

Preliminary	Terminal
child 25, 79, 159, 247, 251, 295, 1359, 1515	berild 762
⎰ffikenhild 647	child 648
⎱fikenhild 1449	ffikenild 26
harild 761	Godhild 1360
Rymenhild 947	Mild 160
	myld 80
	Rymenhild 248, 1450
	reynild 1516
	wild 252, 296, 948

Total: 12

Word	Recurrence	#	%
child	9	9	75
wild	3	1	8
f(f)ikenhild	3	1	8
Rymenhild	3	0	Ø

(12.5%) <u>SUBGROUP</u>: <u>Major</u>: child (75%)
<u>Minor</u>: wild, fikenhild (16%)

Comment: The <u>harild/berild</u> rhyme (ll. 761/762) seems
a clear and valid exception (8%).
It should be noted that six proper names
all ending in (H)ild (OE "war") recur a
total of ten times; the suffix itself may
be considered a "formulaic" rhyme element
in this cluster and can be taken to account
for the four couplets (25%) that do not employ
<u>child</u>.   221

Preliminary	Terminal
bringe 641, 979	blessing 156, 1530
comynge 1093	bringe 582, 1094
derling 723	derling 488
dubbing 487, 629	dubbing 438, 564
erndinge 581	euening 206
fissing 1149	fundlyng 220
fiȝtinge 817	gleowinȝe 1468
⌈king 31, 155, 437, 925,	huntinge 646
1507, 1529	⌈king 424
⟨kinge 843	⟨kinge 4, 496, 642, 1288,
⌊kyng 147, 195, 205, 219,	1428
341, 805, 981	⟨kyng 782
knewelyng 781	⌊kynge 212
⌈(gold)ring 563	lokyng 342
⟨ringe 613, 1381, 1483	Niþing ("villain") 196
⌊rynge 873	noþing 1150
Rymenhilde 1287*	⌈pleing 630
singe 3, 129, 1467,	⌊pleȝing 32
springe 211, 495, 593,	⌈rimenilde 614*
645, 1017, 1229,	⟨Rymenhild 1034*
1427	⌊Rymenhilde 874, 1484*
þing 443	risinge 844
wedding 423, 1033	singe 594, 1382
	springe 130, 818
	sweuening 724
	swoȝning 444
	teching 1508
	⌈tiþing 982
	⟨tiþinge 1230
	⌊tyþyng 806 .
	⌈wedding 926
	⟨weddinge 1018
	wiþering 148
	wringe 980

Total: 43

Word	Recurrence	#	%
(y)			
king(e)	22	22	51
springe	9	6	14
(-)ringe	5	5	12
(i)			
Rymenhild(e)*	5	1	2
singe	5	1	2
bringe	4	3	7
dubbing	4	2	5
wedding(e)	4	0	Ø
(y)(y)			
tiþing(e)	3	0	Ø
blessing	2	0	Ø
derling	2	1	2
(no)þing	2	2	5
ple(ʒ)ing	2	0	Ø

(10%)<u>SUBGROUP</u>:   <u>Major</u>:· kinge (51%)
                 <u>Minor</u>:   springe, ringe, Rymenhilde*,
                          singe, bringe, dubbing, derling,
                          þing (49%)

<u>Comment</u>:   This INGE cluster represents the single
          most recurrent rhyme sound in the C MS.;
          here, unlike the L or O MSS., there can be
          no question that -<u>inge</u> and -<u>ing</u> were con-
          sidered exact equivalents.
          Note that <u>ringe</u> was employed only in pre-
          liminary lines. <u>Rymenhilde</u>, the "off-rhyme"
          element in this subgroup, is peculiar as
          such, but note that it "accounts for" only
          one new couplet which might as readily
          have been attributed to <u>wedding</u>. No doubt,

<u>Comment (cont.)</u>: phonic allowances for the heroine's
           proper name were made. Cf. ILD (III).
           Although the -<u>ing</u> suffix provides one of the
           most readily available rhymes in English,
           it is not necessary to include all participles
           and gerunds as a single "rhyme element" so
           that the established criteria might be
           satisfied. Nevertheless, it should be
           noted that such verbals do recur 24 times
           in the above cluster.

Preliminary	Terminal

```
  aliue 107, 619            ⌠ariue 1296
⌠ariue 179, 923, 1505       ⌡aryue 778
⌡ariued 807*                ⌠driue 1424
  bliue 721                 ⌡dryue 796
  driue 1333                 fiue 808
  fiue 1295, 1423            kniue 108
⌠lyue 559, 777              ⌠liue 1334
⌡(on)lyue 131, 693          ⌡lyue 180
  wyue 795                   ryue 132
                            sire 1506*
                            þriue 620
                            wyue 560, 694, 722, 924
```

Total: 15

Word	Recurrence	#	%
(-)liue	8	8	53
ariue(d)	6	4	27
wyue	4	2	13
driue	3	1	7

(13%)SUBGROUP: <u>Major</u>: liue, ariue (80%)
               <u>Minor</u>: wyue, driue (20%)

MS. C   Rhyme Element: <u>OȝTE</u>

Preliminary	Terminal
biþoȝte 411	boȝte 884, 1388
broȝte 883	broȝte 40, 466, 600
doster (sic., daughter) 249	lofte 904
doȝter 903	miȝte 412
soȝte 465, 599	þoȝte 250, 1274
isoȝte 39	þuȝte 278
þoȝte 277	
wroȝte 1387	
iwroȝte 1273	

Total: 10

Word	Recurrence	#	%
broȝte	4	4	40
(-)þoȝte	4	4	40
doȝter	2	1	10
(-)wroȝte	2	1	10
(i)soȝte	3	0	Ø

(20%)<u>SUBGROUP</u>: Major: broȝte, þoȝte (80%)
                   Minor: doȝter, wroȝte (20%)

Comment: All three recurrences of <u>(i)soȝte</u> are as
          a matched pair with <u>broȝte</u>.

Preliminary	Terminal
anhonde 1109	fonde 730, 832
fond 151	fondede 1514*
honde 81, 215, 1137, 1299,	honde 60, 112, 152, 266,
1327, 1413, 1499	338, 400, 598
hunde 831*	londe 36, 82, 126, 216,
husebonde 415, 735, 1039	416, 754, 810, 870,
londe 59, 511, 701, 713,	934, 1022, 1040,
729, 753	1110, 1180, 1300,
sonde 265, 809, 933	1328, 1414
stonde 399, 597, 869, 1021,	schonde 702, 714
1179	stonde 512
stronde 35, 111, 125	stronde 1138, 1500
wonde 337	wonde 736
yrlonde 1513	

Total: 32

Word	Recurrence	#	%
(yr)londe	23	22	69
(an)honde	15	8	25
stonde	6	0	Ø
stronde	5	0	Ø
fonde	4	1	3
husebonde	3	1	3
sonde	3	0	Ø
schonde	2	0	Ø
wonde	2	0	Ø

(6%)SUBGROUP: Major: londe, honde (94%)
                   Minor: fonde, husebonde (6%)

Preliminary	Terminal
anon 45, 285, 1231	anon 1352
gon 1351	icome 1448*
gone 611	⎧done 784
⎧one 527	⎨idone 446, 484
⎨alone 1025, 1113	⎩vndone 1238
⎩al one 833	gomes 22*
none 801	gon 46, 286, 1232
slone 43	mone (comrade) 528
sone (soon) 357, 445, 483,	ymone ("?, complaint?) 834
783, 1237	mone (share) 1114
sone (son) 1447	⎧on 820
sones 21*	⎨alone 74
stone 73	⎨al one 612
þurston 819	⎩none 358
	sone (soon) 802
Total: 20	stone 1026
	vpon 44

Word	Recurrence	#	%
(-)one	9	9	45
sone ("soon")	6	4	20
(-)done	4	0	Ø
anon	4 ⎫		
gon	4 ⎬	4	20
sone(s) ("son")	2	20	10

(10%)SUBGROUP: Major: one, sone ("soon") (65%)
              Minor: done, gon/anon, sone ("son")(30%)

Comment: The slone/upon (ll. 43/44) rhyme is a clear
          variant (5%); it implies, primarily since
          slone is the preliminary element, that the
          ONE and ON rhyme elements should be considered
          a single cluster, according to our general
          criteria. If, however, we separate these
          groupings into two distinct clusters and
          include lines 43-44 in the ON category

Comment (cont.): as an "off-rhyme," then the per-
        centages given above would increase pro-
        portionate to the reduction of the cluster's
        total number of couplets to fourteen. The
        subsequently generated ON cluster would
        consist of six couplets; in it, anon pairs
        exclusively with gon four times accounting
        for 67% of the cluster.

        Another peculiarity of the ONE cluster as
        recorded above, is that the minor element
        sone ("son") is used only in "off-rhymes,"
        which may also be considered excludable as
        such (10%).

Preliminary	Terminal
{ fonge 327, 719, 737 { vnderuonge 239 longe 303 ringe 565, 1187* songe 1097 wronge 905 ȝonge 127, 279, 547	anhonge 328 bringe 280* longe 720, 738, 1098 songe 240 isprunge 548* stronge 304 tiþinge 128* vnderfonge 906 ȝonge 566, 1188

Total: 12

Word	Recurrence	#	%
(vnder)fonge ᵘ	5	5	42
ȝonge	5	5	42
longe	4	2	16
ringe	2	0	Ø
songe	2	0	Ø

(12.5%)SUBGROUP: fonge, ȝonge, longe (100%)

Comment: Cf. ONG (I), INGE (III), and UNGE (I).

MS. C   Rhyme Element: <u>(O)UNDE</u>

Preliminary	Terminal

cunde 421, 1377   {bunde 422
funde (hasten) 103, 133   {ibunde 1116
{ifounde 773   funde (discover, reach) 882
{ifunde 955   ifunde (hasten) 1280
grunde 639, 1115   grunde 104, 134, 334, 740,
hundes 881   1160
stunde 167, 333, 739,   londe 168*
     1159, 1279   {stunde 956
                                   {astunde 774
                                    þende 1378*
                                    wunde 640

Total: 14

Word	Recurrence	#	%
grunde	7	7	50
stunde	7	4	29
(i)f(o)unde	3	1	7
ibunde	2	1	7
cunde	2	1	7

(18%)<u>SUBGROUP</u>: <u>Major</u>: grunde, stunde (79%)
                   <u>Minor</u>: funde, bunde, cunde (21%)

Comment: Cf. UND (I) and ONDE (II).

Preliminary	Terminal
⎰bur 325 ⎱bure 269, 649, 695, 709, 1161, 1223 flur 15 sture 685 ture 1091, 1437 vre 393, 813	⎰auenture 650 ⎱mesauenture 326 ⎰messauenture 710 bure 394, 686, 1438 colur 16 couerture 696 foure 1162 lure 270 pure 1092 ture 1224 ᴣoure 814

Total: 13

Word	Recurrence	#	%
bur(e)	10	10	77
(-)auenture	3	0	Ø
ture	3	1	8
ure	2	1	8

(11.5%)SUBGROUP: Major: bure (77%)
                  Minor: ture, ure (16%)

Comment: The flur/colur couplet (ll. 15/16) is the only
          exception in the above cluster (8%). It should
          be noted, however, that this "exception" is
          a unique example of an exact UR rhyme without
          final e's. Nevertheless, since bur rhymes
          with mesauenture (ll. 325/326), it seems invalid
          to subdivide this cluster into separate UR
          and URE groupings.

Rhyme Element: __OWE__

Preliminary	Terminal
blowe 1009, 1371	droȝe 1006
boȝe 1227	flowe 632
buȝe 427*	gloue 794
⎰todroȝe 181	knowe 418, 670, 1090, 1206
⎱wiþ droȝe 1399	iknowe 1372
felawe 1089*	louȝe 1480*
flowe 117, 1095, 1503	(his) oȝe 984
iknowe 983	⎰inoȝe 182
inoȝe 857, 1005	⎰Inoȝe 1228
lowe 417	⎱ynoȝe 1400
loȝe 1079	rowe 118, 1096
⎰(Min) oȝe 335	Rowe 1504
⎱þinowe 669	rowe ("queue") 1080
⎱þinoȝe 1205	iswoȝe 428, 858
proue 545	þrowe 1490
Rowe 631	þroȝe 336, 1010
a rowe ("queue") 1489	woȝe 546, 970
yswoȝe 1479	
þroȝe 969	
woȝe ("woo") 793	

Total: 24

Word	Recurrence	#	%
knowe (y)	6	6	25
inoʒe	5	5	21
flowe	4	4	17
rowe	4		
(-)oʒe (w)	4	1	4
proʒe	4	3	13
(-)dro e	3	0	Ø
iswoʒe	3	2	8
woʒe	3	2	8
lowe	2	1	4
rowe ("queue")	2	0	Ø

(19%)<u>SUBGROUP</u>:   <u>Major</u>:   knowe, inoʒe, flowe/rowe,
                         oʒe, prowe (80%)
              <u>Minor</u>:   iswoʒe, woʒe, lowe (20%)

Comment: Clearly -OʒE and -OWE are equivalents
           (ll. 1009/1010, 983/984, 1079/1080, 1205/
           1206); similiarly -OʒE and -OUE are equiva-
           lents (ll. 545/546, 793/794). Cf. O (I).
           Note the unique spelling of <u>felawe</u> (rather
           than <u>felaʒe</u>) when it conjoins with primary
           element of this OWE cluster. For this (albeit
           minimal) reason, the preliminary rhyme of
           lines 1089/1090 has not determined the place-
           ment of the couplet; transferring this coup-
           let to MS. C's AʒE cluster, however, would
           merely increase the recurrence of one of its
           subgroup's major rhymes. Cf. AʒE (II).

APPENDIX B

THE END-RHYMES OF KING HORN, MS. L

Category I: Rhyme elements that occur in less than three couplets of MS. L.

Rhyme Element	Preliminary	Terminal
ABLE	stable 715 table 585	fable 716 stable 586
ACCHE	cacche 1227	vacche 1228
ACE	g/ra̅/ce 569 la̅ce 719	place 570, 720
ADDE	hadde 21	ladde 22
ADDEN	hadden 597	ladden 598
AHTE	bycahte 663 lahte 249	lahte 664 taht 250
AKEDE	crakede 1083	rakede 1084
AL	þral 423	al 424
ALE	sale 1109 tale 1043	ale 1110 brudale 1044
AME	name 205	game 206
AN	man 793 þeran 573	cam 794* lemman 574
ANNE	wymmanne 71	þanne 72
APE	slape 1315	yshape 1316
ARME	arme 705	barme 706
ARPE	harpe 237	sharpe 238
AS	was 13	glas 14
ASSE	c/ri̅/stemasse 805	lasse 806
ATERE	watere 1029	latere 1030

235

MS. L

Rhyme Element	Preliminary	Terminal
AYDE	sayde 277, 405	mayde 278, 406
AYLEN	asaylen 863	faylen 864
AYLY	asayly 633	fayly 634
EAREN	earen 969	tearen 970
ECCHE	kecche 1377 fecche 357	yrecche 358 vecche 1378
ED	bed 1435	adred 1436
EF	þef 331	lef 332
ENTE	hente 443 bywente 329	trente 434 shende 330*
EON	fleon 887 teon 723	seon 724 teon 888
EOSE	forleose 665	cheose 666
EOTEN	fleoten 159	weopen 160
EPE	wepe 655	yslepe 656
EPEST	kepest 1319	slepest 1320
ER	þer 509	Aylmer 510
ERDE	ferde 757 herde 945	ferde 946 herde 758
EREN	leren 247 weren 1249	feren 248, 1250
ERKE	derke 1451	werke 1452
ERNDE	ernde 1239	bernde 1240
ERSTE	ferste 661	berste 662
ER(I)S	harperis 1493	fyþelers 1494
EH	heh 1095	neh 1096

MS. L

Rhyme Element	Preliminary	Terminal
ELD	sheld 515	feld 516
ELE	g/ra͞/uele 1487 dȧmoisele 1173	castele 1488 palmere 1174*
ELVE	tuelue 493	selue 494
EME	reme 1525	streme 1526
EMEÐ	quemeþ 489	bysemeþ 490
EN	men 897 fyhten 1385	eueruchen 898 ohtoun 1386*
ENCH	þench 1163	drench 1164
ENTEN	senten 1347	wenten 1348
ERTE	herte 1503 sherte 935	smerte 1504 derste 936*
ERVE	serue 921 sterue 781	serue 782 sterue 922
ERVEN	keruen 241	seruen 242
ESTES (Cf. ESTE III)	gestes 1225	festes 1226
ET	net 683	sumwet 684
ETTEN	fletten 763	setten 764
EÐE	eþe 61, 843	deþe 62, 844
EUÐE	reuþe 415, 675	treuþe 416, 676
EVED	heued 617	byreued 618
EVENE	steuene 667	sweuene 668
EVERE	euere 1105	neuere 1106
EYDE	seyde 693, 1257	leyde 694 wreyede 1258*
EYȜEN	eyȝen 755	yseyȝen 756

237

MS. L

Rhyme Element	Preliminary	Terminal
EYNE	tweyne 891	beyne 892
EYR	feyr 911	heyr 912
EYSE	eyse 1265	paleyse 1266
HEDE	þralhede 443	knyhthede 444
IBBE	libbe 67 ribbe 323	libbe 324 sibbe 68
ICKE	þicke 1247	nycke 1248
IDDE	bydde 1183	bitidde 1184
IKE	byswyke 669	lyke 670
IKEN	lyken 429	syken 430
ILDE	childe 301 wylde 1045	Remenylde 1046 wilde 302
ILEN	milen 327	bigilen 328
ILTE	pylte 1433	hylte 1434
INDE	bynde 199 sittynde 649	bihynde 200 wepynde 650
IPE	gripe 55, 603	smyte 56* wype 604
IPPE	scrippe 1069 skippe 1361	clippe 1362 lippe 1070
IRSTE	firste 1197	berste 1198*
IS	reynis 959 ywis 519	enimis 960 ys 520
ISSH	fyssh 1145	dyssh 1146
ISTE	kyste 1217	lyste 1218
ITE	ibite 1131 wryte 939	lyte 940 white 1132

MS. L

Rhyme Element	Preliminary	Terminal
ITEN	flyten 855	smiten 856
ITTE	sitte 623, 1089	mitte 624 wytte 1090
LO	slo 91	flo 92
LOUR	flour 15	colour 16
LY	reuly 1057	bitterly 1058
OD	mod 257	god 258
OF	drof 123	of 124
OHTEN	sohten 43	brohten 44
OKE	forsoke 751	loke 752
OLD	Admyrold 95 bold 17	bold 96 old 18
OLE	fole 587	cole 588
OM	nom 583	com 584
OMEN	gomen 169	ycomen 170
ONDER	honder 1339	wonder 1340
ONES	fones 23	gomes 24*
ONG	sprong 497 strong 99	long 100, 498
OPPE	coppe 453, 1125	uppe 454, 1126**
ORD	bord 259	word 260
OREWE	amorewe 407, 845	sorewe 408, 846
ORNE	horne 337, 1147	orne 1148 unorne 338
OS	aros 1325	agros 1326
OTE	hote 773 yhote 209	bote 210, 774

239

MS. L

Rhyme Element	Preliminary	Terminal
OUDE	croude 1301	loude 1302
OUN	galoun 1123	glotoun 1124
OUNES	dounes 161	tounes 162
OUSE	house 1003	spouse 1004
OUÞE	couþe 359	mouþe 360
OVE	houe 1277 proue 543	proue 1278 wowe 544*'
OWEN	wowen 779	glouen 780
REDE	adrede 297	rede 298
UNDER	under 1439	wonder 1440
URCHE	wurche 1391	chyrche 1392*
URE	sture 1445	cure 1446
URSTE	furste 885 vurste 1119	afurste 1120 huerte 886*
UR(R)Y	Murry 873 mury 1345	sturdy 874* hardy 1346*
US	Aþelbrus 231, 1521	hous 1522 þus 232
USTE	custe 403 puste 1079	fluste 1080 luste 404
VISE	deuyse 243	seruise 244
WARD	styward 455 ʒateward 1073	foreward 456 froward 1074
YE	enuye 689	folye 690
YN	arnoldyn 1463 myn 397	cosyn 1464 þyn 398

240

Category II: Rhyme elements
that occur in three to
nine couplets of MS. L.   Rhyme Element: __ADE__

Preliminary	Terminal
feyrhade 89	felaurade 174
lade 1409	made 90, 1410
made 173	

Total: 3

Word	Recurrence	#	%
made	3	3	100

(17%)SUBGROUP: made (100%)

MS. L   Rhyme Element: ___AGE___

Preliminary	Terminal
baronage 1517	age 1334
heritage 1289	page 1290
passage 1333	t/ru/age 1518

Total: 3

Word	Recurrence	#	%
0	0	0	Ø

SUBGROUP: No discernible recurrence.

Comment: The relative smallness of this cluster and,
          conversely, the frequent use of the relatively
          available suffix -age (4 of the 6 words above
          employ it) may explain the absence of any
          discernible subgroup.

MS. L   Rhyme Element: <u>AKE</u>

Preliminary	Terminal
blake ("black") 1331 make 1427, 1473 spake 535 take 551, 1209 ytake 1317	awake 1318 blake ("dirt") 1210 forsake 1332 make 552 sake 1474 take 536, 1428

Total: 7

Word	Recurrence	#	%
(-)take	5	5	71
make	3	1	14

(21%)<u>SUBGROUP</u>: take, make (86%)

Comment: . Perhaps, <u>sake</u> (1. 1474) should be included
with <u>forsake</u> (1. 1332). We have not done
so because of the contradictory meanings
of "to <u>forsake</u>" and "for the <u>sake</u> of."
Similarly, the recurrence of <u>blake</u> (in 1.
1331 as a plural adjective; in 1. 1210 as
a singular substantive) might be counted
as a single rhyme word--which would thus
become a <u>minor</u> member of the cluster's
subgroup <u>(14%)</u>. As with homonyms, however,
we have here opted for maximum distinction
among semantic units. Cf. the comment on
<u>croune</u> in the OUNE cluster (ii) of this MS.

MS. L   Rhyme Element: <u>ARE</u>

Preliminary	Terminal
aylmare 1251 þare 471, 1365	care 1252 yfare 472, 1366

Total: 3

Word	Recurrence	#	%
þare	2 ⎫	2	67
yfare	2 ⎭		

(33%)<u>SUBGROUP</u>: þare/yfare (67%)

Comment: The <u>aylmare</u>/<u>care</u> (ll. 1251/1252) couplet seems
          a clear and valid exception.

244

MS. L   Rhyme Element: <u>ASTE</u>

Preliminary	Terminal
{ caste 849 { ycaste 659 maste 1023	caste 1024 faste 850 laste 660

Total: 3

Word	Recurrence	#	%
(-)caste	3	3	100

(17%)<u>SUBGROUP</u>:   caste (100%)

MS. L   Rhyme Element: <u>AWE</u>

Preliminary	Terminal
{drawe 867, 1297, 1461 {ydrawe 1313 felawe 1093, 1437 have 1005* shewe 1481* yslawe 913	dawe 914 drawe 1438 felawe 1006, 1298, 1462, 1482 lawe 1314 plawe 1094 slawe 868

Total: 9

Word	Recurrence	#	%
felawe	6	6	67
(-)drawe	5	2	22
(-)slawe	2	1	11

(17%)<u>SUBGROUP</u>: <u>Major</u>: felawe, (-)drawe (86%)
                   <u>Minor</u>: slawe (14%)

MS. L   Rhyme Element: __AY__

Preliminary	Terminal
ay 1543	away 732
{ day 31, 1421	day 918, 956
{ godneday 731	lay 1544
lay 1499	may 32, 1422
may 917, 955	weylaway 1500

Total: 7

Word	Recurrence	#	%	
(-)day	5	5	71	
may	4	0	Ø	
lay	2	2	29	

(14%)SUBGROUP: Major: day 71% (day/may 57%)
                Minor: lay 29%

Comment: We have not considered weylaway (1. 1500)
          and away (1. 732) a recurrence.

247

MS. L   Rhyme Element: ___E___

Preliminary	Terminal
he 503	be 268, 560, 824, 920
fre 267	solempnite 504
þe 559, 919	
þre 823	

Total: 5

Word	Recurrence	#	%
be	4	4	80
þe	2	0	Ø

(10%)SUBGROUP: be (80%)

Comment: The he/solempnite (ll. 503/504) couplet seems
          a clear and valid exception (20%). It might
          be possible, however, to consider the homo-
          phonic personal pronouns (i.e., he and þe,
          but also me, we, e, hey) as a single rhyme
          "word" which would recur three times in this
          cluster and account for the remaining 20% of
          its couplets.

248

MS. L   Rhyme Element: <u>ECHE</u>

Preliminary	Terminal

cleche 963
{ seche 177
  biseche 457
speche 317, 389
{ teche 1379
  byteche 577
þorhreche 1291
	seche 318
	speche 178, 458, 578, 964,
	    1380
	teche 390
	wreche 1292

Total: 8

Word	Recurrence	#	%
speche	7	7	88
(-)seche	3	0	Ø
(-)teche	3	0	Ø

(6%)<u>SUBGROUP</u>: speche (88%)

Comment: The <u>þorhreche</u>/<u>wreche</u> (ll. 1291/1292) couplet
          seems a clear and valid exception.

MS. L   Rhyme Element: __EDDE__

Preliminary	Terminal
bedde 847, 1201 hedde 1169 sredde 589 wedde 957	bedde 958 adredde 1170 fedde 590 gredde 1202 shredde 848

Total: 5

Word	Recurrence	#	%
bedde	3	3	60
s(h)redde	2	1	20

(20%)<u>SUBGROUP</u>: bedde, s(h)redde (80%)

Comment: The <u>hedde/adredde</u> (ll. 1169/1170) couplet
          seems a clear and valid exception (20%).

MS. L   Rhyme Element: <u>ELLE</u>

Preliminary	Terminal
belle 1263	felle 66
felle 1157	fulfulle 1264*
quelle 65	quelle 614
spelle 951	spelle 1040
telle 613, 1039	telle 952, 1158

Total: 6

Word	Recurrence	#	%
telle	4	4	67
felle	2	1	17
quelle	2	0	Ø
spelle	2	0	Ø

(17%)<u>SUBGROUP</u>: <u>Major</u>: telle (67%)
                    <u>Minor</u>: felle (17%)

Comment: <u>Spelle</u> rhymes exclusively with <u>telle</u> forming
          two matched pairs. The inclusion of <u>felle</u>
          in the subgroup, rather than <u>quelle</u> is
          determined solely by their alphabetical order.
          Cf. ALLE (III) in which <u>(-)fulle</u> occurs as an
          "off-rhyme" with <u>palle</u> (ll. 413/414); perhaps,
          we should establish an ULLE group to be
          included in Category I.

MS. L   Rhyme Element: <u>ENCHE</u>

Preliminary	Terminal
⎧benche 1107 ⎨abenche 1497 ⎩obenche 373 adrenche 109 ouerblenche 1429	clenche 1498 adrenche 1430 shenche 374, 1108 þenche 110

Total: 5

Word	Recurrence	#	%
(-)benche	3	3	60
adrenche	2	2	40
shenche	2	0	Ø

(20%)<u>SUBGROUP</u>: (-)benche, adrenche (100%)

MS. L   Rhyme Element: __ENDE__

Preliminary	Terminal
ende 737	wodes ende ("wood's end")
hende 375, 1117, 1137	1220
rende 727	sende 728, 738
sende 527	shende 682, 1418
wende 681, 1219, 1417	pende 1138
	wende 376, 528, 1118

Total: 9

Word	Recurrence	#	%
wende	6	6	67
(-)sende	4	2	22
hende	3	1	11
ende	2	0	Ø
shende	2	0	Ø

(17%)__SUBGROUP__: __Major__: wende, sende (89%-)
                    __Minor__: hende (11%)

MS. L   Rhyme Element: ENE

Preliminary	Terminal
fyftene 41	bene 8, 1542
grene 959	kene 42, 172, 860, 1128
kene 97	ysene 686
quene 7, 1541	shene 98
tene 685	
þrettene 171	
wene 1127	

Total: 8

Word	Recurrence	#	%
kene	5	5	63
quene	2 ⎫	2	25
bene	2 ⎭		

(19%)SUBGROUP: Major: kene (63%)
                 Minor: quene/bene (25%)

Comment: The tene/ysene (ll. 685/686) rhyme seems a
          clear and valid exception (12%).

MS. L   Rhyme Element: <u>ENNE</u>

Preliminary	Terminal

kenne 875, 995
menne 629
sudenne 149, 183, 1275,
      1375, 1539
	kenne 150, 184, 630, 1276,
	     1540
	yrisshemenne (Irish men)
	     1376
	sudenne 876, 996

Total: 8

Word	Recurrence	#	%
kenne	7	7	86
sudenne	7	1	14
(-)menne	2	0	Ø

(12.5%)<u>SUBGROUP</u>:   kenne, sudenne (100%)

MS. L   Rhyme Element: <u>ERDE</u>

Preliminary	Terminal
yherde 45	yherde 208
sherte 1485*	orde 620*
suerde 619	suerde 1486
onsuerede 207	onsuerede 46

Total: 4

Word	Recurrence	#	%
yherde	2	2	50
onsuerede	2	1	25
suerde	2	1	25

(37.5%) <u>SUBGROUP</u>:   yherde, onsuerede, suerde (100%)

Comment: This is a very unstable cluster. The <u>sherte/</u>
            <u>suerde</u> (ll. 1485/1486) and <u>suerde/orde</u>
            (ll. 619/620) couplets seem excludable as
            "off-rhymes"; all the rest of the cluster
            seems to consist of "near rhymes" ([ɛr·də]and
            [ɛr·ə·də]). The cluster should perhaps be
            divided among the ERTE (I), ORDE (II), and
            EDE (III) clusters.

MS. L   Rhyme Element: ERIE

Preliminary	Terminal
sterye 147 werie 791, 1399	derye 148, 792 merye 1400

Total: 3

Word	Recurrence	#	%
werie	2	2	67
derye	2	1	33

(33%)SUBGROUP: werie, derye (100%)

MS. L   Rhyme Element: <u>ERNE</u>

Preliminary	Terminal
erne 889	forberne 692
werne 691	werne 890, 924, 1420
3erne 923, 1419	

Total: 4

Word	Recurrence	#	%
werne	4	4	100
3erne	2	0	Ø

(12.5%)<u>SUBGROUP</u>: werne (100%)

MS. L   Rhyme Element: ETE

Preliminary	Terminal
lete 1495	ete 1268
sete 1253	forlete 224
shete 947	lete 1254
suete 223, 1267, 1425	mete 948, 1426
	sete 1496

Total: 6

Word	Recurrence	#	%
(-)lete	3	3	50
suete	3	2	33
mete	2	0	Ø
sete	2	1	17

(25%)SUBGROUP: Major: (-)lete, suete (83%)
                 Minor: mete (17%)

259

MS. L   Rhyme Element: __ETTE__

Preliminary	Terminal
flette 713	fette 1398
grette 1397	flette 1412
mette 1037	grette 386, 1038
sette 385, 1411, 1207	kepte 1208*
	sette 714

Total: 6

Word	Recurrence	#	%
sette	4	4	67
grette	3	2	33
flette	2	0	Ø

(17%)SUBGROUP: sette, grette (100%)

260

MS. L   Rhyme Element: __EVE__

Preliminary	Terminal
bileue 367 leue 467, 745	byleue 746 eue 368, 468

Total: 3

Word	Recurrence	#	%
eue leue bileue	2 2 2	3	100

(50%)SUBGROUP: bileue, leue, eue 100%

Preliminary	Terminal
fewe 59	arewe 382
knewe 1459	hewe 1324
shewe 1323	yknewe 646
trewe 381, 749, 1175	newe 750, 1460
vntrewe 645	schrewe 60
	brewe 1176

Total: 7

Word	Recurrence	#	%
(-)trewe	4	4	57
(-)knewe	2	1	14
newe	2·	0	Ø

(14%)SUBGROUP: Major: trewe (57%)
                 Minor: knewe (14%)

Comment: The fewe/schrewe (ll. 59/60) and shewe/hewe
           (ll. 1323/1324) rhymes seem clear and valid
           exceptions to this cluster (29%).

MS. L   Rhyme Element: __E**ʒ**E__

Preliminary	Terminal
deʒe 1191	eʒe 1048
dreʒe 1047	leʒe 1160
seʒe 1159	preʒe 1192

Total: 3

Word	Recurrence	#	%
0	0	0	Ø

SUBGROUP: Ø

Comment: No discernible subgroup in this cluster;
           rather, it demonstrates "maximum variety"
           among its rhyming vocabulary.

MS. L   Rhyme Element: <u>ICHE</u>

Preliminary	Terminal
riche 345 yliche 19, 295, 321	ryche 20, 322 ylyche 346 suyke 296

Total: 4

Word	Recurrence	#	%
yliche	4	4	100
riche	3	0	Ø

(12.5%)<u>SUBGROUP</u>: yliche (100%)

Comment: <u>Riche</u> rhymes exclusively with <u>yliche</u> to form
            three matched pairs.

264

MS. L   Rhyme Element: __IHT__

Preliminary	Terminal
knyht 451	fourteniht 452
myht 483	knyht 484, 508
nyht 127	lyht 128
wiht 507	

Total: 4

Word	Recurrence	#	%
knyht	3	3	75
(-)nyht	2	1	25

(25%)SUBGROUP: knyht, (-)nyht (100%)

Comment: Cf. YHTE (III).

MS. L   Rhyme Element: __ILD__

Preliminary	Terminal
Abyld 767 ⎧child 27, 85, 167, 253, ⎨ 1369 ⎩chyld 1537 ffykenild 1469	beryld 768 ermenyld 1538 fykenyld 28 godyld 1370 myld 86, 168 rymenyld 254, 1470

Total: 8

Word	Recurrence	#	%
(y) child	6	6	75

(6%)<u>SUBGROUP</u>:   child (75%)

Comment: The <u>Abyld</u>/<u>beryld</u> (ll. 767/768) and <u>ffykenild/</u>
           <u>rymenild</u> (ll. 1469/1470) couplets seem clear
           and valid exceptions to the cluster (25%).
           As with Ms. C, however, it is possible to
           conceive of a "proper name" rhyme "word" which
           recurs eight times in this cluster and which
           with <u>child</u> accounts for 100% of these couplets.

MS. L   Rhyme Element: ILE

Preliminary	Terminal
gyle 1179	amyle 594
sumwhile 1329	gyle 968, 1472
⎰ whyle 593	myle 1180
⎱ while 967, 1471	yle 1330

Total: 5

Word	Recurrence	#	%	
(y)				
(-)while	4	4	80	
gyle	3	1	20	

(20%)SUBGROUP: while, gyle (100%)

267

MS. L   Rhyme Element: __ILLE__

Preliminary	Terminal

{ ille 1327
{ ylle 677
stille 215, 293, 305,
     539, 1009
wille 201, 369
	hulles 216*
	spille 202
	stille 678
	telle 370*
	wille 294, 306, 540,
	    1010, 1328

Total: 9

Word	Recurrence	#	%
wille	7	7	78
stille	6	2	22
(y.) ille	2	0	Ø

(11%)SUBGROUP: wille, stille (100%)

Comment: The stille/hulles (ll. 215/216) and wille/
          telle (ll. 369/370) couplets may be
          considered excludable as "off-rhymes;
          cf. ELLE (II).

MS. L   Rhyme Element: <u>IME</u>

Preliminary	Terminal
ryme 1373	byme 534
{tyme 533	p/ri7me 976
{bitime 975	ryme 812
paynyme 811	time 1374

Total: 4

Word	Recurrence	#	%
(-)time	3	3	75
ryme	2	1	25

(25%)<u>SUBGROUP</u>: (-)time, ryme (100%)

MS. L   Rhyme Element: __INE____

Preliminary	Terminal
myne 1061	pelryne 1156
pyne 263, 631	pyne 538
ryne 11	shyne 12
þyne 537	syne 264
wyne 1155	þyne 632, 1062

Total: 6

Word	Recurrence	#	%
pyne	3	3	50
þyne	3	1	17

(17%)SUBGROUP: pyne, þyne (67%)

Comment: The ryne/shyne (ll. 11/12) and wyne/pelryne
          (ll. 1155/1156) couplets seem clear and
          valid exceptions to this cluster (33%).

MS. L   Rhyme Element: INKE

Preliminary	Terminal
brynke 145	drynke 1154
drynke 1063	adrynke 146
adrynke 979	þinke 980, 1064
þynke 1153	

Total: 4

Word	Recurrence	#	%
(-)drynke	4	4	100
þynke	3	0	Ø

(12.5%)SUBGROUP: (-)drynke (100%)

Comment: Seventy-five percent of this cluster con-
          sists of the matched pair, drynke/þynke.

MS. L   Rhyme Element: __INNE__

Preliminary	Terminal

agynne 1285   blynne 1002
{ inne 1143   gynne 1476
  ynne 1475   { inne 602
  lynne 319   { ynne 320, 1078, 1368
{ wynne 601, 1001, 1367   wynne 1144, 1286
{ ywynne 1077

Total: 8

Word	Recurrence	#	%
(-)wynne	6	6	75
(y) inne	6	2	25
(-)gynne	2	0	Ø

(12.5%)SUBGROUP: wynne, inne (100%)

MS. L   Rhyme Element: __ISE__

Preliminary	Terminal
agryse 877 wyse 365, 937, 999	aryse 366, 878 deuyse 938 seruice 1000*

Total: 4

Word	Recurrence	#	%
wyse	3	3	75
aryse	2	1	25

(25%)SUBGROUP: wyse, aryse (100%)

273

MS. L   Rhyme Element: <u>ISSE</u>

Preliminary	Terminal
cusse 435*	blisse 420
wisse 125, 419, 1477	blysse 1242
ywisse 1241	misse 126, 1478
	wisse 436

Total: 5

Word	Recurrence	#	%
(-)wisse	5	5	100
misse	2	0	Ø
(y)			
blisse	2	0	Ø

(10%)<u>SUBGROUP</u>: wisse (100%)

Comment: <u>Wisse</u> occurs in two sets of matched pairs
           with <u>misse</u> and <u>blisse</u> for 80% of this
           cluster.

           Cf. the recurrence of <u>cusse</u> (1. 581) in ESSE
           (III).

MS. L   Rhyme Element: <u>ISTE</u>

Preliminary	Terminal
c/r̄i/st 83* {līste 1321 {listes 239, 1479* miste 1371	c/r̄i/ste 1322 {nuste 84* (ne wiste) {wiste 1372, 1480 wystest 240*

Total: 5

Word	Recurrence	#	%
(-)wiste(st)	4	4	80
liste(s)	3	1	20
crist(e)	2	0	Ø

(20%)<u>SUBGROUP</u>:   (-)wiste, liste (100%)

MS. L   Rhyme Element: <u>IÞE</u>

Preliminary	Terminal
blyþe 1, 361, 475, 977, 1233, 1357 ⎧suyþe 279 ⎩swyþe 411, 797	blyþe 280, 798 lyþe 412 ylyþe 2 olyue 362* ⎧suyþe 978 ⎩swyþe 476, 1234 syþe 1358

Total: 9

Word	Recurrence	#	%
blyþe	8	8	89
(u) swyþe	6	1	11

(11%)<u>SUBGROUP</u>: blyþe, swyþe (100%)

Comment: The <u>blyþe/olyue</u> couplet (ll. 361/362) may be
           excluded as an "off-rhyme"; if so, cf. IVE
           (III) where <u>(-)lyue</u> functions as the primary
           rhyme word of that subgroup.

MS. L   Rhyme Element: <u>ODE</u>

Preliminary	Terminal
blode 185	blode 1424
flode 143, 1189	fode 1350
gode 81, 151, 1349	forbode 82
mode 287, 1423	gode 144, 186, 288, 1190
	moder 152*

Total: 8

Word	Recurrence	#	%
gode	7	7	88
blode	2	1	12
flode	2	0	Ø

(12.5%)<u>SUBGROUP</u>:   <u>Major</u>:   gode (88%)
                     <u>Minor</u>:   blode (12%)

MS. L   Rhyme Element: <u>OFTE</u>

Preliminary	Terminal
dohter 699*	dohter 392*
{so/t̸/te 391	ofte 700, 1076
{softe 1075	

Total: 3

Word	Recurrence	#	%
ofte	2	2	66
softe	2	1	33
dohter	2	0	Ø

(33%)<u>SUBGROUP</u>: ofte, softe (100%)

Comment: Since there is only one exact rhyme (ll. 1075/
           1076) in this entire cluster, the six couplets
           above might more accurately be divided into
           two separate clusters--that is OHTER and OFTE,
           both belonging to Category I. As such, the
           lack of a clear subgroup for either cluster
           would be ignorable. But, according to our
           established criteria, the <u>dohter/softe</u> (ll.
           699/670) couplet precludes such a splitting
           of the above "cluster."

278

MS. L   Rhyme Element: ___OHTE___

Preliminary	Terminal
dohter 255*	abohte 1402
{ sohte 469	brohte 470
{ bysohte 283	ohte 418
byþohte 417	þohte 256, 284, 1282
wrohte 1281, 1401	

Total: 6

Word	Recurrence	#	%
(-)þohte	4	4	67
wrohte	2	1	16.5
(-)sohte	2	1	16.5

(25%)SUBGROUP: Major: (-)þohte (67%)
                Minor: wrohte, (-)sohte (33%)

Comment: The dohter/þohte (ll. 255/256) may be con-
          sidered excludable as an "off-rhyme"; cf.
          OFTE (II).

MS. L   Rhyme Element: <u>OKE</u>

Preliminary	Terminal
bitoke 1103 forsoke 69 loke 1141	loke 1104 toke 70, 1142

Total: 3

Word	Recurrence	#	%
(-)toke	3	3	100
loke	2	0	Ø

(17%)<u>SUBGROUP</u>:   (-)toke (100%)

Comment: <u>Loke</u> rhymes exclusively with <u>toke</u>, forming
two matched pairs. Since <u>toke</u> recurs one time
more often, <u>loke</u> does not appear in this sub-
group according to our established procedures.
But cf. MS. C OKE (II) where <u>loke</u> does account
for couplets in its own right and, thus,
appears as an operative member of that subgroup

Rhyme Element: __OLDE__

Preliminary	Terminal
bolde 379 golde 463 {holde 1259 {biholde 599 molde 325 olde 1407 {wolde 1167 {nolde 1049 ȝolde 639	bolde 600 golde 1050, 1168 holde 380, 1408 sholde 326, 1260 woldest 640* yȝolde 464

Total: 9

Word	Recurrence	#	%
(-)holde	4	4	44
golde	3	3	33
(ne)wolde(st)	3	1	11
sholde	2	1	11
(-)ȝolde	2	0	Ø

(22%) <u>SUBGROUP</u>: <u>Major</u>: holde, golde, wolde (88%)
<u>Minor</u>: sholde (11%)

Comment: There seems to be an extraordinary variety of
rhyming vocabulary in this cluster. Yet,
<u>holde</u> and <u>golde</u> alone account for 77% of the
cluster. The remaining 23% of the couplets
may be attributed to the readily available
rhymes provided in English by its modals.

MS. L

Rhyme Element: <u>OME</u>

Preliminary	Terminal
come 985 nome 1177 ylome 197	{come 1178 {ycome 198 gome 986

Total: 3

Word	Recurrence	#	%
(y)come	3	3	100

(17%)<u>SUBGROUP</u>: (y)come (100%)

MS. L   Rhyme Element: <u>ON</u>

Preliminary	Terminal
anon 49, 291	anon 1022
{gon 1021	{gon 50, 292, 822
{bygon 927	{ygon 648
on 647, 821	non 928
slon 47	on 48, 828
ston 905	won 906
þurston 827	

Total: 9

Word	Recurrence	#	%
(-)gon	6	6	67
on	4	2	22
anon	3	0	Ø

(11%)<u>SUBGROUP</u>: (-)gon, on (89%)

Comment: The <u>ston</u>/<u>won</u> (ll. 905/906) couplet seems a
          clear and valid exception to this cluster (11%).

          Thirty-three percent of this cluster consists
          of the three matched pairs made by rhyming
          <u>anon</u> exclusively with <u>gon</u>.

MS. L   Rhyme Element: OND

Preliminary	Terminal
hond 87, 871	hond 900, 1528
lond 899, 1279, 1527	lond 88, 872
vnderstond 245	song 246*
	strong 1280*

Total: 6

Word	Recurrence	#	%
lond	5	5	83
hond	4	0	Ø

(8%)SUBGROUP: lond (83%)

Comment: The vnderstond/song (ll. 245/246) couplet
           seems an exception (17%); it and the lond/
           strong (ll. 1279/1280) couplet may, how-
           ever, be considered excludable as "off-rhymes."
           Cf. ONGE (III).

MS. L   Rhyme Element: <u>ONNE</u>

Preliminary	Terminal
bigonne 1453 sonne 565, 651	byronne 652 conne 566 sonne 1454

Total: 3

Word	Recurrence	#	%
sonne	3	3	100

(17%)<u>SUBGROUP</u>:   sonne (100%)

MS. L   Rhyme Element: __ORDE__

Preliminary	Terminal
borde 117, 835, 1507 worde 461	{ suorde 1508 { sworde 462 { worde 118 { wordes 836

Total: 4

Word	Recurrence	#	%
borde	3	3	75
worde(s)	3	1	25
(u)			
sworde	2	0	Ø

(25%)<u>SUBGROUP</u>: borde, worde (100%)

Comment: The <u>borde/wordes</u> (ll. 835/836) couplet seems
         somewhat anomolous, but hardly may be con-
         sidered excludable as an "off-rhyme."

MS. L   Rhyme Element: ORE

Preliminary	Terminal
flore 709	hore 710
lore 1531	lore 446
more 445, 1199	more 74, 76
ore 653	sore 654, 1120
sore 73, 75, 1091	þore 1092, 1532

Total: 8

Word	Recurrence	#	%
sore	5	5	63
more	4	1	13
lore	2	1	13
þore	2	0	Ø

(19%)SUBGROUP: Major: sore, more (76%)
                 Minor: lore (13%)

Comment: The flore/hore (ll. 709/710) couplet seems
           a clear and valid exception to this cluster
           (12%).

MS. L   Rhyme Element: __ORN__

        Preliminary | Terminal
_____|_____

horn 9, 141, 511, 531 | ⎧born 10,
                               | ⎨yborn 142, 512
                               | ⎩biforn 532

Total: 4

_____
      Word | Recurrence | # | %
_____|_____|_____|_____

horn | 4 | 4 | 100
(-)born | 3 | 0 | Ø

(12.5%)SUBGROUP: horn (100%)

Comment: (-)born rhymes exclusively with horn, forming
           three matched pairs which may themselves be
           considered to account for 75% of this cluster.

                              288

MS. L   Rhyme Element: OÞE

Preliminary	Terminal
{ cloþe 1223 { cloþes 1067 loþe 1203 oþe 353 soþe 449	boþe 1204 loþe 1068 oþe 450 wroþe 354, 1224

Total: 5

Word	Recurrence	#	%
oþe	2	2	40
loþe	2	2	40
wroþe	2	1	20
cloþe(s)	2	0	Ø

(30%) SUBGROUP: oþe, loþe, wroþe (100%)

289

MS. L   Rhyme Element: OÞER

Preliminary	Terminal
broþer 575, 1299 oþer 195, 289, 829	broþer 290, 830 oþer 576, 1300 roþer 196

Total: 5

Word	Recurrence	#	%
oþer	5	5	100
broþer	4	0	Ø

(10%)SUBGROUP: oþer (100%)

Comment: Broþer rhymes exclusively with oþer, forming
four matched pairs which may themselves be
considered to account for 80% of this cluster.

MS. L   Rhyme Element: __OUNE__

Preliminary	Terminal
coroune ("crown") 479	adoune 1510
croune ("head") 1041,	broune 1122
1509	roune 1294
doune 1121	toune 218, 480, 1042
soune 217	
toune 1293	

Total: 6

Word	Recurrence	#	%
toune	4	4	67
(-)doune	2	2	33
croune	2	0	∅

(17%)SUBGROUP: Major: toune (67%)
                  Minor: (-)doune (33%)

Comment: It seems likely that c(o)roune could be
           considered a single rhyme word in this
           cluster, recurring three times and thus
           becoming a major item of its subgroup.
           But since the MS itself seems to maintain
           a distinction between the respective spel-
           lings and meanings of "crown," so have we.
           As with homonyms, we have consistently
           sought to maintain semantic distinctions.
           Compare the comments on sake and blake in
           the AKE cluster (II) of this MS.

MS. L   Rhyme Element: __OURE__

Preliminary	Terminal
boure 275, 333, 697, 1165, 1231 oure 395 stoure 687, 1455	couertoure 698 boure 396, 688, 1456 foure 1166 loure 276, 1232 shoure 334

Total: 8

Word	Recurrence	#	%
boure	8	8	100
loure	2	0	Ø
stoure	2	0	Ø

(6%)SUBGROUP: boure (100%)

MS. L   Rhyme Element: <u>OUTE</u>

Preliminary	Terminal
aboute 349, 1087 oute 251, 1403	aboute 252, 1404 doute 350 snoute 1083

Total: 4

Word	Recurrence	#	%
aboute	4	4	100
oute	2	0	Ø

(12.5%)<u>SUBGROUP</u>: aboute (100%)

293

MS. L   Rhyme Element: OWEN

Preliminary	Terminal
flowen 121, 1523 rowen 627	byflowen 628 rowen 122, 1524

Total: 3

Word	Recurrence	#	%
flowen ⎫ rowen ⎭	3	3	100

(33%)SUBGROUP: flowen/rowen (100%)

Comment: Cf. OWE (III).

MS. L   Rhyme Element: ___UGGE___

Preliminary	Terminal
abuggen 1081	brugge 1082
legge 1065*	rugge 1066
lygge 1283*	sugge 1284

Total: 3

Word	Recurrence	#	%
0	0	0	Ø

SUBGROUP: Ø

Comment: The <u>abugge/brugge</u> (ll. 1081/1082) couplet is
           the only exact rhyme in this cluster, and
           the "cluster" itself should perhaps be
           subdivided into three Category I entries.

           Cf. also MS. O's cluster IGGE (II).

MS. L   Rhyme Element: __URNE__

Preliminary	Terminal
hurne 1383 turne 703, 973	murne 974 sturne 704 ȝurne 1384

Total: 3

Word	Recurrence	#	%
turne	2	2	67

(17%)SUBGROUP: turne (67%)

Comment: The hurne/ȝurne (ll. 1383/1384) couplet seems
a clear and valid exception to this cluster
(33%); cf. ERNE (II) for the recurrence of
ȝerne.

Category III: Rhyme elements
that occur in ten or more
couplets of MS. L   Rhyme Element: ALLE

Preliminary	Terminal

alle 179, 371
calle 907
{falle 459
{byfalle 103
halle 77, 229, 261, 785,
     903, 1053, 1229,
     1395
	alle 78, 104, 230, 262,
	     622, 904, 908
	{falle 786, 1230
	{byfalle 180
	halle 372, 460
	walle 1054, 1396

Total: 14

Word	Recurrence	#	%
halle	11	11	79
alle	9	3	21
(-)falle	5	0	Ø
walle	2	0	Ø

(7%)SUBGROUP: halle, alle (100%)

MS. L   Rhyme Element: <u>EDE</u>

Preliminary	Terminal
dede 1545	bede 466
feryhede 803	dede 834
hede 1255	falssede 1256
nede 473	glede 506
rede 191, 833, 1059	lede 192, 1546
spede 465, 1405	mede 474, 1406
stede 51, 505, 717	nede 52
	shredde 718*
	spede 804
	wede 1060

Total: 12

Word	Recurrence	#	%
stede	3	3	25
rede	3	3	25
spede	3	3	25
lede	2 ⎫	1	8
dede	2 ⎭		
nede	2 ⎫	1	8
mede	2 ⎭		

(21%)<u>SUBGROUP</u>: <u>Major</u>: stede, rede, spede (75%)
                <u>Minor</u>: lede, dede, nede, mede (17%)

Comment: The <u>hede/falssede</u> (ll. 1255/1256) rhyme seems
          a clear and valid exception (8%), but the
          availability of the <u>-hede</u> suffix may make
          this an "easy," or common, rhyme.
          Cf. EDDE (II).

MS. L   Rhyme Element: __EIE__

Preliminary	Terminal
bytreye 1261	beye 114
deȝe 113*	deye 1356
galeye 193	galeye 1018
pleye 25, 351	leye 308, 1262
preye 769, 1243	pleye 194
tueye 307, 1355	seye 770
weye 765, 1017	tueye 26, 352, 766
	weye 1244

Total: 11

Word	Recurrence	#	%
tueye	5	5	50
weye	3	2	20
pleye	3	1	10
preye	2	1	10
leye	2	1	10
galeye	2	0	Ø

(28%)SUBGROUP: Major: tueye, weye, pleye (80%)
                Minor: preye, leye (20%)

Comment: Cf. E3E (II)

MS. L   Rhyme Element: <u>ELDE</u>

Preliminary	Terminal

aquelde 881   aquelde 998
{ felde 425, 853   { felde 556, 1312
{ afelde 997   { yfelde 58
bihelde 1149   { helde 314
shelde 57, 555, 1311 { byhelde 854
welde 313, 485   kelde 1150
           shelde 882
           welde 426
           ȝelde 486

Total: 10

Word	Recurrence	#	%
(-)felde	6	6	60
shelde	4	1	10
welde	3	2	20
(-)helde	3	1	10
aquelde	2	0	Ø

(20%) <u>SUBGROUP</u>: <u>Major</u>: (-)felde, shelde (70%)
         <u>Minor</u>: welde, (-)helde (30%)

Rhyme Element: <u>ERE</u>

Preliminary	Terminal
beere ("beer") 1113	Aylmere 1514
beggere 1133	bere ("to bear") 568
chayere 1271	bere ("bier") 902
chere 401, 901, 1071	⎰dere 1130, 1213
⎰dere 679, 795	⎱duere 228
⎱duere 437	eere 316
fere ("whole") 155	yfere ("companion") 394
⎧fere ("companion") 501,	fysshere 1134
⎪ 747, 949, 1359	⎰here ("hear") 680
⎬yfere ("companion") 227,	⎱yhere ("hear") 1272
⎪ 1129	here ("here") 156, 796,
⎩yfere ("together") 1363	950, 1360
here ("hear") 965, 1491	lere 234
here ("here") 233, 393	nere ("near") 966
mestere 235, 547	manere 548
suere 1211	ryuere 236
þere 525, 735, 771, 925,	skyere 1114
1139, 1513	⎰suere 402
⎰were 303, 315, 567, 1171	⎱swere 748, 1072
⎱nere ("ne were") 93, 909	þere 304, 1172
	⎧were 94, 438, 772, 910,
	⎨ 1364, 1492
	⎩ywere 502
	ȝere 526, 736, 926, 1140

Total: 36

Word	Recurrence	#	%
(ne)were	13	11	31
(y)fere	8	6	17
þere	8	5	14
d(u)ere	6	3	8
here ("here")	6	2	5
(y)here ("hear")	4	2	5
(w)suere	4	2	5
ʒcre	4	0	Ø
chere	3	1	3
mestcre	2	2	5

(13%)<u>SUBGROUP</u>: <u>Major</u>: were, fere, þere (62%)
<u>Minor</u>: dere, here, here, suere, chere, mestere (32%)

Comment: The <u>beere/skyere</u> (11. 1113/4) and <u>beggere/fysshere</u> (11. 1133/4) couplets seem clear and valid variants.(6%). The frequent recurrence of the -<u>er</u> agent suffix (an "easy" rhyme) should a<u>l</u>so be noted in the above cluster.

Lines 93/94 and 909/910 offer rare instances of a rhyme element joining with itself to make couplets (i.e., in the positive and negative). The pairings of ʒ<u>ere</u>/<u>bere</u> (4x) and <u>chere/suere</u> (2x) should a<u>l</u>so be noted.

MS. L   Rhyme Element: __ESSE__

Preliminary	Terminal
blesse 553	blesse 166, 582
cusse 581*	eftnesse 954
feirnesse 221	kesse 1216
gesse 1187	mildenesse 1516
passe 759*	pruesse 554
westnesse 165, 929, 953,	sorewenesse 930
1215, 1515	westnesse 222, 760, 1188

Total: 10

Word	Recurrence	#	%
westnesse	8	8	80
blesse	3	2	20

(10%)SUBGROUP: __Major__: westnesse (80%)
                 __Minor__: blesse (20%)

Comment: The frequent recurrence (12x) of the __-ness__
          suffix makes this cluster one of the "easier"
          rhyme links in the romance; nevertheless,
          if __westnesse__ is excluded, the suffix itself
          accounts for none of the above couplets.

303

MS. L   Rhyme Element: __ESTE__

Preliminary	Terminal
beste 29, 611, 1007, 1483	beste 182, 478, 776, 808,
feste 481, 807	832, 1136, 1182, 1336
geste 523	feste 524
keste 1195	geste 482
leste 477	⎧leste 612, 870
reste 409, 869	⎨yleste 6
strongeste 831	lyste 410*
weste 5, 775, 1135, 1181,	reste 1196
1335	treweste 1008
wyseste 181	werste 30*
	weste 1484

Total: 18

Word	Recurrence	#	%
beste	11	11	69
weste	6	1	6
(-)leste	4	1	6
feste	3	2	12
geste	2	0	Ø
reste	2	1	6

(14%)_SUBGROUP_: Major: beste, weste (75%)
                          Minor: leste, reste, feste (25%)

Comment: Geste rhymes exclusively with _feste_, forming
           two matched pairs.

           Cf. ISTE (II) & ESTES (I).

MS. L   Rhyme Element: <u>ICTE</u>

Preliminary	Terminal
bryhte 1449	bryhte 384
fyhte 819, 1013, 1341	flyhte 1414
knyhte 439, 495, 517,	fyhte 838
549, 943, 1221	fyþte 550*
lyhte 521	knyhte 522
⎰mihte 1353	knyhtes 820*
⎱myhte 1413	lyhte 388, 1014, 1222
⎰nyhte 265, 1205	myhte 266, 440, 944, 1206,
⎱midnyhte 1307	1342
plyhte 311	nyhte 1450
ryhte 383, 837	⎰rihte 1308
syhte 387	⎱ryhte 312, 518, 1354
wyhte 673	syhte 496
	yplyhte 674

Total: 21

Word	Recurrence	#	%
(y)			
mihte	7	7	37
knyhte	6	4	21
(i)			
ryhte	6	4	21
(-)nyhte	4	1	5
lyhte	4	2	11
bryhte	2	0	∅
syhte	2	0	∅
(-)plyhte	2	1	5
fyhte	3	0	∅

(23%)<u>SUBGROUP</u>: <u>Major</u>: mihte, knyhte, ryhte (79%)
                              <u>Minor</u>: nyhte, fyhte, bryhte, syhte,
                                    plyhte (21%)

Rhyme Element: <u>IDE</u>

Preliminary	Terminal
abyde 1033	abide 1466
glide 1055	abyde 862, 1056
ride 1443	bridel 778*
ryde 777	ryde 36, 140, 542, 754,
side 35, 211, 1305	858, 1306
syde 139	side 962, 1444
biside 861	syde 644, 972, 984, 1034
stryde 753	bitide 212
tide 857	
tyde 1465	
bitide 541, 971	
wide 983	
wyde 643, 961	

Total: 17

Word	Recurrence	#	%
(y) (-)side	11	11	69
(y) ride	7	3	19
(y) (-)tide	5	1	6
(y) abide	4	1	6
(y) wide	3	0	Ø

(12%)<u>SUBGROUP</u>: <u>Major</u>: (-)side, ride (88%)
<u>Minor</u>: (-tide, abide (12%)

Preliminary	Terminal
brynge 637, 989	⎧bringe 286
comynge 1097	⎩brynge 580, 1098
derlyng 725	derlyng 492
dobbyng 491	dobbyng 442, 562, 626
endyng 579	fundlyng 226, 708
fyhtynge 925	ofysshyng 658
fysshyng 1151	gleynge 1490
knelyng 787	hontynge 642
⎧kyng 33, 153, 163, 203,	⎧kyng 428, 788
⎪ 213, 225, 347, 441,	⎨kinge 4
⎨ 707, 1529	⎩kynge 220, 378, 500, 638,
⎪kynge 813, 851, 991	1028, 1296, 1448
⎩kynges 933*	lokyng 348
metyng 657	⎧nobyng 1152
pleyyng 625	⎩nybyng 204
⎧rynge 563, 609, 883, 1193,	pley3yng 34
⎨ 1393, 1505	rysynge 852
⎩goldring 561	synge 592, 1394
singe 3, 133, 1489	⎧sp/ri/nge 134
⎧springe 591	⎩vpsp/ri/nge 826
⎨sp/ri/nge 219, 499, 641,	techyng 1530
1237, 1447	sweuenyng 726
weddyng 427	swowenynge 448
3ynge 131, 285, 377, 447,	⎧tidynge 814, 992
1027, 1295	⎩tydynge 132, 1238
	tymyng 164
	weddynge 934
	wrynge 990
	wytherlyng 154
	⎧3yng 214
	⎩3ynge 564, 610, 884, 1194,
	1506

Total: 48

Word	Recurrence	#	%
(y)			
king(e)(s)	24	24	50
ӡyng(e)	12	8	17
(-)springe	8	5	10
(y)			
ring(e)	7	2	4
(y)			
bringe	5	3	6
(y)			
singe	5	1	2
dobbyng	4	2	4
(y)			
tidynge	4	0	Ø
derlyng	·2	1	4
(-)fysshyng	2	2	4
fundlyng	2	0	Ø
(y)			
nobyng	2	0	Ø
pley(ӡ)yng	2	0	Ø
(-)springe	2	0	Ø
weddyng(e)	2	0	Ø

(9%)<u>SUBGROUP</u>:   <u>Major</u>: ·kinge (50%)
                 <u>Minor</u>: ӡynge, springe, ringe, bringe,
                        singe,··bobbyng, derlyng, fysshyng
                        (50%)

<u>Comment</u>:   With its 48 couplets, ING(E) is the single
           most recurrent rhyme sound in the L MS. There
           are strong indications that this cluster might
           be divisable into separate ING and INGE group-
           ings; for example, <u>fysshyng</u> and <u>dobbyng</u> complete
           only ING couplets, while <u>springe</u> and <u>singe</u>
           are employed only in INGE links. But the most
           recurrent member of the subgroup appears in
           both <u>king</u> and <u>kinge</u> forms, as does <u>ӡyng(e)</u>
           and <u>ring(e)</u>. Although the <u>endyng</u>/<u>brynge</u>
           couplet (11. 579-580) seems to be the only

Comment (cont.):   example of ING actually rhyming with
          INGE, we have considered it sufficient to pre-
          clude the subdivision of this cluster.

          It would seem logical to assume that the avail-
          ability of rhymes which the -ing suffix produces
          in English would make the subgroup of systematic
          rhyme words indicated above largely unneces-
          sary. Nevertheless, kinge, ʒynge and springe
          alone (which are neither participals nor
          gerunds) may be taken to account for 77% of
          the above cluster.

Preliminary	Terminal
dryue 1343	dryue 730, 802, 1442, 1534
fyue 1303, 1441	fyue 816
lyue 557, 695	knyue 112
alyue 111, 135, 783, 1457	lyue 188, 616, 1344
⌠to ryue 1533	⌠to ryue 136
⎰aryue 187, 815, 931	⎱aryue 784, 1304, 1458
⌊oryue 615	wyue 558, 696, 932, 414
st/ri̅7ue 729, 413	
wyue 801	

Total: 17

Word	Recurrence	#	%
(-)lyue	9	9	53
(-)ryue	9	4	23
dryue	5	3	18
wyue	5	1	6
fyue	3	0	Ø
striue	2	0	Ø

(12%)SUBGROUP: (-)lyue, (-)ryue, dryue, wyue (100%)

MS. L   Rhyme Element: __O__

Preliminary	Terminal
bo 299	do 274, 282
go 101, 105	so 102, 106, 894
so 605	to 606
to 273	þo 38, 120, 270
tuo 37, 53	wo 54
wo 119, 269, 281, 893	ygo 300

Total: 11

Word	Recurrence	#	%
wo	5	5	45
so	4	3	27
þo	3	1	9
(-)go	3	1	9
do	2 ⎫		
to	2 ⎬	1	9
tuo	2	0	Ø

(27%)<u>SUBGROUP</u>: <u>Major</u>: wo, so, þo, go (90%)
               <u>Minor</u>: do, to (10%)

Comment: There seems to be an extraordinary variety
           of rhyming vocabulary in this relatively
           "easy" cluster. Yet, it should also be
           noted that the four major elements of the
           subgroup alone account for 90% of the
           couplets though they comprise only 18% of
           the cluster's maximum vocabulary.

MS. L   Rhyme Element: ___ONDE___

Preliminary	Terminal
fonde 157	fonde 734, 1536
honde 817, 1113, 1309,	honde 64, 116, 158, 272,
1337, 1431, 1519	344, 400
hosebonde 421, 739, 1051	⌠londe 40, 130, 176, 422, 818,
⌠londe 63, 513, 701, 733,	⎜ 880, 942, 1012, 1032,
⎨ 1273	⎨ 1052, 1114, 1310, 1338,
⎩yrlonde 1535	⎜ 1432
sonde 271, 941, 987, 1011	⎩olonde 762
stonde 175, 399, 761, 879,	shonde 702
1031, 1185	stonde 514
stronde 39, 115, 129	vnderstonde 1274
wonde 243	⌠stronde 988, 1186
	⎩st/ro/nde 1529
	wonde 740

Total: 30

Word	Recurrence	#	%
(-)londe	21	21	70
honde	12	6	20
(-)stronde	8	1	3
stonde	6	1	3
sonde	4	0	Ø
hosebonde	3	1	3
fonde	3	0	Ø
wonde	2	0	Ø

(8%)SUBGROUP: Major: londe, honde (90%)
               Minor: stonde, stronde, hosebonde, (10%)

MS. L   Rhyme Element: __ONE__

Preliminary	Terminal
gone 607	bone 916
kyngessone 1467	{done 488, 712, 790
{ one 529, 915, 1035	{vndone 1246
{ alone 841	{one 80, 608
{ none 809	{none 364
sone ("soon") 363, 487,	quene 356*
711, 789, 1245	sone 810
stone 79	stone 1036
teone 355	welcome 1468*
	ymone 530, 842

Total: 14

Word	Recurrence	#	%
(-)one	8	8	57
sone	6	4	29
(-)done	4	0	Ø
stone	2	0	Ø
ymone	2	0	Ø

(7%)SUBGROUP: (-)one, sone (86%)

Comment: The rhymes kyngessone/welcome (ll. 1467/1468)
          and teone/quene (ll. 355/356) are exceptions
          to this cluster (14%), but they may be con-
          sidered excludable as "off-rhymes"; cf. OME
          (II) and ENE (II).

313

MS. L   Rhyme Element: <u>ONGE</u>

Preliminary	Terminal
{ fonge 721, 741	honge 336
{ vnderfonge 335, 571	longe 722, 742, 1102
longe 309	{ songe 1270
songe 1101	{ ysonge 1026
stonge 1385	stronge 310
tonge 1269	yspronge 546
yronge 1025 ("rung")	wronge 572 ("wrong")
ȝonge 545	ȝonge 1386

Total: 10

Word	Recurrence	#	%
(-)fonge	4	4	40
longe	4	2	20
ȝonge	2	2	20
(-)songe	3	2	20

(20%)<u>SUBGROUP</u>:   <u>Major</u>: (-)fonge, longe (-)songe (80%)
                        <u>Minor</u>: ȝonge (20%)

MS. L   Rhyme Element: (O)UNDE

Preliminary	Terminal

⎧founde 107, 137
⎨yfounde 779
⎩grounde 595, 635, 1115
houndé 839
sounde 1351
⎧stounde 895
⎨astounde 339, 743, 1161,
       1287
	ybounde 1116
	founde 840, 1288
	grounde 108, 138, 340, 744,
	       896, 1162
	hounde 596
	⎧stounde 636
	⎨astounde 780
	wounde 1352

Total: 13

Word	Recurrence	#	%
grounde	9	9	69
(-)stounde	7	2	15
(-)founde	5	1	8
hounde	2	0	Ø

(11.5%)SUBGROUP: grounde, stounde, foundë (92%)

Comment: The sounde/wounde (ll. 1351/1352) couplet
          seems a clear and valid exception to this
          cluster (8%).

315

MS. L   Rhyme Element: ___OWE___

Preliminary	Terminal
arowe ("in order") 1511	drowe 1016, 1388
blowe 1019, 1381	⎰knowe 672
bowe 1235	⎱yknowe 1382
vnbowe 431	lowe 1502
drowe 189, 1415	owe 994, 1214
flowe 1099	rowe ("rank") 1086
⎰biknowe 993	rowe ("to row") 1100
⎱yknowe 1213	þrowe 342, 1020, 1512
lowe 1085	wowe 982
owe 341, 671	ynowe 190, 1236, 1416
slowe 1387	yswowe 432, 866
þrowe 981	
ynowe 865, 1015	
yswowe 1501	

Total: 18

Word	Recurrence	#	%
ynowe	5	5	28
drowe	4	1	5
(-)knowe	4	4	22
owe	4	1	5
þrowe	4	3	17
yswowe	3	2	11
blowe	2	0	Ø
lowe	2	1	5
(a)rowe	2	0	Ø

(19%)<u>SUBGROUP</u>: <u>Major</u>: ynowe, drowe, knowe, owe,
                                þrowe, yswowe (89%)
                  <u>Minor</u>: lowe (5%)

Comment: The <u>flowe/rowe</u> couplet (ll. 1099/1100) is the
single exception in this cluster; here, it
seems a clear and valid variant. But cf. OWEN
(II), a cluster consisting entirely of this
matched pair.

Note also the pairings of <u>ynowe/drowe</u> (four
times) and of <u>owe/knowe</u> (three times).

316

APPENDIX C

THE END-RHYMES OF <u>KING</u> <u>HORN</u>, MS. O

Category I: Rhyme elements that occur in less than
             three couplets of MS. O.

Rhyme Element	Preliminary	Terminal
ABLE	stable 736 table 599	fable 737 stable 600
ACE	g/r̄a̱/ce 585 lacē 740	place 586, 741
ADE (cf. EDE III)	made 175, 1394	calde 176 rede 1395*
ALE	stale 383 tale 1072	ale 384 bridale 1073
ALKE	halke 1128	stalke 1129
AME	name 207	game 208
AN	gan 119 man 816	cam 817* wan 200
ARD	gateward 1108	hard 1109
ARE	ȝare 1396	fare 1397
ARME	arme 726	barme 727
ARPE	harpe 242	sharpe 243
ARPEN	harpen 244	seruen 245*
AS	was 13	glas 14
ATERE	wat/ēr̲/e 1058	lat/ēr̲/e 1059
AUD	amyraud 95	baud 96
E	þe 61 þre 842	be 843 deye 62
EAUME	reaume 1550	streume 1551*
ED	bed 1236 ded 1226	bed 1227 leyd 1237*

MS. O

Rhyme Element	Preliminary	Terminal
EDES	dedes 553	seydes 554*
EF	þef 336	lef 337
EL	g/r̄a/uel 1514	castel 1515
ELLEN	bellen 1294	fullen 1295*
ELVE	xij 509	felue 510
EME	queme 505	seme 506
EN	ten 742	sen 743
ENGÞE	strengþe 940	lengþe 941
ENY	reny 994	enemy 995*
ENYE	brenye 605	denye 606
EPE (Cf. ETE II)	slepe 1346 wepe 673	mete 1347* slepe 674
EPPE	steppe 1392	cleppe 1393
ERCHEN	werchen 1422	cherchen 1423
ERES	harperes 1520	fiþeleres 1521
ERKE	derke 1458	werke 1459
ERSTE	ferste 1232	berste 1233
ERTE	girde 517* herte 1530	h/ēr/te 518 smerte 1531
ERVE	s/ēr/ue 950 st/er/ue 804	berwe 951* s/er/ue 508
ERYE	werye 814, 1430	derye 815 merye 1431
ESE	forlese 683	chese 684
EST	fayrest 183 lest 499	makedest 500 wisest 184

MS. O

Rhyme Element	Preliminary	Terminal
ESTEN	westen 5	lesten 6
ETEN	heten 1280	leten 1281
EÐE	heþe 862	deþe 863
EUED	heued 635	reued 636
EUENE	steuene 685	sweuene 686
EUERE	eu/ē͞r⁊e 1142	neu/ē͞r⁊e 1143
IRTE	gyrte 1512	schirte 1513
ISE	wise 1013	seruyse 1031
ISTES	listes 246	vistes 247
ITE	bite 1166 write 974	lite 975 wite 1167
ITH (Cf. IT I, ICTE III)	with 523	knict 524*
ITTE	sitte 641, 1124	mitte 642 witte 1125
IȜCTE (Cf. ITE I)	ryȝcte 858, 1020	fyȝcte 859 knyte 1021*
IȜYCTE	fiȝycte 1372	miȝte 1373*
IKE	lyke 447 swike 687	syke 448 like 688
LAWE	felawe 1130	lawe 1131
LEY	salyley 195	pleye 196*
ME	tyme 551	me 552
OD	god 81	forbod 82
ODY	mody 1282	blody 1283
OF	drof 127	of 128

MS. O

Rhyme Element	Preliminary	Terminal
OFTE (Cf. OUTER II)	softe 401, 1110	douter 402* ofte 1111
OKEN	forsoken 69	token 70
OLD	bold 17	hold 18
OLE	dole 1092 fole 601	cole 602 sole 1093
OM	nom 597	com 598
OME	grome 171 nome 1212	come 1213 ycome 172
EWÐE	rewþe 431, 693	trewþe 432, 694
EXE	wexe 101, 1452	nexte 102* twexe 1453
EXTE	nexte 960 syxe 403*	nexte 404 sexte 961
EYEN	wreyen 1292	leyen 1293
EYNE (Cf. INE II)	reyne 11 seyne 700	bleine 701 schine 12*
EYRES	heryes 938	boneyres 939
EYSE	heyse 1298	paleyse 1299
HEDE	þralhede 459	hede 460
IBBE	libbe 67 ribbe 328	libbe 329 sibbe 68
IT	nict 131*	lyt 132
IDDE	bidde 1218	tidde 1219
IE	envie 706 lye 1498	folye 707 twye 1499
IN	arnoldyn 1490 wyn 1190	cosyn 1491 pyle/gr/im 1191*

MS. O

Rhyme Element	Preliminary	Terminal
INDE	binde 201	hinden 202*
INGEN	ryngen 1424	syngen 1425
INGES	kynges 968	weddinges 969
IPE	gripe 55, 621	smyte 56* wipe 622
IPPE	scrippe 1104	lippe 1105
IRE	syre 1552	yre 1553
IRIE	stirie 149	derie 150
IRKE	kyrke 932	werke 933*
OND	hond 1546	strond 1547
ONDER	ond⟨er⟩ 1474 wond⟨er⟩ 918	hond⟨er⟩ 919 wond⟨er⟩ 1475
ONES	sones 23	gomes 24*
ONG	strong 99	long 100
OPPE	coppe 469, 1160	oppe 470, 1161
ORD	bord 121	word 122
ORNE	torne 722	Mourne 723*
ORTE	schorte 970	dorste 971*
ORY	Mory 892, 1376	stordy 893, 1377*
OT	smot 623	hot 624
OTE	hote 211, 796	bote 212, 797
OTES	fotes 521	botes 522
OUDE	croude 1334	loude 1335
OUNDEN	hounden 912	founden 913
OUR	flour 15	colur 16*

321

MS. O

Rhyme Element	Preliminary	Terminal
OUS	aybrous 235, 1548	hous 236, 1549
OUE(D)	ȝoue 1310	proued 1311*
OUSE	house 1034	spuse 1035*
OUTEN	fouten 1414	ouȝten 1415*
OWEN	awowen 822 flowen 125	glouen 823 rowen 126
OWNE	crowne 1536 towne 163	adowne 1537 downe 164
OWTEN	sowten 1418	brouten 1419
OWÐE	cowþe 365	mouþe 366
RECHE	reche 1326	wreche 1327
REWE	arewe 1538	þrewe 1539
ROS	ros 1354	agros 1355
TEN	cleten 1428	wenten 1429
ULTE	pulte 1470	hylte 1471*
UN	galun 1158	glotoun 1159*
UNDRED	hundred 1370	wonder 1371*
UNE	tune 1328	owne 1329*
URNE	turne 1008, 1114	morne 1009* spurne 1115
VISE	deuise 248	seruise 249
WARD	styward 471	foreward 472
YE	drye 1488	weye 1489

322

Category II: Rhyme elements
that occur in three to
nine couplets of MS. O.

Rhyme Element: __ADDE__

Preliminary	Terminal
hadde 21, 615, 1084, 1204	dradde 1205 ladde 22, 616, 1085

Total: 4

Word	Recurrence	#	%
hadde	4	4	100
ladde	3	0	Ø

(12.5%)SUBGROUP: hadde (100%)

MS. O   Rhyme Element: <u>AGE</u>

<div align="center">Preliminary</div>	<div align="center">Terminal</div>
barnage 1544 h/er/itage 1324 passage 1364	age 1365 page 1325 t/ru/age 1545

Total: 3

Word	Recurrence	#	%
0	0	0	Ø

SUBGROUP: No discernible recurrence.

Comment: The relative smallness of this cluster and,
          conversely, the frequent use of the relatively
          available suffix -<u>age</u> (4 of the 6 words above
          employ it) may explain the absence of any
          discernible subgroup.

MS. O   Rhyme Element: AKE

Preliminary	Terminal
attegate 1088*	awake 1349
blake 1360	blake 1245
krake 1118	forsake 570, 1361
make 1464, 1500	rake 1089, 1119
speke 555*	sake 1501
take 569, 1244, 1348	take 556, 1465

Total: 9

Word	Recurrence	#	%
take	5	5	56
rake	2	2	22
forsake	2	2	22
make	2	0	Ø
blake	2	0	Ø

(17%)SUBGROUP: Major: take (56%)
                 Minor: rake, forsake (44%)

Comment: Perhaps, sake (l. 1501) should be included
           with the occurrences of forsake; this con-
           junction would raise the triple recurrence
           of (--)sake to a major element of the sub-
           group. We have not done so because of the
           contradictory meanings of "to forsake" and
           "for the sake of."

325

MS. O   Rhyme Element: ___ASTE___

Preliminary	Terminal
caste 868	faste 869
haste 631	kaste 1053
maste 1052	leste 632*

Total: 3

Word	Recurrence	#	%
(k) caste	2	2	67

(17%)SUBGROUP: caste (67%)

Comment: The exclusion of the haste/leste "off-rhymes"
          (11. 631/ 632) from this cluster would
          increase the double recurrence of caste
          to 100% of the remaining couplets, but
          reduce the cluster itself to a Category I
          entry.
          Cf. ESTE (III).

326

MS. O   Rhyme Element: AUCTE

Preliminary	Terminal
laucte 254, 681, 914	kaucte 682 kaute 915* taucte 255

Total: 3

Word	Recurrence	#	%
laucte	3	3	100
kau(c)te	2	0	Ø

(17%)SUBGROUP: laucte (100%)

Preliminary	Terminal
d/r̄ā/we 886	drawe 1473, 1541
drāwe 1344, 1508	felawe 1037, 1509
felawe 1472	lawe 1345
haue 1036*	slawe 887
yslawe 1540	

Total: 6

Word	Recurrence	#	%
drawe	5	5	83
felawe	3	1	27
(y)slawe	2	0	Ø

(17%)<u>SUBGROUP</u>: drawe, felawe (100%)

MS. O   Rhyme Element: ___AY___

Preliminary	Terminal
day 31, 754	awey 755*
lay 1526	may 32
	weylawey 1527*

Total: 3

Word	Recurrence	#	%
day	2	2	67

(17%)SUBGROUP: day (67%)

Comment: The -ey variant for -ay is probably merely
          orthographic. It also seems unlikely that
          weylawey ("And reynyld makede weylaway")
          and awey ("For nov ich founde awey") are
          conjoinable into another element of the sub-
          group; (--)awey would account for the remaining
          33% of the cluster, but would make the subgroup
          itself greater than 25% of the max. vocab.

329

MS. O   Rhyme Element: ___AYLE__

Preliminary	Terminal
{assayle 882	batayle 588
{a saylen 651	fayle 652, 883, 1051
fayle 587	
seyle 1050*	

Total: 4

Word	Recurrence	#	%
fayle	4	4	100
a()sayle(n)	2	0	Ø

(12.5%)SUBGROUP: fayle (100%)

MS. O   Rhyme Element: <u>EDDE</u>

Preliminary	Terminal
bedde 310, 866	bedde 993
schredde 603	fedde 604
wedde 992	schredde 867
	wedde 311

Total: 4

Word	Recurrence	#	%
bedde	3	3	75
schredde	2	1	25
wedde	2	0	Ø

(25%)<u>SUBGROUP</u>: bedde, schredde (100%)

331

MS. O   Rhyme Element: __EIDE__

Preliminary	Terminal
seyde 282, 419, 710, 936,	leyde 711
1288, 1312	makede 420*
	mede 283*
	rede 937*
	treyde 1313
	wreyde 1289

Total: 6

Word	Recurrence	#	%
seyde	6	6	100

(8%)SUBGROUP: seyde (100%)

Comment: This EIDE cluster may, be a sub-cluster of
          EDE (III) if the two rhyme elements are
          themselves allophonic; certainly, they
          overlap as "near" rhymes. But the distinct-
          ness of their respective subgroups seems
          to argue for their own separateness.

MS. O   Rhyme Element: ELLE

Preliminary	Terminal
felle 65, 986, 1510	pelle 1511
fulle 1192*	quelle 66
telle 1068	spelle 1069
	telle 987, 1193

Total: 5

Word	Recurrence	#	%
felle	3	3	60
telle	3	2	40

(20%)SUBGROUP: felle, telle (100%)

333

MS. O   Rhyme Element: __ENCHE__

Preliminary	Terminal

{ abenche 381
{ benche 1144, 1524
  blenche 1466
  drenche 1014

adrenche 1467
clenche 1525
schenche 382, 1145
þinche 1015*

Total: 5

Word	Recurrence	#	%
(-)benche	3	3	60
(-)drenche	2	2	40

(20%)<u>SUBGROUP</u>: benche, drenche (100%)

Rhyme Element: <u>ENNE</u>

Preliminary	Terminal
⎧ ma/n̄/ne 613* ⎨ me/n̄/ne 647 ⎩ wi/m̄/menne 71 ⎰ sodenne 151, 185, 1562 ⎱ sode/n̄/ne 1308, 1404	godeme/n̄/ne 186 ⎰ kenne 614 ⎱ ke/n̄/ne 648 kinne 152* kunne 1309, 1563* me/n̄/ne 1405 o/n̄/ne 72*

Total: 8

Word	Recurrence	#	%
sodenne (a)	5	5	63
(-)menne	4	3	37
kenne	2	0	Ø

(12.5%)<u>SUBGROUP</u>: sodenne, menne (100%)

Comment: The disproportionately large number of "off-
rhymes" above (four of the eight couplets)
make this a rather unstable cluster; cf. INNE
(III) and ONNE (II).
In the <u>(-)menne</u> element of the subgroup, we
have included the singular <u>manne</u> (1. 613)
and, less probably, the "compound" <u>wimmenne</u>
("wif+man," 1. 71). They may, however, be
considered excludable; in which case, the
subgroup accounts for only 76% of this cluster.

335

MS. O   Rhyme Element: <u>ENTE</u>

Preliminary	Terminal
dunte 625*	dunte 891*
hente 890	re⟨n⟩te 955
rente 750	sente 751
sente 1378	{ wente 626
wente 954	{ we⟨n⟩te 1379

Total: 5

Word	Recurrence	#	%
wente	3	3	60
dunte	2	1	20
rente	2	0	Ø
sente	2	1	20

(20%)<u>SUBGROUP</u>: wente, sente (80%)

Comment: <u>Dunte</u> indeed accounts for 20% of this cluster,
          but, since it is not an exact rhyme, we have
          not included it in the subgroup. An alterna-
          tive would be to remove lines 625/6 and 890/1
          from this cluster as an UNTE group in Category
          I.

MS. O   Rhyme Element: <u>ERDE</u>

Preliminary	Terminal
answerede 209*	answerede 46*
ferde 780	herde 210, 781
yherde 45	horde 638*
swerde 637	

Total: 4

Word	Recurrence	#	%
(-)herde	3	3	75
answerede	2	0	∅

(12.5%)<u>SUBGROUP</u>:   (-)herde (75%)

Comment: The <u>swerde/horde</u> (ll. 637/638) couplet is the
          <u>single exception</u> in this cluster (25%), but
          may be considered excludable as an "off-rhyme";
          cf. ORDE (II).

MS. O   Rhyme Element: __EREN__

Preliminary	Terminal
eren 1004	dere 124, 232*
feren 123, 231	feren 253
leren 252	teren 1005

Total: 4

Word	Recurrence	#	%
feren	3	3	75
dere	2	0	Ø

(12.5%)SUBGROUP: feren (75%)

Comment: Cf. ERE (III).
           The eren/teren couplet (ll. 1004/1005) seems
           a clear and valid variant.

MS. O   Rhyme Element: ___ESSE___

Preliminary	Terminal
agesce 1222	blisse 168*
c/ri/stemesse 826	estnesse 989
estnesse 1250	kusse 1251*
fayrnesse 223	lesse 827
westnesse 167, 964, 988	sorwenesse 965
	westnesse 224, 1223

Total: 7

Word	Recurrence	#	%
westnesse	5	5	71
estnesse	2	1	14

(14%)SUBGROUP: <u>Major</u>: westnesse (71%)
              <u>Minor</u>: estnesse (14%)

Comment: Cf. ISSE (II).
           The <u>cristemesse</u>/<u>lesse</u> couplet (ll. 826/827)
           seems a clear and valid variant. Actually,
           the very common -<u>nesse</u> suffix is the most
           recurrent element of this cluster; it is
           employed in nine of the fourteen instances
           above, and itself can be taken to account
           for 86% of the cluster's couplets.

339

MS. O   Rhyme Element: __ETE__

Preliminary	Terminal
flete 161	hete 1301
grete 928	lete 228, 929
lete 1522	mete 1463
swete 227, 1300, 1462	sete 1523
	wepe 162*

Total: 6

Word	Recurrence	#	%
lete	3	3	50
swete	3	2	33

(17%)<u>SUBGROUP</u>: lete, swete (83%)

Comment: The <u>flete/wepe</u> couplet (ll. 161/162) is the
          sole exception in this cluster and may be
          considered excludable as an "off-rhyme";
          cf. EPE (I) and ETTE (II).

340

MS. O   Rhyme Element: <u>ETTE</u>

Preliminary	Terminal
flette 732, 786	{ grette 396
mette 1066	{ g/re̱/tte 1067
sette 395, 1242	hette 733
	lette 1243
	sette 787

Total: 5

Word	Recurrence	#	%
sette	3	3	60
grette	2	1	20
flette	2	1	20

(30%)<u>SUBGROUP</u>: sette, grette, flette (100%)

Comment: The relative size of this subgroup (30% of
          the max. vocab.) seems somewhat unsatisfac-
          tory. Such variety is atypical, but may not
          simply be ignored. The rhyme sound, <u>-ette</u>,
          may itself be considered a readily available
          rhyme in English--particularly among the past
          tenses of verbs. Nevertheless, we acknowledge
          that labelling a specific rhyme sound as
          "easy" hardly explains such exceptions from
          the norm.   341

MS. O   Rhyme Element: __EVE__

Preliminary	Terminal
leue 375, 481, 768, 1362	eue 482 heue 376, 769 reue 1363

Total: 4

Word	Recurrence	#	%
leue	4	4	100
heue	2	0	Ø

(12.5%)SUBGROUP: leue (100%)

342

MS. O   Rhyme Element: ___EWE___

Preliminary	Terminal
fewe 59	fleme 1315*
knewe 1486, 1566	hewe 1353, 1487
rewe 1314	leue 578*
schewe 1352	rewe 392
trewe 391, 577, 772, 1210	srewe 60
	trewe 1567
	þrewe 1211
	wiue 773*

Total: 9

Word	Recurrence	#	%
trewe	5	5	56
hewe	2	2	22
rewe	2	1	11
knewe	2	0	Ø

(17%)SUBGROUP: Major: trewe (56%)
                 Minor: hewe, rewe (33%)

Comment: The fewe/srewe couplet (ll. 59/60) seems a
           clear and valid variant, but 33% of this
           cluster consists of "off-rhyme" couplets;
           cf. EME (I), EUE (II), and IUE (III).

MS. O   Rhyme Element: __ICHE__

Preliminary	Terminal
{ yliche 19 { ylyche 300 riche 326, 351	{ liche 352 { yliche 327 riche 20 swike 301*

Total: 4

Word	Recurrence	#	%
(y) (y)liche riche	4 3	4 0	100 Ø

(12.5%)SUBGROUP: yliche (100%)

Preliminary	Terminal
abygge 1116 legge (lay) 1100, 1445, 1502* ligge (lie) 1318	b/ri̅/gge 1117 bri̅gge 1447, 1503 rigge 1101 sigge 1319

Total: 5

Word	Recurrence	#	%
legge*	3	3	60
brigge	3	1	20

(20%)SUBGROUP: legge, brigge (80%)

Comment: · The ligge/sigge (ll. 1318/1319) couplet
seems a clear and valid variant. If,
however, we consider the transitive verb
"legge" and the intransitive "ligge" (which
are still so readily interchanged) to be
a single rhyme unit, its recurrence becomes
four and it would account for 80% of the
cluster. This interpretation might also
explain the curious use of an off-rhyme
as the cluster's most recurrent element.

Rhyme Element: __IȝTE__

Preliminary	Terminal
bryȝte 1456	dyȝcte 875*
fyȝte 840, 874, 1044	knyctes 841*
{ knyte 467*	myȝte 1241
{ knyȝtes 1256*	{ niȝte 1457
{ niȝte 1338	{ nyȝte 468
{ /nyȝte/ 1240	{ ryhcte 317*
plyȝte 316	{ ryȝte 1339
	wyȝte 1045, 1257

Total: 9

Word	Recurrence	#	%
(y)			
niȝte	4	4	44
(c)			
kny(ȝ)te(s)	3	1	11
fyȝte	3	3	33
(ȝ)			
ryhcte	2	1	11
wyȝte	2	0	Ø

(22%) SUBGROUP: Major: niȝte, knyȝte, fyȝte (89%)
                 Minor: ryȝte (11%)

Comment: Cf. ICTE (III).

Preliminary	Terminal
childe 306, 1560 hylde 1074	h/er/menylde 1561 reymylde 1075 wilde 307

Total: 3

Word	Recurrence	#	%
childe	2	2	67

(17%)SUBGROUP: childe (67%)

Comment: The hylde/reymylde couplet (ll. 1074/1075)
           seems a clear and valid variant. Although
           the coinage of proper names may generate more
           readily available rhymes than is usual, it
           is probably the minimal size of this Category
           II cluster that provides the primary reason
           for the relatively small percentage of coup-
           lets which its subgroup accounts for.

347

MS. O   Rhyme Element: ILE

Preliminary	Terminal
⌠ gile 1002	amyle 1215
⌡ gyle 1214	bigile 333
mile 332	mile 610
⌠ wile 609	wile 1003
⌡ wyle 1358	yle 1359

Total: 5

Word	Recurrence	#	%
(y)			
(bi)gile	3	3	60
(y)			
wile	3	2	40
mile	2	0	Ø

(20%)SUBGROUP: (-)gile, wile (100%)

348

MS. O   Rhyme Element: __ILLE__

Preliminary	Terminal
snille 217	dwelle 338*
stille 298, 387, 557,	hulle 218*
695, 1040	spille 204, 696
wille 203, 377	telle 378*
ylle 1356	wille 299, 558, 1041, 1357

Total: 9

Word	Recurrence	#	%
wille	6	6	67
stille	5	2	22
spille	2	0	Ø

(11%)<u>SUBGROUP</u>: wille, stille (89%)

Comment: Cf. ELLE (II).
         The single exception (11%) in this cluster is
         the <u>snille</u>/<u>hulle</u> couplet (ll. 217/218) which
         may, however, be considered excludable as
         an "off-rhyme."

349

MS. O   Rhyme Element: __IME__

Preliminary	Terminal
paynime 832	p/r̄i/me 1011
rime 1402	r̄ime 833
tyime 1010*	tyme 1403

Total: 3

Word	Recurrence	#	%
rime	2	2	67
ty(i)me	2	1	33

(33%)<u>SUBGROUP</u>: rime, tyme (100%)

Comment: The disproportionately large size of the sub-
           group (33% of the cluster's max. vocab.) may
           be attributed primarily to the minimal size
           of the cluster itself.

MS. O   Rhyme Element: __INE__

Preliminary	Terminal
pyne 270, 649 sclauyne 1096	fine 271 myne 1097 þine 650

Total: 3

Word	Recurrence	#	%
pyne	2	2	67

(17%)<u>SUBGROUP</u>: pyne (67%)

MS. O   Rhyme Element: __INKE__

Preliminary	Terminal
{drinke 1098 {adrinke 111 þynke 1188	drynke 1189 þinke 112, 1099

Total: 3

Word	Recurrence	#	%
(y) (a)drinke (y) pinke	3 } 3	3	100

(33%)SUBGROUP: (-)drinke/þinke (100%)

Comment: This entire cluster consists of the triple
          recurrence of a single matched pair. Although
          the two words of the subgroup, thus, exceed
          33% of the cluster's max. vocab., either one
          of them alone (17% of the max. vocab.) may be
          considered to account for 100% of the couplets.

MS. O   Rhyme Element: __IS__

Preliminary	Terminal
⎧ wis (adv.) 537	blys 1277
⎨ hywys (adv.) 1276	hys 538
⎩ ywis ("I know": adv.	ymis 130
"certainly") 129	

Total: 3

Word	Recurrence	#	%
(y) (y)wis	3	3	100

(17%)<u>SUBGROUP</u>: (y)wis (100%)

Comment: For examples of the orthographic mutability
          of our single "rhyme word" <u>ywis</u>, compare:
          ⎰ "Bo seyde þe king wel <u>sone wis</u>" MS. O, l. 537
          ⎱ "Aylmer seide ful <u>ywis</u>" MS. L, l. 519
          ⎰ "Of tok he horn <u>hy wys</u>" MS. O, l. 1276
          ⎱ "he oftok him <u>ywisse</u>" MS. L, l. 1241

MS. O   Rhyme Element: __ISE__

Preliminary	Terminal
g/ri͞/se 896 wi͞se 371, 972	deuise 973 {ryse 897 {aryse 372

Total: 3

Word	Recurrence	#	%
wise	2	2	67
(a)ryse	2	1	33

(33%)SUBGROUP: wise, (a)ryse (100%)

Comment: The disproportionate size of this cluster's
          subgroup must, again, be attributed to the
          minimal size of this Category II cluster
          itself.

MS. O   Rhyme Element: _ISSE_

Preliminary	Terminal
blisse 571	blisse 436, 596
fyȝsse (v. "fish") 1180*	disse 1181
kusse 595*	misse 1505
wisse 435, 782, 1504	pruesce 572*
	westnisse 783

Total: 6

Word	Recurrence	#	%
wisse	3	3	50
blisse	3	2	33

(17%)<u>SUBGROUP</u>:   wisse, blisse (83%)

Comment: If the yogh in fyȝsse (l. 1180) is silent and
           does not lengthen the preceeding vowel, its
           rhyming with disse (l. 1181) may be considered
           a valid variant (17%). Otherwise, the couplet
           may be considered excludable as an "off-rhyme."

MS. O   Rhyme Element: <u>ISTE</u>

Preliminary	Terminal
c/r̄i̲/ste 83 kīste 417 lyste 1350, 1506	c/r̄i̲/ste 1351 lūste 418* wiste 84, 1507

Total: 4

Word	Recurrence	#	%
(u) lyste wiste c/r̄i̲/ste	 3 2 2	 3 1 0	 75 25 Ø

(25%)<u>SUBGROUP</u>: lyste, wiste (100%)

MS. O   Rhyme Element: __IÐE__

Preliminary	Terminal
⎰ bliþe 1, 489 ⎱ blyþe 367, 1012, 1268, 　　　1388 　swiþe 284, 427, 820	⎰ bliþ 285* ⎱ blyþe 821 　liþe 2, 428 ⎰ swiþe 368, 490 ⎱ swyþe 1013, 1269 　syþe 1389

Total: 9

Word	Recurrence	#	%
(y) bliþ(e)	8	8	89
(y) swiþe	7	1	11
liþe	2	0	Ø

(11%)SUBGROUP: bliþe, swiþe (100%)

357

MS. O   Rhyme Element: __O__

Preliminary	Terminal
go 103, 107	also 108
to 278	do 279, 287
ii ("two") 53	so 104
tvo 37	þo 38, 120, 275
wo 119, 274, 286	wo 54

Total: 8

Word	Recurrence	#	%
wo	4	4	50
þo	3	1	12.5
do	2	1	12.5
go	2	2	25
tvo (ii)	2	0	Ø

(25.5%) SUBGROUP: Major: wo, þo (63%)
                    Minor: go, do (37%)

Comment: The subgroup equals exactly 25% of the clus-
          ter's max. vocab.; so and also might be counted
          as a recurrence as well. And it should be
          acknowledged that this cluster exhibits
          unusual variety for its size. Perhaps, the
          rhyme itself could be considered "easy," but
          it might also be noted that wo and go alone
          account for 75% of the cluster's couplets.

MS. O   Rhyme Element: __ODE__

Preliminary	Terminal
blode 187, 920	gode 148, 188, 293, 917,
flode 147, 1224	1225
gode 153, 1380	fode 1381
mode 292	mod/er̄/ 154
stode 916	wodē 921

Total: 8

Word	Recurrence	#	%
gode	7	7	88
blode	2	1	12
flode	2	0	Ø

(12.5%)SUBGROUP: Major: gode (88%)
                      Minor: blode (12%)

MS. O   Rhyme Element: __OKE__

Preliminary	Terminal
forsoke 774	loke 775, 1141
loke 1176	toke 1177
toke 1140	

Total: 3

Word	Recurrence	#	%
loke	3	3	100
toke	2	0	Ø

(17%)<u>SUBGROUP</u>: loke (100%)

Comment: <u>Toke</u> rhymes exclusively with <u>loke</u> to form two
           matched pairs. Since, however, <u>loke</u> takes
           priority--according to our established criteria--
           by also rhyming with <u>forsoke</u>, <u>toke</u> does not
           here seem to be an operative member of the
           subgroup. Compare the equivalent subgroup for
           MS. L, and contrast that of MS. C.

MS. O   Rhyme Element: ON

Preliminary	Terminal
anon 49, 296	alon 628
gon 627	flon 92
slon 47, 91	gon 50, 297
þurston 848	on 48, 849

Total: 6

Word	Recurrence	#	%
gon	3	3	50
on	2	2	33
slon	2	1	17
anon	2	0	Ø

(25%)SUBGROUP: gon, on, slon (100%)

MS. O   Rhyme Element: <u>ONNE</u>

Preliminary	Terminal
go⌐n̄⌐ne 1460 { so⌐n̄⌐ne 581 { sonne 669	konne 582 ronne 670 so⌐n̄⌐ne 1461

Total: 3

Word	Recurrence	#	%
sonne	3	3	100

(17%)<u>SUBGROUP</u>:   sonne (100%)

MS. O   Rhyme Element: ORDE

Preliminary	Terminal
borde 264, 856, 1534	swerde 1535* worde 265, 857

Total: 3

Word	Recurrence	#	%
borde	3	3	100
worde	2	0	Ø

(17%)<u>SUBGROUP</u>: borde (100%)

Comment: Cf. ERDE (II).

MS. O   Rhyme Element: <u>ORE</u>

Preliminary	Terminal
flore 730	bour/e̯7 1483*
lore 1556	hore 731
ore 671	lore 462
more 461, 1234	more 74, 76
sore 73, 75	sore 672, 1235
store 1482	þore 1557

Total: 8

Word	Recurrence	#	%
more	4	4	50
sore	4	1	12.5
lore	2	1	12.5

(19%) <u>SUBGROUP</u>: Major: more, sore (62.5%)
                      <u>Minor</u>: lore (12.5%)

Comment: The <u>flore/hore</u> (ll. 730/731) rhyme link seems
          a clear and valid variant, but the <u>store/</u>
          <u>boure</u> (ll. 1482/1483) exception may be con-
          sidered excludable as an "off-rhyme."

MS. O   Rhyme Element: ___ORN___

Preliminary	Terminal
horn (proper name) 9, 145,	born 10, 530
342, 529, 549	yborn 146
horn (drinking horn) 1182	⎰bi forn 550
	⎱biforn 343
	ȝouren 1183*

Total: 6

Word	Recurrence	#	%
horn	5	5	83
(y)born	3	0	Ø
biforn	2	0	Ø

(8%)<u>SUBGROUP</u>: horn (83%)

Comment: It is possible that <u>horn</u> as a proper name
           (five times) and as a common noun (one time)
           may be considered a single rhyming item, in
           which case it would account for 100% of this
           cluster. Or, the <u>horn</u>/<u>ȝouren</u> (ll. 1182/1183)
           exception may be considered excludable as an
           "off-rhyme" (17%).

MS. O   Rhyme Element: __ORWE__

Preliminary	Terminal
{ morwe 864 { amorwe 421 sorwe 425	morwe 426 sorwe 422, 865

Total: 3

Word	Recurrence	#	%
(a)morwe sorwe	3 } 3 }	3	100

(33%)<u>SUBGROUP</u>: (a)morwe/sorwe (100%)

Comment: This entire cluster consists of the triple
          recurrence of a single matched pair. Either
          <u>morwe</u> or <u>sorwe</u> alone may be considered the
          cluster's systematic rhyme word--a decision
          which would reduce the size of the subgroup
          to only 17% of the cluster's max. vocab.

Rhyme Element: <u>OþE</u>

Preliminary	Terminal
boþe 449	boþe 1239
⎰cloþe 1258	loþe 1103
⎱cloþes 1102*	yswowe 450*
loþe 1238	wroþe 360, 1259
oþe 359	

Total: 5

Word	Recurrence	#	%
boþe	2	2	40
cloþe(s)	2	2	40
wroþe	2	1	20
loþe	2	0	∅

(30%)<u>SUBGROUP</u>: boþe, cloþe, wroþe (100%)

Comment: It might be possible to consider boþe and
          cloþe alone as the subgroup; in which case,
          only 20% of the max. vocab. would account
          for 80% of the cluster's rhymes. But it
          must be remembered that "#" is an arbitrary
          (i.e. alphabetical) determination when the
          priority of words is not indicated by any
          differences among their recurrence.

MS. O   Rhyme Element: __ODER__

Preliminary	Terminal
anoþer 294 broþer 589 oþer 197, 850	broþer 295, 851 a noþer 590 roþer 198

Total: 4

Word	Recurrence	#	%
(an)oþer	4	4	100
broþer	3	0	Ø

(12.5%)<u>SUBGROUP</u>: (an)oþer (100%)

Preliminary	Terminal
founde 802, 1000	founde 1323
sounde 1384	{ grounde 1197
stounde 346, 1196, 1322	{ grunde 347*
	stounde 803, 1001
	wounde 1385

Total: 6

Word	Recurrence	#	%
stounde	5	5	83
founde	3	0	Ø
gr(o)unde	2	0	Ø

(8%)SUBGROUP: stounde (83%)

Comment: Cf. UNDE (II).
          The sounde/wounde (ll. 1384/1385) couplet
          seems a clear and valid variant (17%).

MS. O   Rhyme Element: <u>OUNE</u>

Preliminary	Terminal
{ corune 495* { croune 1070 a doune 1156 toune 219	broune 1157 soune 220 toune 496, 1071

Total: 4

Word	Recurrence	#	%
toune	3	3	75
c(o)r(o)une	2	0	Ø

(12.5%) SUBGROUP: toune (75%)

Comment: The <u>doune</u>/<u>broune</u> (ll. 1156/1157) couplet seems
a clear and valid variant (25%). Any etymo-
logical link between the adv. "down" and the
n. "town" at the time of this MS. seems highly
tenuous, but if we considered a <u>doune</u> a fourth
recurrence of <u>toune</u> (as it might have once
been), the subgroup would have accounted for
100% of this cluster.

370

MS. O   Rhyme Element: __OUTE__

Preliminary	Terminal
aboute 355, 1122	aboute 257, 1433, 1435
oute 256, 1434	doute 356
wroute 288, 1316, 1432	ferde 981*
þoute 433, 980	myȝte 434*
	snowte 1123*
	þoute 289, 1317

Total: 9

Word	Recurrence	#	%
aboute	5	5	56
þoute	4	4	44
wroute	3	0	Ø
oute	2	0	Ø

(11%) SUBGROUP: aboute, þoute (100%)

Comment: Cf. ERDE (II) and OWTE (II).

MS. O   Rhyme Element: __OUTER__

Preliminary	Terminal
⎧ dout⟨er⟩ 260, 944	oft⟨e⟩ 717*
⎩ douter 716	softe 945*
	þoute 261

Total: 3

Word	Recurrence	#	%
douter	3	3	100

(17%)SUBGROUP: douter (100%)

Comment: Cf. OUTE (II) and OFTE (I).

MS. O   Rhyme Element: <u>OWTE</u>

Preliminary	Terminal
browte 922 sowte 43, 483	bowten 923* {broucte 44* {browte 484

Total: 3

Word	Recurrence	#	%
(u) brow(c)te sowte	3 2	3 0	100 Ø

(17%)<u>SUBGROUP</u>: browte (100%)

MS. O   Rhyme Element: __UNDE__

Preliminary	Terminal
grunde 653, 1150 sto⌐n⌐nde ("stand") 109* stunde ("astound") 766	bounde 1151* grunde 110 gru⌐n⌐de 767 stounde ("⌐in a little⌐ while") 654

Total: 4

Word	Recurrence	#	%
grunde	4	4	100

(12.5%)SUBGROUP: grunde (100%)

Comment: , Cf. OUNDE (II) and ONDE (III).

MS. O   Rhyme Element: <u>URSTE</u>

<u>Preliminary</u>	<u>Terminal</u>
furste 679, 904, 1154	berste 680* herte 905* þerste 1155*

Total: 3

Word	Recurrence	#	%
furste	3	3	100

(17%)<u>SUBGROUP</u>: furste (100%)

Comment: If lines 904 and 905 were conjoined with
          the ERTE (I) cluster, it would become a
          Category II entry in which <u>herte</u> would ac-
          count for 100% of its couplets.

MS. O   Rhyme Element: USTE

Preliminary	Terminal
kuste 1230, 1252	beste 494*
luste 493	luste 1253
	reste 1231*

Total: 3

Word	Recurrence	#	%
kuste	2	2	67
luste	2	1	33

(33%)SUBGROUP: kuste, luste (100%)

Comment: Cf. ESTE (III).

Category III: Rhyme elements
that occur in ten or more
couplets of MS. O.

Rhyme Element: __ALLE__

Preliminary	Terminal

alle 181
ou/er/alle 1426
falle 105, 473
halle 77, 233, 266, 639,
    808, 934, 1086, 1264
palle 413
þralle 441
	alle 78, 106, 234, 267,
	   640, 935
	falle 182, 442, 809, 1265
	fulle 414*
	halle 474
	walle 1087, 1427

Total: 14

Word	Recurrence	#	%
halle	9	9	64
(--)alle	8	3	21
falle	6	1	7
walle	2	0	Ø

(4%)SUBGROUP: halle, alle, falle (93%)

Comment: The palle/fulle (ll. 413/414) couplet is
the sole exception in this cluster (7%),
but may be considered excludable as an
"off-rhyme."

MS. O   Rhyme Element: __ECHE__

Preliminary	Terminal
feche 363	drenche 1199*
keche 1262	keche 323
reche 998	mete 983*
seche 179, 982, 1198	reche 364
speche 322, 399	speche 180, 592, 999, 1409
teche 591, 1408	teche 400, 1263

Total: 10

Word	Recurrence	#	%
speche	6	6	60
teche	4	1	10
seche	3	2	20 (both off-rhymes)
reche	2	1	10
keche	2	0	Ø

(20%)__SUBGROUP__: __Major__: speche, teche (70%)
                 __Minor__: seche, reche (30%)

Comment: It is curious that the less recurrent element
          of this cluster's subgroup, __seche__, should
          account for double the couplets of a "major"
          element, __teche__; but it should also be noted
          that __seche__'s recurrence is primarily (i.e.,
          67%) in "off-rhyme" couplets.

MS. O   Rhyme Element: ___EDE___

Preliminary	Terminal
bede 948 dede 1568 drede 302 fayrhede 89 lede 1442 makede 1286 nede 487 prede 1438 rede 193, 854, 1094 spede 479 stede 51, 268, 519, 738	bede 480 dede 855 falsede 1287 glede 520 lede 194, 949, 1569 made 90, 1443* (?) meche 269* mede 488, 1439 nede 52 rede 303 schrede 739 wede 1095

Total: 16

Word	Recurrence	#	%
lede	4	4	25
stede	4	4	25
rede	4	3	19
ma(ke)de ("made")	3	2	13
mede ("reward")	2	2	12
bede	2	1	6
dede	2	0	Ø
nede	2	0	Ø

(19%)SUBGROUP: **Major:** lede, rede, stede, makede (82%)
　　　　　　　　 Minor: mede, bede (18%)

Comment: Scribal abbreviations are not uncommon in MS.
O (cf. the use of Roman numerals in cluster
ENE of this category and ELVE of Category I);
we have interpreted made to be one such
abbreviation for makede, although it is pos-
sible to consider its double recurrence as
a separate "off-rhyme" element.
Cf. ADE (I), ECHE (II), and EIDE (II).

Rhyme Element: __EIE__

Preliminary	Terminal
deye 115	abeye 116
dreye 1078	deye 927, 1387
heye 778	eye 1079
pleye 25, 357	leye 313, 1195
⌠preye 792	seye 779, 793
⌡p/re/ye 1048	⌠tueye 26
seye 1194	⌡tweye 358, 789
tweye 312, 926, 1386	weye 1049
weye 788	

Total: 12

Word	Recurrence	#	%
(u)			
tweye	6	6	50
deye	3	1	8
seye	3	3	25
(h)eye	2	1	8
leye	2	0	Ø
pleye	2	0	Ø
preye	2⌍	1	8
weye	2⌏		

(13%)SUBGROUP: Major: tweye (50%)
                Minor: deye, seye (33%)

Comment: Rather than including eye, preye and weye in
          the subgroup, we have counted the dreye/eye
          (ll. 1078/1079) and preye/weye (ll. 1048/1049)
          rhymes as exceptions (17%; their inclusion
          would increase the size of the subgroup to
          25% of the cluster's max. vocab.

Rhyme Element: <u>ELDE</u>

Preliminary	Terminal
aquelde 900	felde 58, 534, 574, 1343
felde 240, 872	⌠helde ("hold") 319, 502,
helde ("hold") 942	⎱ 1441
helde ("old") 1440	⌡byhelde 873
⌠scelde 533	⌠schelde 901
⎰schelde 573, 1342	⎰shelde 241
⌡selde 57	welde 943
welde 318, 501	

Total: 11

Word	Recurrence	#	%
felde	6	6	55
s(c)(h)elde	6	1	9
(by)helde	5	4	36
welde	3	0	Ø

(13%)<u>SUBGROUP</u>: felde, schelde, helde (100%)

Comment: There seems to be a strong tendency towards
a double system of matched pairs within this
cluster; <u>felde</u> pairs with <u>schelde</u> five times,
and <u>helde</u> with <u>welde</u> three times.

MS. O   Rhyme Element: <u>ENDE</u>

Preliminary	Terminal
hende 385, 760, 1152, 1296	brende 1275
kende 443, 1420	fende 1421
rende 1274	fonde 380*
schende 699	hende 953, 1255
sende 545	heynde ("hind") 662*
sitte⌈n⌉de 667	schende 335, 719
wende 334, 379, 451, 661,	sende 761, 963
718, 952, 962, 1254	trende 452
we⌈n⌉de 1450	welde 444*
	wende 386, 546, 1153, 1451
	wepende 668
	ȝonge 1297*

Total: 18 couplets and 1 odd line (<u>schende</u>, 1. 699)

Word	Recurrence	#	%
wende	13	13	72
hende	6	2	11
schende	3	0	Ø
sende	3	0	Ø
kende	2	2	11

(17%)<u>SUBGROUP</u>:   <u>Major</u>:   wende, hende (83%)
                    <u>Minor</u>:   kende (11%)

Comment: Line 699 in MS. O reads: "Ðy sweuene ich schal
           schende"; MS. L has a parallel line that rhymes
           with the most dominant element of this cluster,
           <u>wende</u> (L, 11. 681-682).   In the O MS., the
           couplet preceding <u>schende</u> is an ERE rhyme,
           while that following is an EINE couplet.

MS. O   Rhyme Element: __ENE__

Preliminary	Terminal
grene 878	bene 8, 528, 1565
kene 527	kene 42, 98, 879, 1163
quene 7, 1564	quene 362
scene 97	schene 174
tene 361, 702	sene 703
wene 1162	
XV 41	
xiij 173	

Total: 10

Word	Recurrence	#	%
kene	5	5	50
bene	3	2	20
quene	3	1	10
sc(h)ene	2	1	10
tene	2	1	10

(25%)SUBGROUP: Major: kene, bene, quene (80%)
              Minor: schene, tene (20%)

Comment: The -teen suffix recurs twice in this cluster
          and might itself be considered a rhyme element,
          but it accounts for no additional couplets
          and, therefore, has been discounted.

Rhyme Element: ERE

Preliminary	Terminal
alym/er/e 1284	aylm/er/e 526, 1543
begger/e/ 1168	dere 1127, 1165, 1247
bere 930, 1148	⎧fare ("journeyed") 486*
chere 415, 1106, 1126	⎩fere ("company") 1285
cheyere 1304	fyӡsser/e/ 1169
damysele 1208*	here ("here") 158, 819,
dere 157, 453, 697, 818	985, 1391
⎧fere ("companion") 770,	here ("hear") 698, 1305
⎨ 984, 1164	lere 238
⎩yfere ("together") 1390	man/er/e 566
here (?"ear") 320	palm/er/e 1209
here ("here") 237, 1174	squiere 1149
⎰here ("hear") 409	stere 454
⎱yhere 1518	swere 416, 771, 1107
mestere 239, 565	þere 309, 795, 931, 1207
swere 1246	ware 94* (?) (subjunctive)
⎧þere 485, 525, 543, 758,	were 321, 410, 1519
⎨ 958	⎰yere 544, 959
⎩þer/e/ 1542	⎱ӡere 759, 1175
⎰were 308, 794, 1206	
⎱nere 93	

Total: 34 (i.e., 33 coup-
       lets and 1 triplet
       ll. 237-239)

Word	Recurrence	#	%
þere	10	10	29
(a)			
(ne) were	8	4	12
dere	7	7	21
here ("here")	6	4	12
(a)			
(y)fere	6	2	6
(y)here			
("hear")	4	1	3
swere	4	2	6
(3)			
yere	4	0	Ø
aylm/er/e	3	0	Ø
chere	3	0	Ø
bere	2	1	3
mestere	2	1	3

(13%)<u>SUBGROUP</u>:   <u>Major</u>: þere, were, dere, here, fere (80%)
                   <u>Minor</u>: here, swere, bere, mestere (15%)

Comment: The <u>damysele/palmere</u> (ll. 1208/9) and <u>beggere/</u>
           <u>fyჳssere</u> (ll. 1168/9) couplets are exceptions
           (5%); the latter seems a clear and valid
           variant, but the former may be considered
           excludable as an off-rhyme. It should also
           be noted that these two exceptions (as well
           as two other couplets and the triplet) employ
           the common agent-suffix, -<u>ER</u>, which might
           itself be considered a rhyming element of the
           subgroup (accounting for 8% of the cluster).

Comment (cont.): Lines 93/94 offer a rare
instance of a word rhyming <u>with</u> <u>itself</u>:
<u>nere/ware</u>. As usual, such a phenomenon
is counted twice under "Recurrence," but
only once under "#."

Although various forms of <u>fere</u> function in
this cluster as nouns, verbs or adverbs,
their semantic uniformity permits them to be
considered a single rhyming element. Con-
trast the various homonyms of "here."

Preliminary	Terminal
derne 1382 erne 906 h/er/ne 956 horne 373* st/er/ne 1412 terne 1480 warne 708* ȝerne 724, 908, 1436	berne 709 sterne 907, 1481 werne 374, 725, 909, 957, 1437 ȝerne 1383, 1413

Total: 10

Word	Recurrence	#	%
(a) werne	6	6	60
ȝerne	5	2	20
sterne	3	2	20

(15%)<u>SUBGROUP</u>: werne, ȝerne, sterne (100%)

Comment: It seems most probable that <u>warne</u> (l. 708) is merely a scribal error rather than an off-rhyme.
Cf. ORNE (I) and ORN (II).

MS. O   Rhyme Element: __ESTE__

Preliminary	Terminal
beste 29, 1038	beste 799, 829, 853, 911,
⎧feste 828, 1444	1217, 1367
⎩festes 497	feste 542, 1171, 1261
gestes 541, 1260	gestes 498
keste 677	lache 678*
reste 423, 888, 910	⎧liste 424*
strengeste 852	⎩luste 889*
weste 798, 1170, 1216,	sette 1445*
1366	treweste 1039
	werste 30*

Total: 16

Word	Recurrence	#	%
beste	8	8	50
feste(s)	6	5	31
weste	4	0	Ø
gestes	3	0	Ø
reste	3	2	13

(9%)SUBGROUP: Major: beste, feste(s) (81%)
              Minor: reste (13%)

Comment: The gestes/feste (ll. 541/542, 1260/1261)
          rhymes demonstrate that ESTE and ESTES may
          not be separated into distinct clusters.
          The keste/lache (ll. 677/678) couplet is
          the cluster's sole exception (6%) but may be
          excludable as an "off-rhyme." Cf. ETE (II)
          and ETTE (II). It should be noted that the
          two couplets which reste accounts for may
          have been the terminal word of these couplets,
          liste, which actually functioned as the sys-
          tematic rhyme. Cf. ISTES (I) and USTE (II).
          It should be also be noted that weste occurs
          three times as a matched pair with beste,
          and that gestes is matched three times with
          feste(s).

388

MS. O

Preliminary	Terminal
{ knicte 455, 511, 535, 567 { knycte 978 lycte 539 nicte 272 { ricte 465, 746 { forþricte 393 { wihcte 397* { wyȝte 691*	{ bricte 476, 747 { briycte 466* { brycte 394 { fycte 568 { fyte 512* knicte 540 licte 398 { micte 273 { myȝte 456, 979* plicte 692 ricte 536

Total: 13

Word	Recurrence	#	%
(y) knicte	7	7	54
bri(y)cte	4	3	23
(--)ricte	4	0	Ø
(yȝ) micte	3	1	8
(ȝ) wihte	2	2	15
fy(c)te	2	0	Ø
(y) licte	2	0	Ø

(15%)SUBGROUP: Major: knicte, bricte (/ricte) (77%)
            Minor: micte, wihte (23%)

Comment: It should be noted that ricte rhymes with
         bricte three times; aside from these matched
         pairs, each rhyme word links with the dominant
         element of this cluster only once. Yet, the
         fact that ricte and bricte do not rhyme ex-
         clusively with one another precludes desig-
         nating ricte a coequal member of the subgroup
         according to our established criteria.
         Cf. IȜTE (II). 389

Rhyme Element: __IDE__

Preliminary	Terminal
abyde 1062	abyde 881, 1091, 1493
glyde 1090	b/ri/del 801*
myde ("with") 304	glīde 144, 1337
⌠Ride 1478	⌠ride 560, 777
⌡ryde 800, 1332	⌡ryde 36, 877
⌠side 143, 880	side 997, 1007, 1063, 1333,
⌡syde 35, 213, 1336	1479
stride 776	tyde 214
⌠tide 1006	ȝede 305*
⌡tyde 559, 876, 1492	
wide 996	

Total: 17

Word	Recurrence	#	%
(y) side	10	10	59
(y) ride	7	4	24
(y) tide	5	1	6
abyde	4	1	6
glide	3	0	Ø

(12%) SUBGROUP: Major: side, ride (83%)
                 Minor: tide, abide (12%)

Comment: The myde/ȝede couplet (ll. 304/305) is the
          sole exception in this cluster (6%) and
          may be considered excludable as an "off-
          rhyme"; cf. EDE (III).

MS. O   Rhyme Element: __ILD__

Preliminary	Terminal
ayld 790	byrild 791
child 27, 85, 169, 258,	child 664
262, 1400	fokenild 28
⎰fikenyld 1496	godild 1401
⎱fokenild 663	mild 86, 170
reymyld 990	⎰Reymyld 1497
	⎱rimenild 259
	wild 263, 991

Total: 10

Word	Recurrence	#	%
child	7	7	70
wild	2	1	10
mild	2	0	Ø
(Proper Names)			
(i) (y)			
reym(en)ild	3	0	Ø
(i) (i)			
fokenyld	3	1	10

(15%)<u>SUBGROUP</u>:   <u>Major</u>:   child (70%)
                  <u>Minor</u>:   wild, fokenyld (20%)

Comment: <u>Ayld/byrild</u> (ll. 790/791) seems a clear and
         valid variant. But it is also possible to
         consider the proper names used in seven of
         these ten couplets as "coinages" with <u>ild</u>
         as the common final syllable to facili<u>tate</u>
         rhyme. In which case, this "proper name
         element" plus <u>child</u> would form a subgroup
         accounting for <u>100%</u> of this cluster.

MS. O   Rhyme Element: __ING__

Preliminary	Terminal
d/ēr/eling 748	derling 508
dubbing 507	dobbing 580, 644
fyssing 1186	king 446, 492, 811
fyȝtyng 846	loking 354
⎧king 155, 165, 205, 215,	meting 749
⎪ 229, 353, 728, 834,	naming 216
⎨ 870	nyþing 206
⎩kyng 1554	rysyng 847, 871
⎰kneuling 491	sweting 230
⎱knewlyng 810	timing 166
pleying 643	tydyng 835, 1555
⎰riᵑg 579, 1228	þyng 1187
⎱Ryng 1532	wendling 729
wedding 445	wiþerling 156
	⎰ȝeng 1229*
	⎱ȝonge 1533*

Total: 21

Word	Recurrence	#	%
(y)			
king	13	13	62
(u)			
dobbing	3	3	14
ring	3	2	10
der(e)ling	2	1	5
(w)			
kneuling	2	0	Ø
rysyng	2	1	5
tydyng	2	0	Ø
(ȝo)			
yenge*	2	0	Ø

(12%) SUBGROUP: Major: king (62%)
                 Minor: dobbing, ring, derling,
                         rysyng (33%)

Comment: Cf. INGE (III). In the O MS. (unlike C or L),
          the ING and INGE clusters never overlap;
          this "division" may explain the discrepancies
          that seem to exist among their subgroups.
          In this MS., the fyssing/þyng couplet (ll.
          1186/1187) seems a clear and valid exception
          (5%).

392

MS. O   Rhyme Element: __INGE__

Preliminary	Terminal
bringe 655, 1024	bringe 291, 594, 1135
cominge 1134	dobbinge 458
endynge 593	fischinge 676
kinge 33, 457, 1026	huntingge 660*
metynge 675	glewinge 1517

Preliminary:

 bringe 655, 1024
 cominge 1134
 endynge 593
 kinge 33, 457, 1026
 metynge 675
 ⌠ringe 629
 ⎱ri∠n⌿ge 902
 ⌡Ringe 583
 ⌠singe 3, 135, 137
 ⌡synge 1516
 ⌠springe 221, 1272
 ⎱spri∠n⌿ge 515
 ⌡sp∠ri⌿nge 607, 659, 1454
 ȝenge 290, 463*

Terminal:

 bringe 291, 594, 1135
 dobbinge 458
 fischinge 676
 huntingge 660*
 glewinge 1517
 ⌠kinge 4, 222, 516, 656
 ⌡kynge ‧1455
 pleyhinge 34
 sp∠ri⌿nge 138
 swohinge 464
 synge 608
 ⌠tidinge 136
 ⎱tydinge 1027
 ⌡tydyngge 1273*
 wringe 1025
 ⌠yenge 584, 630*
 ⌡ȝo∠n⌿ge 903*

Total: 23

Word	Recurrence	#	%
(y)			
kinge	8	8	35
springe	7	4	17
bringe	5	4	·17
(y)			
singe	5	2	9
(ʒo)			
*yenge	5	4	17
ringe	3	0	Ø
(y)(y)			
tidin(g)ge	3	0	Ø

(22%)<u>SUBGROUP</u>:   kinge, springe, bringe, singe, yenge*
                     (96%) .

Comment: Cf. ING (III). The .metynge/<u>fischinge</u> (ll. 675/
           676) couplet seems to be the only exception
           in the above cluster; note too that "fishing"
           occurs as the only "exception" in the ING
           cluster of this MS. and that the L MS. suggests
           <u>fysshyng</u> may be considered an element of the
           subgroup. <u>Yenge</u>, the "off-rhyme" member of
           this subgroup, is particularly noteworthy
           since, as <u>yinge</u>, it may have once provided
           the jongleur with an exact rhyme; here, it
           pairs with <u>ringe</u> three times. Cf. ING (III)
           and ONGE (III) as well.

MS. O   Rhyme Element: __INNE__

Preliminary	Terminal
gynne 1320	⌈hi⟋n̄⟋ne 620
kinne 894	⟨inne 1399
lynne 324	⟨i⟋n̄⟋ne 325, 1113, 1407
pynne 1018	⌊ynne 1019
þerynne 1178	lynne 1033
⌈winne 619	sodenne 895*
⟨wi⟋n̄⟋ne 1032, 1398, 1406	⌈winne 1179
⌊wynne 1112	⌊wynne 1321

Total: 10

Word	Recurrence	#	%
(þer)inne (y)	7	7	70
winne	7	2	20
lynne	2	0	Ø

(10%)<u>SUBGROUP</u>: inne, winne (90%)

Comment: The <u>kinne/sodenne</u> (ll. 894/895) couplet is
          this cluster's sole exception (10%), and may
          be considered excludable as an "off-rhyme";
          cf. ENNE (II).
          The <u>inne/winne</u> combination in itself forms five
          matched pairs, half of the entire cluster.

Rhyme Element: <u>IVE</u>

Preliminary	Terminal

Preliminary:

⎧ aryue 633
⎨ aryuede 966*
⎩ riue ("come") 189
⎩ a ryued 836*
drive 1374
fiue 1476
⎧ liue 113, 344, 575, 712,
⎨   1484
⎩ lyue 806
⎩ oliue 139
st/rī7uc 429, 752
wyue 824

Terminal:

⎧ aryue 807
⎨ ryue ("come") 140
⎩ a Ryue 1485
bilyue ("quickly") 345
cniue 114
⎧ driue 753, 1477
⎨ dryue 825
fyue 837
liue 190, 634, 1375
⎧ wiue 430, 576, 713
⎨ wyue 967

Total: 16

Word	Recurrence	#	%
(y) (o)liue	10	10	63
(y) (a)(-)riue(d)(e)	7	2	13
(y) wiue	5	2	13
(yv) driue	4	2	13
st/rī7ue	2	0	Ø

(13%) <u>SUBGROUP</u>: <u>Major</u>: liue, ariue, wiue (87%)

<u>Minor</u>: driue (13%)

MS. O   Rhyme Element: OLDE

Preliminary	Terminal
bolde 389	bolde 618
golde 477	golde 1081, 1203
holde 617, 1184, 1290	holde 390
molde 330	hyӡolde 478
schulde 407*	kolde 1185
⎰wolde 1202	scholde 1291
⎱nolde 1080 ("ne wolde")	wolde 331, 408, 658
yolde 657	

Total: 10

Word	Recurrence	#	%
(ne)wolde	5	5	50
holde	4	4	40
golde	3	1	10
bolde	2	0	∅
(u) scholde	2	0	∅
(hyӡ) yolde	2	0	∅

(15%)SUBGROUP: wolde, holde, golde (100%)

Comment: Schulde (l. 407) may simply be a scribal
           variant (cf. scholde, l. 1291) rather than
           an actual off-rhyme.

397

MS. O   Rhyme Element: <u>ONDE</u>

Preliminary	Terminal

fonde 141
honde 87, 225, 350, 547,
    1146, 1172, 1340,
    1368, 1468
hosebonde 437, 762, 1082
⎧hyrelonde 1558
⎩londe 63, 531, 720, 756,
    976
sonde 276, 1022, 1042
⎧stonde 177, 411, 898, 1060,
⎨   1220
⎩sto∠n̄∠de 784
stronde 39, 117, 133, 838

fonde 757
grunde 142*
honde 64, 118, 277, 412
londe 40, 88, 178, 226,
    438, 899, 977, 1043,
    1061, 1083, 1147,
    1341, 1369, 1469, 1559
lo∠n̄∠de 839
alonde 134
hirelonde 785
ponde 1173
schonde 721
sto∠n̄∠de 532, 548
stronde 1023, 1221
wonde 763

Total: 31 couplets and 1 odd line (<u>honde</u>, l. 350)

Word	Recurrence	#	%
(--)londe	24	24	77
honde	13	5	16
stonde	8	1	3
stronde	6	1	3
hosebonde	3	0	Ø
sonde	3	0	Ø

(13%)<u>SUBGROUP</u>: <u>Major</u>: londe, honde (93%)
                     <u>Minor</u>: stonde, stronde (7%)

Comment: Line 350 in MS. O reads: "to bringe þe horn
           to honde"; it is preceded by an OWE couplet
           and followed by an ICHE couplet. Clearly,
           a line has been omitted. The L MS. provides
           a preliminary rhyme <u>wonde</u> (ll. 343/344), as
           does the C MS. (ll. 337/338); thus, a thirty-
           second couplet in the above cluster might once
           have been accounted for by <u>honde</u>, increasing
           its "#" to 6.

MS. O   Rhyme Element: __ONE__

Preliminary	Terminal
alone 860, 1064	allone 80
none 830	come 1495*
sone 369, 503, 734, 812,	{done 504, 735, 813
1278, 1494	{ondone 1279
stone 79	mone 861
	none 370
	sone 831
	stone 1065

Total: 10

Word	Recurrence	#	%
sone	7	7	70
(on)done	4	0	Ø
al(l)one	3	3	30
none	2	0	Ø
stone	2	0	Ø

(10%)SUBGROUP: sone, alone (100%)

Comment: Cf. OME (I).
           It may be more accurate to count the three
           recurrence of alone and the two recurrences
           of none together, as five recurrences of (-)one.
           But we thought it an unncecessary complication
           since none itself accounts for no additional
           couplets in this cluster.

Preliminary	Terminal
fonge 159, 250, 340, 744, 764	fonge 947
longe 314, 1306	honde 160*
songe 1138	{ kinge 1057*
{ sp/ro/nge 513	{ kynge 1331
{ sp/ronge/ 1054	{ longe 765, 1139
stonge 1416	{ lo/n/ge 514, 745
tonge 1302	onhonge 341
wronge 946	{ songe 1055, 1303
{ yonge 563	{ so/n/ge 251
{ ʒonge 1056, 1330	spronge 564
	stonge 1307
	stronge 315
	ʒonge 1417

Total: 16

Word	Recurrence	#	%
fonge	6	6	38
longe	6	4	25
songe	4	2	12
(ʒ)			
yonge	4	4	25
spronge	3	0	Ø
stonge	2	0	Ø
(y)			
kinge	2	0	Ø

(13%)SUBGROUP: fonge, longe, songe, yonge (100%)

Comment: It should be noted that kinge pairs exclusively
with yonge for two couplets which may be con-
sidered excludable from this cluster as "off-
rhymes."
Cf. INGE (III) and ONDE (III).

Preliminary	Terminal

```
boure 280, 338, 665, 714,    ⎰auenture 666
      1200                    ⎱mesaue⟨n⟩ture 339
⎰hour⟨e⟩ ("our") 405          boure 406, 705
⎱houre 844                    cou⟨er⟩ture 715
⎰toure 704, 1266             four⟨ē⟩ 1201
⎱tour⟨e⟩ 1132                loure 281
                             lure 1267
                             pour⟨e⟩ 1133
                           ʒyure ("your") 845
```

Total: 10

Word	Recurrence	#	%
boure	7	7	70
toure	3	2	20
houre	2	1	10
(--)auenture	2	0	∅
1(o)ure	2	0	∅

(15%)SUBGROUP: Major: boure (70%)
                 Minor: toure, houre (30%)

Preliminary	Terminal
blowe 1410	drowe 1047
bowe 1270	flowe 612, 646
⎧ cnowe 1028	howe 690
⎩ knowe 1248	knowe 1411
drowe 191, 1448	lowe 1529
flowe 1136	owe 440, 1029, 1077, 1249
howe 348	rowe 1121, 1137
lowe 439, 1120	slawe 925*
nowe (?"mine own"; cf.	swowe 885
comment) 689	þrowe 349
p/r̄o̅/ue 561*	wowe 562, 1017
rowe 611, 645, 924	⎧ ynowe 1271
swowe 1528	⎨ /ynowe/ 1449
þrowe 1016	⎩ hy nowe 192
wowe 1076	
⎧ ynowe ("enough") 884	
⎩ hy nowe 1046	
Total: 20	

Word	Recurrence	#	%
(h)(y)(-)nowe	5	5	25
owe	5	5	25
rowe	5	5	25
(c)			
knowe	3	1	5
drowe	3	0	∅
flowe	3	0	∅
lowe	3	1	5
wowe	3	2	10
howe	2	1	5
swowe	2	0	∅
þrowe	2	0	∅

(18%)SUBGROUP: Major: ynowe, owe, rowe, knowe, lowe
                         wowe (95%)
                 Minor: howe (5%)

Comment: Clearly, ynowe, owe and rowe alone (less than
          8% of the max. vocab.) are the dominant ele-
          ments of the subgroup--together, they alone
          account for 75% of the couplets. But the
          established criteria, based on recurrence,
          forbids them alone to be designated "major"

Comment (cont.): elements. Cf. OUE(D)(I).
Flowe rhymes exclusively with rowe, forming
three matched pairs.   Nowe (l. 689) has been
counted with owe; the MS. reads "my nowe"
(clearly a false breaking of "myn owe").

APPENDIX D

HAVELOK THE DANE: FIVE SAMPLE CLUSTERS AND A METHOD-
OLOGY FOR DISTINGUISHING SYSTEMATIC
END-RHYMES FROM CONVENTIONAL REPETI-
TIONS

In all the preceding appendices, the analysis of
rhyme word repetition focused on the maximum recurrence
of a minimum number of words in each cluster so that
the systematic subgroup for each rhyme element of King
Horn might be determined. But rhyme word repetition
may not in itself be taken as indicative of oral
improvisation anymore than the simple recurrence of
apparently formulaic phrasing. The intent of this
final appendix is to provide a statistical basis for
distinguishing systematic end-rhymes that are indica-
tive of oral improvisation from conventional end-rhymes
that are not. To do so, we have extracted five clusters
from Havelok the Dane as edited by Donald B. Sands in
his Middle English Verse Romances (New York: Holt,
Rinehart & Winston, 1966; pp. 55-129). We have selec-
ted the -ALLE, -EDE, -ERE, -O and -ORE rhyme elements,
more or less, at random. But we have attempted to find
five clusters in Havelok that use a highly repetitious
rhyming vocabulary and that parallel five clusters in
King Horn MS. C whose end-rhymes proved to be somewhat
atypically varied. Our goal has been to contrast
Havelok's seemingly most systematic use of end-rhymes
to Horn's least.

In three of these examples drawn from Havelok the
Dane (i.e., its EDE, ERE, and O clusters), the size of
the proposed subgroups themselves may seem far too large
to have functioned as a jongleur's "readily recalled
rhyming lexicon." EDE requires a total of 11 different
words to account for only 86% of its couplets; similarly,
ERE requires 8 separate words for 95%, while O requires
7 for 99%--whereas 2 to 5 words seemed to be the norm
for subgroups in King Horn. But Table II (Chapter V)
reveals that the EDE subgroups of King Horn contain
as many as 7 words (MS. L), ERE as many as 9 (all three
MSS.), and O as many as 6 (MS. L)--even though the EDE
and O clusters themselves are substantially smaller
in King Horn. Furthermore, the size of these three
subgroups relative to the size of their own clusters
in Havelok the Dane seems satisfactory. EDE's subgroup
equals only 11% of its max. vocab.; ERE's equals 10%,
and O's equals a mere 7%.

A quick perusal of the five clusters in this appen-
dix that represent Havelok (and conventional rhyme

404

thereby) makes it most apparent that the end-rhyme
vocabulary of this later romance seems highly repeti-
tious as well. It must be demonstrated that the type
of rhyme-word repetition in Havelok is both substan-
tially different and statistically distinguishable
from that in Horn. In order to do so, it is neces-
sary to consider a heretofore neglected feature of
each cluster--its actual vocabulary, or the total num-
ber of words that are really (not, like max. vocab.,
hypothetically) used to complete couplets for each
rhyme element. The distinction between conventional
repetitions and systematic repetitions may be made
on the basis of three ratios: 1) the size of a clus-
ter's proposed subgroup (SG) relative to the cluster's
total number of recurrent words (RV; cf. "Recurrence"
in Appendices A, B & C); 2) the size of a cluster's
recurrent vocabulary relative to its actual vocabulary;
and 3) the size of a cluster's actual vocabulary rela-
tive to its max. vocab. The discrepancies that may
be discerned in these ratios for Havelok's clusters
as contrasted to Horn's make it possible to distinguish
the latter's systematic repetition of end-rhymes from
the former's conventional repetitions.

     The data for determining these ratios is provided
in Table VIII below. For the ALLE, EDE, ERE, O and ORE
clusters of both Havelok and King Horn MS. C, we have
listed the number of words that might comprise its
maximum vocabulary (Max. V.), and the number (No.)
of words that comprise its ACTUAL VOCAB.--as well as
the words themselves. We have also noted the number
of words in each cluster's actual vocabulary that are
used more than once as end-rhymes in the respective
romances (Recurrent V.); parenthetically, we indicate
the range of these recurrences--from as seldom as twice
to as frequently as twenty-one times. Finally, we
record the size of each cluster's subgroup (SG) as
determined by our established criteria (cf. "Method-
ology") in the appropriate appendix entries themselves.
We have underlined the members of these subgroups under
"Words" and have also indicated the rhyme words of each
cluster that do not appear more than once with an aster-
isk (*). All of the data given for Havelok the Dane
in Table VIII has been drawn from the five entries that
follow in this appendix, while the data for King Horn
MS. C may be checked against the appropriate entries
in Appendix A.

TABLE VIII

ACTUAL VOCAB.

	Cluster	Max. V.	No.	Words	Recurrent V.	SG
HAVELOK	ALLE	40	6	alle, calle, falle, halle, Galle*, galle*	4 (5x to 17x)	3
	EDE	99	24	bede, beþe, blede, brede*, dede ("did")*, dede, drede, fede, fremede*, glede, gnede*, grede, lede, mede, nede, rede, schrede*, spede, stede, þede*, wede, wede, yede, yemede*	17 (2x to 12x)	11
	ERE	78	20	bere, bere, caysere, dere, dere, dere ("dearth")*, fere*, fishere*, here, here, here, lere, mere*, messegere, spere, suere, tere*, þere, were, yer*	14 (2x to 15x)	8
	O	96	14	do, domino*, flo, fo, fro, go, mo, sho, slo, so, to, tro*, two, wo	12 (2x to 14x)	7
	ORE	64	10	bore*, gore*, more, ore, ore, rore*, sore, swore*, þore, wore	6 (2x to 21x)	3

TABLE VIII (cont.)

ACTUAL VOCAB.

HORN MS. C

Cluster	Max. V.	No.	Words	Recurrent V.	SG
ALLE	26	5	alle, falle, halle, þralle*, walle	4 (3x to 10x)	3
EDE	34	17	bede, dede(s), dede, ("dead")*, drede, fair-hede, lede, makede, mede*, nede, rede, sede(s)*, spede, sprede*, stede, verade*, wede*, ede*	10 (2x to 5x)	7
ERE	76	26	banere*, beggere*, ber*, bere*, chaere*, chere, damesele*, dere, fer*, fere, fisser*, here, here, ire*, lere, luþere*, manere*, mestere, palmere*, riuere*, squier*, stere, swere, þere, were, ere	12 (2x to 11x)	9
O	16	8	also*, do, fro*, go*, to*, þo, two, wo	4 (2x to 4x)	3
ORE	14	6	deole*, lore, more, ore, sore, ere*	4 (2x to 5x)	3

*In Table VIII, the asterisk indicates non-recurrent rhyme words in each cluster, while in the appendix entries themselves the asterisk still signals apparent off-rhymes.

The ERE clusters are almost the same size in both
romances, and the ALLE cluster of Havelok is only
slightly more than half again the size of that in Horn.
But there are notable discrepancies between the sizes
of the three other clusters of Havelok and those of
Horn. The EDE cluster of Havelok is almost three
times as large as that of Horn, while the ORE cluster
of Havelok is more than three times as large as Horn's,
and Havelok's O cluster is exactly six times as large
as that of Horn. It should be recalled, furthermore,
that the romance of Havelok itself is almost twice
as long as King Horn. Our analysis of the ratios that
may be determined within each romance attempts to mini-
mize such discrepancies. But the relative size of a
cluster does seem to effect our statistics and, there-
fore, our conclusions.

It must be noted that the O and ORE clusters of
King Horn are Category II entries; its ALLE, EDE and
ERE clusters belong to Category III. By the same
standards, all five clusters of Havelok should be
considered Category III entries. And even if we
double the size requirement for Category III clusters
in Havelok to twenty rather than ten couplets so that
the doubled size of this romance might be accommodated,
all five sample clusters still attain Category III
status.

It must also be noted that the order of relative
size among these five clusters differs significantly
in the two romances. In King Horn MS. C, the order
of clusters from smallest to largest is: ORE (7 coup-
lets), O (8 couplets), ALLE (13 couplets), EDE (17
couplets), and ERE (38 couplets). In Havelok the Dane,
however, the order is: ALLE (20 couplets), ORE (32
couplets), ERE (39 couplets), O (48 couplets) and EDE
(49 couplets and one odd-line).

These observations regarding the relative size of
each cluster within its own romance will prove signifi-
cant in qualifying the ratios of subgroup size to total
recurrent vocabulary (cf. SG/RV below) in Havelok--but
not in Horn. And cluster size also seems to effect
the ratio of recurrent vocabulary to actual vocabulary
in both Havelok and Horn--but in directly opposite
ways (cf. RV/AV below). These differences will in
themselves be analyzed as statistically consistent
distinctions between Horn's systematic rhyme and
Havelok's conventional rhyme. The ratios of actual
vocabulary to maximum vocabulary (cf. AV/MV below)

do not seem necessarily so effected by cluster size
in either romance--though, of course, there are some
exceptions to be noted. But the normative ratios of
actual vocabulary to maximum vocabulary in Havelok's
clusters are different from those of Horn. So, a com-
parison of these respective ratios in the two romances
provides a third, fairly constant, distinguishing
feature between their respective rhyme-crafts.

1) SG/RV
     The ratios of subgroup size to the total number of
recurrent words in each of the five sample clusters from
King Horn MS. C and from Havelok the Dane are as follows:

	HORN	HAVELOK
ALLE	3/4 (.75)	3/4 (.75)
EDE	7/10 (.70)	11/17 (.65)
ERE	9/12 (.75)	8/14 (.57)
O	3/4 (.75)	7/12 (.58)
ORE	3/4 (.75)	3/6 (.50)

The distinguishing feature to be noted in a comparison
of these two sets of ratios is that, as the size of a
cluster increases in Havelok, the proportion of recur-
rent words that serve as part of the cluster's subgroup
drops off sharply. In Horn, however, this ratio stays
more or less constant (.70 to .75) even though the size
of one cluster (e.g., ERE) may be triple that of another
(e.g., ALLE, O or ORE).

     In other words, there seems to be a basic trend
among Havelok's clusters to the effect that an increas-
ingly large number of rhyme-words will recur in a given
cluster, relative to the size of the cluster itself,
even though such repetitions are not required to account
for the oral completion of any additional couplets by
means of improvisation. Conversely, the broader dis-
tribution of such superfluous recurrences among Havelok's
total rhyming vocabulary may be interpreted as indicative
of an author's wider range of favored rhyme words--
that is, of his conventional links--but not of a per-
former's more restricted system.

     The example of EDE in Havelok prevents our sug-
gesting that the SG/RV ratios of conventional clusters
should be considered directly proportionate to cluster
size since it is higher than that of the smaller O or
ERE clusters. Similarly, the ORE cluster in Havelok
may be considered somewhat anomalous since it has the
lowest SG/RV ratio, even though the cluster itself is
second smallest among our five examples. But both of

these "exceptions" to the idea that there might be a
mathematically precise relation between SG/RV and
cluster size may be taken to support, rather than
contradict, our basic contention--that a jongleur's
improvised repetitions are far more restricted than
those of a writing rhymster. The relatively small
ALLE cluster in Havelok approximates the norm for SG/RV
in Horn, from which EDE's ratio does drop substantially
as might be expected in such a larger cluster. But
the unusually large subgroup of the EDE cluster (which
may be attributed to the accessibility of the rhyme
element in both Havelok and Horn) prevents its SG/RV
ratio from dropping to the size of the O cluster, which
is almost as large as EDE, or even to that of the sig-
nificantly smaller ERE cluster. On the other hand, this
apparent anomaly in the SG/RV ratio of the EDE cluster
of Havelok helps to highlight the marked increase of
non-systematic though recurrent rhyme-words in both its
O and ERE clusters. Furthermore, the extraordinarily
low SG/RV ratio of Havelok's ORE cluster suggests that
even a relatively small cluster in such a composition
may have an exceptional number of (improvisationally
gratuitous) recurrent rhyme words.

In short, even the most revising rhymster--whether
in the twentieth century or the thirteenth--habitually
uses certain words to complete his couplets more often
than others. But such conventional repetitions are
not mandated by the exigencies of oral improvisation
and tend, therefore, to generate a greater number of
recurrent words; the designation of a subgroup among
such recurrences seems purely artificial. The exces-
sive repetition of any one recurrent word in such a
mode of composition could validly be termed "monotonous,"
but an increased number of preferred words achieves
just the opposite of monotony--variety. A jongleur,
however, could not achieve variety in this way, nor
would he want to complexify his improvisational system
by increasing its size. The ideal ratio of SG to RV
for such a jongleur would be one-to-one; a jongleur
might then attain the maximum variety of rhyming vocabu-
lary proper to his own craft by reducing the recurrence
rate of all his non-systematic rhyme words to zero
(cf. AV/MV below).

Such ideals were seldom actually achieved by
jongleurs, it seems--especially in the larger clusters
of their orally performed romances. But then few
writers can attain complete verbal variety for the
end-rhymes of such long poems either. And, quite sim-
ply, the less variety such a writer achieves in his

410

composition, the more conventional his rhymes become,
and, subsequently, the more he deserves to be called
a "hack." The relatively low ratios of SG/RV in
Havelok's larger clusters indicate that its poet does
not deserve this sobriquet. The consistently high
ratios of SG/RV in Horn's larger clusters suggest,
however, that its jongleur was compelled to improvise
his couplets by repeating a fewer number of preferred
(i.e., systematic) end-rhymes more often.

2) RV/AV
     The ratios of the total number of recurrent words
in each of the five sample clusters from King Horn
MS. C and from Havelok the Dane to the number of
words that comprise the actual vocabulary of each
cluster respectively are as follows:

	HORN		HAVELOK	
ALLE	4/5	(.80)	4/6	(.67)
EDE	10/17	(.59)	17/24	(.71)
ERE	12/26	(.46)	14/20	(.70)
O	4/8	(.50)	12/14	(.86)
ORE	4/6	(.67)	6/10	(.60)
COMPOSITE	34/62	(.55)	53/74	(.72)

     These RV/AV ratios may be considered complementary
to the above SG/RV ratios (which focused exclusively
on repeated rhyme words) in that these new statistics
indicate the proportion of non-recurrent rhyme words
in each cluster. In this context, the lower a cluster's
RV/AV ratio, the more varied (i.e., less repetitious)
its total rhyming vocabulary should seem relative to
the recurrence rate of the rhyme element itself. There
appears, at first, to be a rather broad range of dif-
ferences among these RV/AV ratios--relative to cluster
size--in both romances. The highest ratio among the
sample clusters from Horn is that of ALLE (.80), the
lowest is ERE's (.46)--a range of .34. Similarly, the
highest ratio among Havelok's five clusters is that of
O (.86), the lowest is ORE's (.60)--a range of .26. The
difference between these ranges seems negligible. If,
however, we determine an average RV/AV figure for each
romance (cf. COMPOSITE), we may note that the variations
from it in Havelok's clusters are only + .14, but those
in Horn are + .25. This statistic seems slightly more
substantial, but must remain inconclusive till a far
more significant distinction between the types of RV/AV
variations relative to cluster size has been observed
in the respective romances.

     Havelok's two largest clusters (EDE and O) have the
highest RV/AV ratios, and its two smallest clusters (ALLE

and ORE) have the lowest. Again, it is impossible to
suggest an exactly direct proportion between RV/AV and
cluster size in this romance because the ratio of
Havelok's largest sample cluster (EDE) is exceeded by
its second largest (O), while the ratio of its second
smallest sample cluster (ORE) is exceeded by that of
the smallest (ALLE). Even so, a basic trend may be
observed in Havelok to the effect that, as the size
of a cluster increases, the variation of its RV/AV
ratio from the composite norm will increase as well.
Conversely, the smaller a cluster in Havelok, the
lower its RV/AV ratio becomes relative to the com-
posite norm.

     But among Horn's five sample clusters, just the
opposite sort of variation from the composite norm
of RV/AV ratios relative to cluster size seems to occur.
Horn's largest cluster (ERE) has the lowest RV/AV ratio,
while its smallest cluster (ORE) has the highest.
Horn's ALLE and ORE clusters are somewhat problematic,
however.

     ALLE's RV/AV ratio is indeed exceptionally high
given the size of this cluster. Although Horn's
ALLE cluster is almost twice as large as its ORE
cluster, the former's RV/AV ratio remains significantly
higher than the latter's; the number of words that
comprise ALLE's actual vocabulary in Horn proves to
be, in fact, one less than ORE's--despite the marked
difference in the respective sizes of these clusters.
(The actual vocabulary of Havelok's ALLE cluster
seems analogously small. Cf. further comments in the
anomalous nature of Horn's ALLE cluster in the AV/MV
section below.) It is the AV figure of the ALLE clus-
ter relative to the cluster's size that seems atypically
low in King Horn.

     Compared to the RV/AV ratios of the larger EDE
and ERE clusters in King Horn, that of its ALLE clus-
ter may still be considered consistent with the general
type of variation implicitly suggested for such clusters
of systematic end-rhyme--that as the size of such a
cluster decreases its RV/AV ratio will normally increase.
But compared to the RV/AV ratios of Horn's smaller O
and ORE clusters, that of its ALLE cluster must indeed
be considered an exception. This ratio for Horn's ALLE
cluster seems, in fact, far more consistent with the
composite norm of Havelok's ratios; so, the -alle rhymes
in King Horn may also be considered atypically conven-
tional. On the other hand, the anomalously high RV/AV

ratio of Horn's ALLE cluster may be said to highlight
the exceptionally low ratios of its O and ORE clusters.
And much the same might be said of the relation between
the respective RV/AV ratios of these O and ORE clusters
themselves. The RV/AV ratio of Horn's O cluster seems
disproportionately low, but this apparent anomaly may
also be indicative of the fact that even a rather small
cluster of end-rhymes in King Horn may have a relatively
large number of non-recurrent words among its actual
vocabulary.

In general, therefore, the observation seems valid--
with some qualification--that there is both less varia-
tion of RV/AV ratios from a composite norm and a different
sort of variation in the clusters of a romance written
with conventional end-rhymes as opposed to one improvised
around systematic subgroups of rhyme. And this observa-
tion seems thoroughly predictable in terms of our modi-
fied theory. As a jongleur used a given rhyme element
more and more--in other words, as his cluster's size
increased--he might naturally generate a larger number
of non-recurrent end-rhymes in his actual vocabulary,
but the fixed sizes of his subgroups (a significant sub-
set of RV) would thereby become a smaller and smaller
percentage of that vocabulary. A poet who habitually
wrote with certain conventional rhymes, however, would
tend to repeat an increasingly large proportion of a
cluster's actual vocabulary as he wrote more and more
couplets sharing the same rhyme element. The RV/AV
ratios of the larger clusters in such a composition
should, therefore, either exceed those of its smaller
clusters or vary little from a composite norm.

It is true that the sum of the rhyme-words actually,
used in Havelok's five sample clusters (74) is greater
than that of Horn's (62). In terms of such an absolute
comparison, Havelok has slightly more verbal variety
among its end-rhymes than Horn. But if it were anticipated
that the Havelok poet would have generated double the
verbal variety of Horn's jongleur (because Havelok
itself is twice as long as Horn), just the opposite will
prove true in terms of each cluster's maximum potential
for such verbal variety in either romance (cf. AV/MV
below). To defend Havelok's overall variety, an increased
number of rhyme elements themselves may have to be noted.
Nevertheless, a conventional rhymster tends habitually
to repeat the same (albeit larger) group of words in
both lines of his couplets, but a jongleur with his
systematic end-rhyme ready for one line is free to be
unconventional in the other. In fact, among the 377
lines of Havelok represented by the five sample clusters,

413

only twenty-one non-recurrent rhyme words (asterisked
in Table VIII above) may be found. But among the 166
lines of Horn represented by these same clusters, twenty-
seven such non-recurrent words may be found. In short,
44% (27/62) of Horn's actual vocabulary in these five
clusters is non-recurrent, or "unconventional," but only
28% (21/74) of Havelok's is. (These statistics, of course,
are merely the converses of the two romances' respective
RV/AV ratios and will vary in specific clusters accord-
ingly.) These percentages are directly linked to the
differing ratios of actual vocabulary to maximum vocabu-
lary in both romances that will be considered next,
because as the number of such non-recurrent words in a
cluster increases so will the size of its AV relative
to its MV.

3) AV/MV
     The ratios of the total number of words that com-
prise the actual vocabulary used in each of the five
sample clusters from King Horn MS. C and from Havelok
the Dane to the total number of words that might have
been used in each cluster in order to attain maximum
verbal variety are as follows:

	HORN	HAVELOK
ALLE	5/26 (19%)	6/40 (15%)
EDE	17/34 (50%)	24/99 (24%)
ERE	26/76 (34%)	20/78 (26%)
O	8/16 (50%)	14/96 (15%)
ORE	6/14 (43%)	10/64 (16%)
COMPOSITE	62/166 (37%)	74/377 (20%)

     As with the RV/AV ratios above, there seem to be
some notable variations of these AV/MV ratios from a
composite norm. Horn's ratios vary + .18; Havelok's
vary only a third of that figure, + .06. But there
seems to be no correlation--neither by direct proportion
nor in general--between the relative size of each clus-
ter and its resulting AV/MV ratio. In Horn, for example,
the largest sample cluster (ERE) has the second lowest
ratio, while its second largest cluster (EDE, only three
lines less than ERE) shares the same, highest AV/MV ratio
with the romance's second smallest, sample cluster (O).
So too in Havelok, the second largest cluster (O) and
the smallest cluster (ALLE) share the same, lowest AV/MV
ratio among the five selected samples.

     It is the ALLE cluster in King Horn that again seems
to present the most notable exception among the above
ratios; it has the lowest AV/MV ratio (19%) among the
romance's five clusters and the most extreme variation

414

of such (-.18) from the suggested norm (37%). The
sparsity of real verbal variety for this rhyme element
cannot be attributed to the size of the cluster itself.
As a contrast in the same romance, the O cluster uses
60% more words in 38% fewer lines. As a comparison
between romances, Havelok's ALLE cluster is 54% larger
than Horn's, but uses only one more word (albeit three
different words) in its actual vocabulary. Despite the
fact that -alle seems to have been a fairly popular
rhyme element in both romances, the relatively small
actual vocabulary generated for this cluster in both of
the romances must be attributed to an immeasurable pheno-
menon--that of rhyme-word accessibility. In other words,
-alle should be considered a "difficult" rhyme not just
in Horn or in Havelok, but in Middle English.

If we exclude the ALLE cluster from our considera-
tion of both romances' AV/MV ratios, we may refigure
their respective composites. The average AV/MV ratio
among King Horn's remaining four clusters would be
57/140 (41%); that of Havelok's four other clusters
would become 68/337, but remains much the same ratio
(20%). We may also refigure the variation of each ratio
from these new composites and note that Havelok's max-
imum variation is + .06, while Horn's is + .09-- a
negligible difference, apparently not determined by
cluster size. The real difference is that between the
two composite averages of the romances themselves.

Though the general inaccessibility of -alle rhyme-
words in Middle English seems to make the variation of
this cluster's AV/MV ratio from the composite norm of
King Horn's other clusters a real exception (-.22),
it is not such (-.05) in Havelok the Dane. Having
acknowledged that the real exceptions of such "diffi-
cult" clusters as ALLE exist in King Horn--and in sys-
tematically improvised romances thereby--we may then
note that the AV/MV ratios of Horn's other clusters
(as of their composite) consistently double the cor-
responding ratios of Havelok's. In other words, the
jongleur of Horn seems normally to have actualized the
maximum potential for verbal variety in his clusters
twice as much as the poet of Havelok. The relative
variety of Horn's ERE cluster may be considered some-
what weak by this standard of comparison to Havelok's
ERE cluster, but the variety of Horn's O and ORE clus-
ters should seem particularly strong by the same com-
parison. And the AV/MV ratio of Horn's EDE cluster
is almost exactly double that of Havelok's; yet, Havelok's
EDE cluster is itself almost three times as large as
Horn's.

415

Again, our theoretical distinction between the
rhyme techniques of a systematically improvised romance
like Horn and a conventionally composed romance like
Havelok should have made it possible to anticipate such
a statistically consistent discrepancy between their
respective AV/MV ratios. An occasional cluster (like
ALLE) that results from jongleur improvisation may have
also had to be conventional if alternative rhyme words
for its given rhyme element proved difficult for its
performer to recall or its poet to imagine--such rhyme
words are relatively "inaccessible" to author and
jongleur alike. But, in those clusters that have a
more "accessible" rhyme vocabulary, the instant availa-
bility of suitable and systematic end-rhymes for either
line of a jongleur's couplet would normally permit him
to use a more novel link in its other line--at will or
as remembered. And attaining such verbal variety within
the restrictions imposed by uninterrupted live perform-
ance may have been appreciated as one of the jongleur's
primary skills.

    We will not even attempt to provide an acronym for
"the jongleur's maximum verbal variety within the para-
meters of systematic improvisation." But it is possible
to imagine that the ideal AV/MV ratio of clusters at-
taining such variety would somewhat exceed 50%. The
jongleur would be "batting a thousand," as it were, in
that no more than half of his end-rhymes would be sys-
tematic repetitions and the other half would be unique
occurrences--SG, that is, would equal RV. The number
of words in the subgroups themselves plus the vocabulary
of any completely novel couplets (whether rigorous recol-
lections or impromptu innovations) would cause the actual
vocabulary of such clusters to exceed half of their
hypothetical maximum vocabulary.

    In practice, of course, the real jongleurs of King
Horn often repeated even their non-systematic vocabulary.
But it remains statistically observable that as the size
of their clusters increased the jongleurs would (be
forced to) take advantage of those halves of their
increased number of couplets that did not require an
additional, systematic repetition. And these larger
clusters would attain disproportionately larger actual
vocabularies when not deterred from doing so by an
"inaccessibility" of rhyme-words in the language. In
a conventionally composed cluster, however, it may be
observed that as the recurrence rate of its rhyme ele-
ment increases, so does the number of words that achieve
this rhyme, and so does the repetition of a proportion-
ately large number of these words. As has always been

assumed, conventionality in such compositions is a function of "accessibility"; the recurrence rate of a rhyme sound is directly linked to the availability of rhyme words for it, so the variety of rhyme words used in such a cluster remains--often excruciatingly--average.

The basic conclusion to be drawn from our analyses of all three of the above ratios (SG/RV, RV/AV and AV/MV) is that the repetitiveness of the rhyming vocabulary actually used by a conventional poet is far more uniform than that of a jongleur's systematic repetition. The methodology for distinguishing an orally improvised Middle English romance from one that is not requires, therefore, two stages. First, the pervasive repetition of certain rhyme words--those that "account for" the formal completion of a sufficiently large percentage of the romance's couplets--must be observed. Then, whether these "excessive" repetitions are more or less restricted to relatively small (readily recalled) subsets of each rhyme element's actual vocabulary must be determined.

Rhyme-word repetition in itself offers the first suggestion of a jongleur's improvisation, but the substantial difference between systematic and conventional repetitions has been found to be statistically demonstrable. We do not intend, however, that the statistics observed in the above sample ratios should be considered universal or definitive for making this distinction. Such figures would require a far broader survey of medieval poetry. As a start, we may consider the rhyme-indices already available in Ernest Langlois's edition of Le Roman de la Rose (Paris: Librarie de Firmin-Didot et Cie, 1914) and in Henry Cromie's Ryme-Index to the Ellesmere Manuscript of Chaucer's Canterbury Tales, Chaucer Society Publications, First Series XLV-XLVII (London; Kegan Paul, Trench, Trübner & Co., 1875). A quick perusal of the "clusters" in both these indices confirms what we already know--that the works they represent were clearly written compositions. The rhyming vocabulary used in these works seems only slightly repetitious relative to Havelok, not to mention Horn. But in so far as there remain numerous recurrences of a great number of end-rhymes in both these indices, the repetitiveness of their respective works seems conventional rather than systematic.

Preliminary	Terminal
alle 37, 156, 1301, 2028, 2120, 2266, 2692, 2794, 2980	alle 231, 746, 868, 1068, 1695, 2371, 2464, 2859
calle 230, 745, 867, 887, 2370, 2463, 2858	⟨calle 38 ⟨kalle 1358
falle 39, 1357	⟨falle 888, 1302, 2693, 2795 ⟨bifalle 2981
halle 1067, 1694	Galle (name) 2029
	galle (n. "gall") 40
	halle 157, 2121, 2267

Total: 20

Word	Recurrence	#	%
alle	17	17	85
(k) calle	9	2	10
(-)falle	7	1	5
halle	5	0	Ø

(8%) SUBGROUP: alle, calle, falle (100%)

Havelok the Dane   Rhyme Element: __EDE__

Preliminary	Terminal
/bede/ 2548	bede 1665, 2193
{ bepe ("both") 360, 1680*	bepe ("both") 694*
{ bope 2584*	blede 2403
blede 103	brede 98
dede 180, 2902	dede ("did") 185
drede 1169, 1664	{ dede ("deed") 550, 688, 1356
fede 322, 621, 645, 827	{ hand-dede 92
2420	drede 90, 181, 828
glede 91	fede 100, 866, 1170, 1198
gnede 97	fremede 2277*
lede 89, 549, 1684, 2356,	glede 870
2824	grede 96, 2703
mede 685, 2402	{ lede 686
nede 9, 25, 87, 1970, 2894	{ /lede/ 552
rede 118, 184, 687, 693	mede 102, 119, 1635, 2901
2900	nede 646, 2421, 2903
shrede 99	rede 104, 361, 1681, 2585
spede 93, 1197, 1634	stede 10, 26, 88, 622, 1971,
sprede 95	2357, 2549, 2895
stede 2192, 2386, 2640,	wede ("clothing") 94, 323,
2702	2825
þede 105	wede ("gallop") 2387, 2641
wede ("clothing") 861	yede 862, 1685
{ yede 101, 551, 865, 1355	
{ /yede/ 869	
yemede 2276	

Total: 49+1

Word	Recurrence	#	%
stede	12	12	24
fede	9	8	16
rede	9	9	18
nede	8	1	2
lede	7	6	12
yede	7	4	8
(-)dede	6	2	4
mede	6	2	4
drede	5	1	2
(o)			
bepe	4	0	Ø
wede ("clothing")	4	1	2
bede	3	0	Ø
spede	3	0	Ø

Word	Recurrence	#	%
blede	2	0	Ø
glede	2	0	Ø
grede	2	1	2
wede ("gallop")	2	0	Ø

(11%) SUBGROUP: Major: stede, fede, rede, nede, lede, yede (74%)

Minor: dede, mede, drede, wede, grede (14%)

Rhyme Element: ERE

Preliminary	Terminal
bere (n. "bear") 573, 1838, 2448	bere (v. "bear") 488, 974 1317, 1418, 2269, 2653, 2853, 2943
⎧ bere (v. "bear") 378, 623, 805, 1652, 2550, 2552 ⎨ ⎩ forbere 352	kaysere 353
caysere 1316	dere ("dear") 1637, 2293, 2593
dere ("dear") 1213, 2882	dere ("dearth") 824
dere ("to harm") 2310	dere ("to harm") 490, 574, 806
fishere 2230	fere 1214
here ("army") 346, 2942	here ("army") 379, 2153
here ("here") 1636, 2292	here ("to hear") 732
⎧ lere 823, 2592 ⎨ ⎩ /lere/ 731	here ("here") 2883
messe-gere 188	mere 2449
spere 489, 2652	messe-gere 389, 1078, 2217
⎧ suere 388 ⎨ ⎩ swere 487, 1077, 1417, 2216, 2268, 2852	⎧ spere 347, 2299 ⎨ ⎩ sp/er/e 624, 1653, 2551, 2553
were 741, 973, 1003	⎧ suere 189 ⎨ ⎩ swere 2231, 2311
were ("to defend") 2152, 2298	to-tere 1839
yer 1333*	þere 742, 1004
y-here 11 ("hear")	/were/ 1334
	y-lere 12

Total: 39

Word	Recurrence	#	%
bere ("to bear") (w)	15	15	40
suere	10	6	15
spere	8	3	8
dere ("dear")	5	5	13
were	5	3	8

Havelok the Dane   Rhyme Element: ERE (cont.)

Word	Recurrence	#	%
bere (bear n.)	4	3	8
dere ("to harm")	4	0	Ø
here ("army")	4	1	3
(-)lere	4	3	8
messe-gere	4	0	Ø
here ("here")	3	0	Ø
(k)			
caysere	2	0	Ø
(-)here ("hear")	2	0	Ø
þere	2	0	Ø

(10%)SUBGROUP: Major: bere, suere, spere (63%)
               Minor: dere, were, bere, here, lere (32%)

                              Rhyme Element: 0

Preliminary	Terminal
do 17, 252, 412, 525, 713, 1137, 1231	a-two 2643
fo 1363	⎰do 1046, 1805, 1935, 2731, 2863 ⎱undo 2739
fro 1740	/domino/ 20
go 509, 2074, 2688, 2776, 2848	flo 612, 2495
ouer-go 2220	fo 2849
mo 511, 1742, 1846, 2050, 2722, 2740, 2950	fro 2071, 2741
slo 849, 2070, 2166, 2588	go 125, 542, 850, 934, 1741, 2951
so 19, 933, 1822, 2642, 2738, 2960	sho 1138, 1232
⎰to 2136, 2494, 2556, 2744 ⎨þer-to 1045 ⎱un-to 1934	slo 512, 1364, 1745, 2051, 2689, 2723
tro 2862	so 351, 714, 2137, 2557, 2891, 2969
⎰two 350, 1804, 2890, 2968 ⎱on-two 2730	to 18, 253, 413, 526, 1743, 1823, 1847, 2961
wo 124, 541, 611, 1744	wo 510, 2075, 2167, 2221, 2589, 2745, 2777

Total: 48

Word	Recurrence	#	%
(-)to	14	14	29
(-)do	13	7	15
go	12	12	25
so	12	5	10
wo	11	4	8
slo	10	5	10
mo	7	1	2
(-)two	6	0	Ø
fro	3	0	Ø
flo	2	0	Ø
fo	2	0	Ø
sho	2	0	Ø

(7%)SUBGROUP: Major: to, do, go, so, wo, slo (97%)
              Minor: mo (2%)

| Havelok the Dane | Rhyme Element: ___ORE___ |

Preliminary	Terminal
bore 45	more 46, 259, 456, 982, 1034,
gore 2497	1054, 1092, 1701, 2487,
eure-more 683	2569, 2753, 2833
more 210, 653, 787, 921,	ore ("oar") 718
1013, 1866, 2306,	ore ("mercy") 153, 211, 2443,
2334	2797
ore ("oar") 1887	rore 2498
sore 152, 236, 455, 503,	sore 415, 654, 788, 1888
2442, 2568, 2638,	swore 2307
2752, 2796	þore 922, 1014, 2335, 2639,
þore 981, 1033, 2486, 2832	2929
wore 258, 414, 717, 1053,	wore 237, 504, 684, 1867
1091, 1700, 2928	

Total: 32

Word	Recurrence	#	%
(-)more	21	21	66
sore	13	7	22
wore	11	3	9
þore	9	0	Ø
ore ("mercy")	4	0	Ø
ore ("oar")	2	0	Ø

(5%) SUBGROUP: more, sore, wore (97%)